Marley & Me

Marley & Me

Life and Love with
the World's Worst Dog

John Grogan

HODDER

First published in Great Britain in 2006 by Hodder & Stoughton
A division of Hodder Headline

"Saying Farewell to a Faithful Pal" by John Grogan. Reprinted with
permission from the *Philadephia Inquirer*

A Hodder paperback

4

A CIP catalogue record for this title
is available from the British Library

ISBN 978 0340 93684 9 (A)
ISBN 978 0340 92210 1 (B)

Typeset by Hewer Text UK Ltd, Edinburgh
Printed in Great Britain by Clays Ltd, St Ives plc

Hodder Headline's policy is to use papers that are natural, renewable
and recyclable products and made from wood grown in sustainable
forests. The logging and manufacturing processes are expected to
conform to the environmental regulations of the country of origin.

Hodder & Stoughton Ltd
A division of Hodder Headline
338 Euston Road
London NW1 3BH

Dear Reader,

✳ ✳ ✳

When I sat down to write *Marley & Me*, I had no idea what lay ahead. I knew only that there was a story inside me burning to get out, a story I needed to tell. It was the story of my wife, Jenny, and me starting our life together and the big, nutty, incorrigible, lovable dog that changed it all. Changed us, changed our children, changed the family we would become. The first step in that odyssey was a column I wrote in the *Philadelphia Inquirer* on January 6, 2004, saying good-bye to that dog, Marley, a Labrador retriever like no other. That column, which is included at the end of this edition of *Marley & Me*, drew such an overwhelming response, I knew I had touched on something bigger, the story not just of a dog, not just of a family with a dog, but of the journey humans and animals take together—the ups, the downs; the laughter, the tears; the joys and the heartbreaks. A journey worth taking.

For nine months I wrote in solitude, mostly in the pre-dawn darkness, not quite believing anyone would want to read an entire book about my very ordinary life. Then an amazing thing happened. My book was published in the

United States and soon after in many countries: the United Kingdom, Australia, New Zealand, Ireland (especially pleasing) and South Africa — and I was alone no more.

From Los Angeles to London, from the Catskills to the Cotswolds—and eventually the globe—the letters and e-mails and phone calls began arriving. They came from retirees and newlyweds, from police officers and firefighters, from college students and construction workers. They came from soldiers in Iraq and Afghanistan and from children in elementary schools. They came in a daily torrent and many of them said nearly the same thing: "It was like you were describing my life." They, too, had made the journey worth taking. In the very ordinariness of our lives, I had somehow managed to find the universal.

Many of these readers have become like friends, making me laugh out loud and, occasionally, pause to bite my lip. They've embraced me like a member of their own families. One painted a beautiful portrait of Marley in oils and mailed it to me; another sent me songs she composed after the loss of her dog; several baked gourmet treats for our new Lab, Gracie. A K-9 officer in Los Angeles gave me an elaborate framed dog-obedience diploma, complete with a gold paw-print stamp, because the real one had proved so elusive. Many blessed me with their sense of humor, such as the young woman who sent me a photograph with the provocative subject line: "Hot bedroom action." I opened the image to find her under the covers reading *Marley & Me*—with her pet boxer snoozing on top of her, the covers pulled to his chin.

Marleyandme.com has evolved into a sort of boisterous town square populated by thousands of dog lovers and book aficionados sharing stories and photos and advice and consolation. Friendships have been forged, phone numbers exchanged, invitations issued. Some are planning to meet in person. Yet another gift my never-do-well Marley has bestowed upon those he has touched—the gift of community.

Jenny and I have a new dog now, and, yes, it's another yellow Labrador retriever. Her name is Gracie, and she is the anti-Marley—sweet, calm, sedate, focused. Every day I tell her, "Gracie, you're a great dog but don't expect a book about you. You're *too* good." And that makes me smile at the memory of the eternally mischievous Marley who filled our lives with so much joyous havoc. It amuses me no end to think he has become a household name to millions.

Dogs are great. Bad dogs, if we can really call them that, are perhaps the greatest of them all.

—John Grogan
October 2006

In memory of my father, Richard Frank Grogan,
whose gentle spirit infuses every page of this book

Contents

Preface

The Perfect Dog

❊

In the summer of 1967, when I was ten years old, my father caved in to my persistent pleas and took me to get my own dog. Together we drove in the family station wagon far into the Michigan countryside to a farm run by a rough-hewn woman and her ancient mother. The farm produced just one commodity—dogs. Dogs of every imaginable size and shape and age and temperament. They had only two things in common: each was a mongrel of unknown and indistinct ancestry, and each was free to a good home. We were at a mutt ranch.

"Now, take your time, son," Dad said. "Your decision today is going to be with you for many years to come."

I quickly decided the older dogs were somebody else's charity case. I immediately raced to the puppy cage. "You want to pick one that's not timid," my father coached. "Try rattling the cage and see which ones aren't afraid."

I grabbed the chain-link gate and yanked on it with a loud clang. The dozen or so puppies reeled backward, collapsing on top of one another in a squiggling heap of fur. Just one remained. He was gold with a white blaze on his chest, and he charged the gate, yapping fearlessly. He jumped up and excitedly licked my fingers through the fencing. It was love at first sight.

I brought him home in a cardboard box and named him Shaun. He was one of those dogs that give dogs a good name. He effortlessly mastered every command I taught him and was naturally well behaved. I could drop a crust on the floor and he would not touch it until I gave the okay. He came when I called him and stayed when I told him to. We could let him out alone at night, knowing he would be back after making his rounds. Not that we often did, but we could leave him alone in the house for hours, confident he wouldn't have an accident or disturb a thing. He raced cars without chasing them and walked beside me without a leash. He could dive to the bottom of our lake and emerge with rocks so big they sometimes got stuck in his jaws. He loved nothing more than riding in the car and would sit quietly in the backseat beside me on family road trips, content to spend hours gazing out the window at the passing world. Perhaps best of all, I trained him to pull me through the neighborhood dog-sled-style as I sat on my bicycle, making me the hands-down envy of my friends. Never once did he lead me into hazard.

He was with me when I smoked my first cigarette (and my last) and when I kissed my first girl. He was right there beside me in the front seat when I snuck out my older brother's Corvair for my first joyride.

Shaun was spirited but controlled, affectionate but calm. He even had the dignified good manners to back himself modestly into the bushes before squatting to do his duty, only his head peering out. Thanks to this tidy habit, our lawn was safe for bare feet.

Relatives would visit for the weekend and return home determined to buy a dog of their own, so impressed were they with Shaun—or "Saint Shaun," as I came to call him. It was a family joke, the saint business, but one we could almost believe. Born with the curse of uncertain lineage, he was one of the tens of thousands of unwanted dogs in America. Yet by some stroke of almost providential good fortune, he became wanted. He came into my life and I into his—and in the process, he gave me the childhood every kid deserves.

The love affair lasted fourteen years, and by the time he died I was no longer the little boy who had brought him home on that summer day. I was a man, out of college and working across the state in my first real job. Saint Shaun had stayed behind when I moved on. It was where he belonged. My parents, by then retired, called to break the news to me. My mother would later tell me, "In fifty years of marriage, I've only seen your father cry twice. The first time was when we lost Mary Ann"—my sister, who was stillborn. "The second time was the day Shaun died."

Saint Shaun of my childhood. He was a perfect dog. At least that's how I will always remember him. It was Shaun who set the standard by which I would judge all other dogs to come.

CHAPTER 1

And Puppy Makes Three

We were young. We were in love. We were rollicking in those sublime early days of marriage when life seems about as good as life can get. We could not leave well enough alone.

And so on a January evening in 1991, my wife of fifteen months and I ate a quick dinner together and headed off to answer a classified ad in the *Palm Beach Post*.

Why we were doing this, I wasn't quite sure. A few weeks earlier I had awoken just after dawn to find the bed beside me empty. I got up and found Jenny sitting in her bathrobe at the glass table on the screened porch of our little bungalow, bent over the newspaper with a pen in her hand.

There was nothing unusual about the scene. Not only was the *Palm Beach Post* our local paper, it was also the source of half of our household income. We were a two-newspaper-career couple. Jenny worked as a feature writer in the *Post*'s "Accent" section; I was a news reporter at the competing paper in the area, the South Florida *Sun-Sentinel*, based an hour south in Fort Lauderdale. We began every morning poring over the newspapers, seeing how our stories were played and how they stacked up to the competition. We circled, underlined, and clipped with abandon.

But on this morning, Jenny's nose was not in the news pages but in the classified section. When I stepped closer, I saw she was feverishly circling beneath the heading "Pets—Dogs."

"Uh," I said in that new-husband, still-treading-gently voice. "Is there something I should know?"

She did not answer.

"Jen-Jen?"

"It's the plant," she finally said, her voice carrying a slight edge of desperation.

"The plant?" I asked.

"That dumb plant," she said. "The one we killed."

The one *we* killed? I wasn't about to press the point, but for the record it was the plant that *I* bought and *she* killed. I had surprised her with it one night, a lovely large dieffenbachia with emerald-and-cream variegated leaves. "What's the occasion?" she'd asked. But there was none. I'd given it to her for no reason other than to say, "Damn, isn't married life great?"

She had adored both the gesture and the plant and thanked me by throwing her arms around my neck and kissing me on the lips. Then she promptly went on to kill my gift to her with an assassin's coldhearted efficiency. Not that she was trying to; if anything, she nurtured the poor thing to death. Jenny didn't exactly have a green thumb. Working on the assumption that all living things require water, but apparently forgetting that they also need air, she began flooding the dieffenbachia on a daily basis.

"Be careful not to overwater it," I had warned.

"Okay," she had replied, and then dumped on another gallon.

The sicker the plant got, the more she doused it, until finally it just kind of melted into an oozing heap. I looked at its limp skeleton in the pot by the window and thought, *Man, someone who believes in omens could have a field day with this one.*

Now here she was, somehow making the cosmic leap of logic from dead flora in a pot to living fauna in the pet classifieds. *Kill a plant, buy a puppy.* Well, of course it made perfect sense.

I looked more closely at the newspaper in front of her and saw that one ad in particular seemed to have caught her fancy. She had drawn three fat red stars beside it. It read: "Lab puppies, yellow. AKC purebred. All shots. Parents on premises."

"So," I said, "can you run this plant-pet thing by me one more time?"

"You know," she said, looking up. "I tried so hard and look what happened. I can't even keep a stupid houseplant alive. I mean, how hard is *that*? All you need to do is water the damn thing."

Then she got to the real issue: "If I can't even keep a plant alive, how am I ever going to keep a baby alive?" She looked like she might start crying.

The BabyThing, as I called it, had become a constant in Jenny's life and was getting bigger by the day. When we had first met, at a small newspaper in western Michigan, she was just a few months out of college, and serious adulthood still seemed a far distant concept. For both of us, it was our first professional job out of school. We ate a lot of pizza, drank a lot of beer, and gave exactly zero thought to the possibility of someday being anything other than young, single, unfettered consumers of pizza and beer.

But years passed. We had barely begun dating when various job opportunities—and a one-year postgraduate program for me—pulled us in different directions across the eastern United States. At first we were one hour's drive apart. Then we were three hours apart. Then eight, then twenty-four. By the time we both landed together in South Florida and tied the knot, she was nearly thirty. Her friends were having babies. Her body was sending her strange messages. That once seemingly eternal window of procreative opportunity was slowly lowering.

I leaned over her from behind, wrapped my arms around her shoulders, and kissed the top of her head. "It's okay," I said. But I had to admit, she raised a good question. Neither of us had ever really nurtured a thing in our lives. Sure, we'd had pets growing up, but they didn't really count. We always knew our parents would keep them alive and well. We both knew we wanted to one day have children, but was either of us really up for the job? Children were so . . . so . . . scary. They were helpless and fragile and looked like they would break easily if dropped.

A little smile broke out on Jenny's face. "I thought maybe a dog would be good practice," she said.

As we drove through the darkness, heading northwest out of town where the suburbs of West Palm Beach fade into sprawling country properties, I thought through our decision to bring home a dog. It was a huge responsibility, especially for two people with full-time jobs. Yet we knew what we were in for. We'd both grown up with dogs and loved them immensely. I'd had Saint Shaun and Jenny had had Saint Winnie, her family's beloved English setter. Our happiest childhood memories almost all included those dogs. Hiking with them, swimming with them, playing with them, getting in trouble with them. If Jenny really only wanted a dog to hone her parenting skills, I would have tried to talk her in off the ledge and maybe placate her with a goldfish. But just as we knew we wanted children someday, we knew with equal certainty that our family home would not be complete without a dog sprawled at our feet. When we were dating, long before children ever came on our radar, we spent hours discussing our childhood pets, how much we missed them and how we longed someday—once we had a house to call our own and some stability in our lives—to own a dog again.

Now we had both. We were together in a place we did not plan to leave anytime soon. And we had a house to call our very own.

It was a perfect little house on a perfect little quarter-acre fenced lot just right for a dog. And the location was just right, too, a funky city neighborhood one and a half blocks off the Intracoastal Waterway separating West Palm Beach from the rarified mansions of Palm Beach. At the foot of our street, Churchill Road, a linear green park and paved trail stretched for miles along the waterfront. It was ideal for jogging and bicycling and Rollerblading. And, more than anything, for walking a dog.

The house was built in the 1950s and had an Old Florida charm—a fireplace, rough plaster walls, big airy windows, and French doors leading to our favorite space of all, the screened back porch. The yard was a little tropical haven, filled with palms and bromeliads and avocado trees and brightly colored coleus plants. Dominating the property was a towering mango tree; each summer it dropped its heavy fruit with loud thuds that sounded, somewhat grotesquely, like bodies being thrown off the roof. We would lie awake in bed and listen: *Thud! Thud! Thud!*

We bought the two-bedroom, one-bath bungalow a few months after we returned from our honeymoon and immediately set about refurbishing it. The prior owners, a retired postal clerk and his wife, loved the color green. The exterior stucco was green. The interior walls were green. The curtains were green. The shutters were green. The front door was green. The carpet, which they had just purchased to help sell the house, was green. Not a cheery kelly green or a cool emerald green or even a daring lime green but a puke-your-guts-out-after-split-pea-soup green accented with khaki trim. The place had the feel of an army field barracks.

On our first night in the house, we ripped up every square inch of the new green carpeting and dragged it to the curb. Where the carpet had been, we discovered a pristine oak plank floor that, as best we could tell, had never suffered the scuff of a single shoe. We painstakingly sanded and varnished it to a high sheen. Then we went out and blew the better part of two weeks' pay for a handwoven Persian rug, which we unfurled in the living room in front of the fireplace. Over the months, we repainted every green surface and replaced every green accessory. The postal clerk's house was slowly becoming our own.

Once we got the joint just right, of course, it only made sense that we bring home a large, four-legged roommate with sharp toenails, large teeth, and exceedingly limited English-language skills to start tearing it apart again.

"Slow down, dingo, or you're going to miss it," Jenny scolded. "It should be coming up any second." We were driving through inky blackness across what had once been swampland, drained after World War II for farming and later colonized by suburbanites seeking a country lifestyle.

As Jenny predicted, our headlights soon illuminated a mailbox marked with the address we were looking for. I turned up a gravel drive that led into a large wooded property with a pond in front of the house and a small barn out back. At the door, a middle-aged woman named Lori greeted us, a big, placid yellow Labrador retriever by her side.

"This is Lily, the proud mama," Lori said after we introduced ourselves. We could see that five weeks after birth Lily's stomach was still swollen and her teats pronounced. We both got on our knees, and she happily accepted our affection. She was just what we pictured a Lab would be—sweet-natured, affectionate, calm, and breathtakingly beautiful.

"Where's the father?" I asked.

"Oh," the woman said, hesitating for just a fraction of a second. "Sammy Boy? He's around here somewhere." She quickly added, "I imagine you're dying to see the puppies."

She led us through the kitchen out to a utility room that had been drafted into service as a nursery. Newspapers covered the floor, and in one corner was a low box lined with old beach towels. But we hardly noticed any of that. How could we with nine tiny yellow puppies stumbling all over one another as they clamored to check out the latest strangers to drop by? Jenny gasped. "Oh my," she said. "I don't think I've ever seen anything so cute in my life."

We sat on the floor and let the puppies climb all over us as Lily happily bounced around, tail wagging and nose poking each of her offspring to make sure all was well. The deal I had struck with Jenny when I agreed to come here was that we would check the pups out, ask some questions, and keep an open mind as to whether we were ready to bring home a dog. "This is the first ad we're answering," I had said. "Let's not make any snap decisions." But thirty seconds into it, I could see I had already lost the battle. There was no question that before the night was through one of these puppies would be ours.

Lori was what is known as a backyard breeder. When it came to buying a purebred dog, we were pure novices, but we had read enough to know to steer clear of the so-called puppy mills, those commercial breeding operations that churn out purebreds like Ford churns out Tauruses. Unlike mass-produced cars, however, mass-produced pedigree puppies can come with serious hereditary problems, running the gamut from hip dysplasia to early blindness, brought on by multigenerational inbreeding.

Lori, on the other hand, was a hobbyist, motivated more by love of the breed than by profit. She owned just one female and one male. They had come from distinct blood-lines, and she had the paper trail to prove it. This would be Lily's second and final litter before she retired to the good life of a countrified family pet. With both parents on the premises, the buyer could see firsthand the lineage—although in our case, the father apparently was outside and out of pocket.

The litter consisted of five females, all but one of which already had deposits on them, and four males. Lori was asking $400 for the remaining female and $375 for the males. One of the males seemed particularly smitten with us. He was the goofiest of the group and charged into us, somersaulting into our laps and clawing his way up our shirts to lick our faces. He gnawed on our fingers with surprisingly sharp baby teeth and stomped clumsy circles around us on giant tawny paws that were way out of proportion to the rest of his body. "That one there you can have for three-fifty," the owner said.

Jenny is a rabid bargain hunter who has been known to drag home all sorts of things we neither want nor need simply because they were priced too attractively to pass up. "I know you don't golf," she said to me one day as she pulled a set of used clubs out of the car. "But you wouldn't believe the deal I got on these." Now I saw her eyes brighten. "Aw, honey," she cooed. "The little guy's on clearance!"

I had to admit he was pretty darn adorable. Frisky, too. Before I realized what he was up to, the rascal had half my watchband chewed off.

"We have to do the scare test," I said. Many times before I had recounted for Jenny the story of picking out Saint Shaun when I was a boy, and my father teaching me to make a sudden move or loud noise to separate the timid from the self-assured. Sitting in this heap of pups, she gave me that roll of the eyes that she reserved for odd Grogan-family behavior. "Seriously," I said. "It works."

I stood up, turned away from the puppies, then swung quickly back around, taking a sudden, exaggerated step toward them. I stomped my foot and barked out, "Hey!" None seemed too concerned by this stranger's contortions. But only one plunged forward to meet the assault head-on. It was Clearance Dog. He plowed full steam into me, throwing a cross-body block across my ankles and pouncing at my shoelaces as though convinced they were dangerous enemies that needed to be destroyed.

"I think it's fate," Jenny said.

"Ya think?" I said, scooping him up and holding him in one hand in front of my face, studying his mug. He looked at me with heart-melting brown eyes and then nibbled my nose. I plopped him into Jenny's arms, where he did the same to her. "He certainly seems to like us," I said.

And so it came to be. We wrote Lori a check for $350, and she told us we could return to take Clearance Dog home with us in three weeks when he was eight weeks old and weaned. We thanked her, gave Lily one last pat, and said good-bye.

Walking to the car, I threw my arm around Jenny's shoulder and pulled her tight to me. "Can you believe it?" I said. "We actually got our dog!"

"I can't wait to bring him home," she said.

Just as we were reaching the car, we heard a commotion coming from the woods. Something was crashing through the brush—and breathing very heavily. It sounded like what you might hear in a slasher film. And it was coming our way. We froze, staring into the darkness. The sound grew louder and closer. Then in a flash the thing burst into the clearing and came charging in our direction, a yellow blur. A very *big* yellow blur. As it galloped past, not stopping, not even seeming to notice us, we could see it was a large Labrador retriever. But it was nothing like the sweet Lily we had just cuddled with inside. This one was soaking wet and covered up to its belly in mud and burrs. Its tongue hung out wildly to one side, and froth flew off its jowls as it barreled past.

In the split-second glimpse I got, I detected an odd, slightly crazed, yet somehow joyous gaze in its eyes. It was as though this animal had just seen a ghost—and couldn't possibly be more tickled about it.

Then, with the roar of a stampeding herd of buffalo, it was gone, around the back of the house and out of sight. Jenny let out a little gasp.

"I think," I said, a slight queasiness rising in my gut, "we just met Dad."

CHAPTER 2

Running with the Blue Bloods

Our first official act as dog owners was to have a fight. It began on the drive home from the breeder's and continued in fits and snippets through the next week. We could not agree on what to name our Clearance Dog. Jenny shot down my suggestions, and I shot down hers. The battle culminated one morning before we left for work.

"*Chelsea?*" I said. "That is *such* a chick name. No boy dog would be caught dead with the name Chelsea."

"Like he'll really know," Jenny said.

"Hunter," I said. "Hunter is perfect."

"*Hunter?* You're kidding, right? What are you, on some macho, sportsman trip? Way too masculine. Besides, you've never hunted a day in your life."

"He's a male," I said, seething. "*He's supposed to be masculine*. Don't turn this into one of your feminist screeds."

This was not going well. I had just taken off the gloves. As Jenny wound up to counterpunch, I quickly tried to return the deliberations to my leading candidate. "What's wrong with Louie?"

"Nothing, if you're a gas-station attendant," she snapped.

"Hey! Watch it! That's my grandfather's name. I suppose we should name him after your grandfather? 'Good dog, *Bill*!' "

As we fought, Jenny absently walked to the stereo and pushed the play button on the tape deck. It was one of her marital combat strategies. When in doubt, drown out your opponent. The lilting reggae strains of Bob Marley began to pulse through the speakers, having an almost instant mellowing effect on us both.

We had only discovered the late Jamaican singer when we moved to South Florida from Michigan. In the white-bread backwaters of the Upper Midwest, we'd been fed a steady diet of Bob Seger and John Cougar Mellencamp. But here in the pulsing ethnic stew that was South Florida, Bob Marley's music, even a decade after his death, was everywhere. We heard it on the car radio as we drove down Biscayne Boulevard. We heard it as we sipped *cafés cubanos* in Little Havana and ate Jamaican jerk chicken in little holes-in-the-wall in the dreary immigrant neighborhoods west of Fort Lauderdale. We heard it as we sampled our first conch fritters at the Bahamian Goombay Festival in Miami's Coconut Grove section and as we shopped for Haitian art in Key West.

The more we explored, the more we fell in love, both with South Florida and with each other. And always in the background, it seemed, was Bob Marley. He was there as we baked on the beach, as we painted over the dingy green walls of our house, as we awoke at dawn to the screech of wild parrots and made love in the first light filtering through the Brazilian pepper tree outside our window. We fell in love with his music for what it was, but also for what it defined, which was that moment in our lives when we ceased being two and became one. Bob Marley was the soundtrack for our new life together in this strange, exotic, rough-and-tumble place that was so unlike anywhere we had lived before.

And now through the speakers came our favorite song of all, because it was so achingly beautiful and because it spoke so clearly to us. Marley's voice filled the room, repeating the chorus over and over: "Is this love that I'm feeling?" And at the exact same moment, in perfect unison, as if we had rehearsed it for weeks, we both shouted, "Marley!"

"That's it!" I exclaimed. "That's our name." Jenny was smiling, a good sign. I tried it on for size. "Marley, come!" I commanded. "Marley, stay! Good boy, Marley!"

Jenny chimed in, "You're a cutie-wootie-woo, Marley!"

"Hey, I think it works," I said. Jenny did, too. Our fight was over. We had our new puppy's name.

The next night after dinner I came into the bedroom where Jenny was reading and said, "I think we need to spice the name up a little."

"What are you talking about?" she asked. "We both love it."

I had been reading the registration papers from the American Kennel Club. As a purebred Labrador retriever with both parents properly registered, Marley was entitled to AKC registration as well. This was only really needed if you planned to show or breed your dog, in which case there was no more important piece of paper. For a house pet, however, it was superfluous. But I had big plans for our Marley. This was my first time rubbing shoulders with anything resembling high breeding, my own family included. Like Saint Shaun, the dog of my childhood, I was a mutt of indistinct and undistinguished ancestry. My lineage represented more nations than the European Union. This dog was the closest to blue blood I would ever get, and I wasn't about to pass up whatever opportunities it offered. I admit I was a little starstruck.

"Let's say we want to enter him in competitions," I said. "Have you ever seen a champion dog with just one name? They always have big long titles, like Sir Dartworth of Cheltenham."

"And his master, Sir Dorkshire of West Palm Beach," Jenny said.

"I'm serious," I said. "We could make money studding him out. Do you know what people pay for top stud dogs? They all have fancy names."

"Whatever floats your boat, honey," Jenny said, and returned to her book.

The next morning, after a late night of brainstorming, I cornered her at the bathroom sink and said, "I came up with the perfect name."

She looked at me skeptically. "Hit me," she said.

"Okay. Are you ready? Here goes." I let each word fall slowly from my lips: "Grogan's . . . Majestic . . . Marley . . . of . . . Churchill." *Man,* I thought, *does that sound regal.*

"Man," Jenny said, "does that sound dumb."

I didn't care. I was the one handling the paperwork, and I had already written in the name. In ink. Jenny could smirk all she wanted; when Grogan's Majestic Marley of Churchill took top honors at the Westminster Kennel Club Dog Show in a few years, and I gloriously trotted him around the ring before an adoring international television audience, we'd see who would be laughing.

"Come on, my dorky duke," Jenny said. "Let's have breakfast."

CHAPTER 3

Homeward Bound

❖

While we counted down the days until we could bring Marley home, I belatedly began reading up on Labrador retrievers. I say *belatedly* because virtually everything I read gave the same strong advice: *Before* buying a dog, make sure you thoroughly research the breed so you know what you're getting into. Oops.

An apartment dweller, for instance, probably wouldn't do well with a Saint Bernard. A family with young children might want to avoid the sometimes unpredictable chow chow. A couch potato looking for a lapdog to idle the hours away in front of the television would likely be driven insane by a border collie, which needs to run and work to be happy.

I was embarrassed to admit that Jenny and I had done almost no research before settling on a Labrador retriever. We chose the breed on one criterion alone: curb appeal. We often had admired them with their owners down on the Intracoastal Waterway bike trail—big, dopey, playful galumphs that seemed to love life with a passion not often seen in this world. Even more embarrassing, our decision was influenced not by *The Complete Dog Book*, the bible of dog breeds published by the American Kennel Club, or by any other reputable guide. It was influenced by that other heavyweight of canine literature, ''The Far Side'' by Gary Larson. We were huge fans of the cartoon. Larson filled his panels with witty, urbane Labs doing and saying the darnedest things. Yes, they talked! What wasn't to like? Labs were immensely amusing animals—at least in Larson's hands. And who couldn't use a little more amusement in life? We were sold.

Now, as I pored through more serious works on the Labrador retriever, I was relieved to learn that our choice, however ill informed, was not too wildly off the mark. The literature was filled with glowing testimonials about the Labrador retriever's loving, even-keeled personality, its gentleness with children, its lack of aggression, and its desire to please. Their intelligence and malleability had made them a leading choice for search-and-rescue training and as guide dogs for the blind and handicapped. All this boded well for a pet in a home that would sooner or later likely include children.

One guide gushed: ''The Labrador retriever is known for its intelligence, warm affection for man, field dexterity and undying devotion to any task.'' Another marveled at the breed's immense loyalty. All these qualities had pushed the Labrador retriever from a specialty sporting dog, favored by bird hunters because of its skill at fetching downed pheasants and ducks from frigid waters, into America's favorite family pet. Just the year before, in 1990, the Labrador retriever had knocked the cocker spaniel out of the top spot on the American Kennel Club registry as the nation's most popular breed. No other breed has come close to overtaking the Lab since. In 2004 it took its fifteenth straight year as the AKC's top dog, with 146,692 Labs registered. Coming in a distant second were golden retrievers, with 52,550, and, in third place, German shepherds, with 46,046.

Quite by accident, we had stumbled upon a breed America could not get enough of. All those happy dog owners couldn't be wrong, could they? We had chosen a proven winner. And yet the literature was filled with ominous caveats.

Labs were bred as working dogs and tended to have boundless energy. They were highly social and did not do well left alone for long periods. They could be thick-skulled and difficult to train. They needed rigorous daily exercise or they could become destructive. Some were wildly excitable and hard for even experienced dog handlers to control. They had what could seem like eternal puppyhoods, stretching three years or more. The long, exuberant adolescence required extra patience from owners.

They were muscular and bred over the centuries to be inured to pain, qualities that served them well as they dove into the icy waters of the North Atlantic to assist fishermen. But in a home setting, those same qualities also meant they could be like the proverbial bull in the china closet. They were big, strong, barrel-chested animals that did not always realize their own strength. One owner would later tell me she once tied her male Lab to the frame of her garage door so he could be nearby while she washed the car in the driveway. The dog spotted a squirrel and lunged, pulling the large steel doorframe right out of the wall.

And then I came across a sentence that struck fear in my heart. "The parents may be one of the best indications of the future temperament of your new puppy. A surprising amount of behavior is inherited." My mind flashed back to the frothing, mud-caked banshee that came charging out of the woods, the night we picked out our puppy. *Oh my,* I thought. The book counseled to insist, whenever possible, on seeing both the dam and the sire. My mind flashed back again, this time to the breeder's ever-so slight hesitation when I asked where the father was. *Oh . . . he's around here somewhere.* And then the way she quickly changed the topic. It was all making sense. Dog buyers in the know would have demanded to meet the father. And what would they have found? A manic dervish tearing blindly through the night as if demons were close on his tail. I said a silent prayer that Marley had inherited his mother's disposition.

Individual genetics aside, purebred Labs all share certain predictable characteristics. The American Kennel Club sets standards for the qualities Labrador retrievers should possess. Physically, they are stocky and muscular, with short, dense, weather-resistant coats. Their fur can be black, chocolate brown, or a range of yellows, from light cream to a rich fox red. One of the Labrador retriever's main distinguishing characteristics is its thick, powerful tail, which resembles that of an otter and can clear a coffee table in one quick swipe. The head is large and blocky, with powerful jaws and high-set, floppy ears. Most Labs are about two feet tall in the withers, or top of the shoulders, and the typical male weighs sixty-five to eighty pounds, though some can weigh considerably more.

But looks, according to the AKC, are not all that make a Lab a Lab. The club's breed standard states: "True Labrador retriever temperament is as much a hallmark of the breed as the 'otter' tail. The ideal disposition is one of a kindly, outgoing, tractable nature, eager to please and non-aggressive towards man or animal. The Labrador has much that appeals to people. His gentle ways, intelligence and adaptability make him an ideal dog."

An ideal dog! Endorsements did not come much more glowing than that. The more I read, the better I felt about our decision. Even the caveats didn't scare me much. Jenny and I would naturally throw ourselves into our new dog, showering him with attention and affection. We were dedicated to taking as long as needed to properly train him in obedience and social skills. We were both enthusiastic walkers, hitting the waterfront trail nearly every evening after work, and many mornings, too. It would be just natural to bring our new dog along with us on our power walks. We'd tire the little rascal out. Jenny's office was only a mile away, and she came home every day for lunch, at which time she could toss balls to him in the backyard to let him burn off even more of this boundless energy we were warned about.

A week before we were to bring our dog home, Jenny's sister, Susan, called from Boston. She, her husband, and their two children planned to be at Disney World the following week; would Jenny like to drive up and spend a few days with them? A doting aunt who looked for any opportunity to bond with her niece and nephew, Jenny was dying to go. But she was torn. "I won't be here to bring little Marley home," she said.

"You go," I told her. "I'll get the dog and have him all settled in and waiting for you when you get back."

I tried to sound nonchalant, but secretly I was overjoyed at the prospect of having the new puppy all to myself for a few days of uninterrupted male bonding. He was to be our joint project, both of ours equally. But I never believed a dog could answer to two masters, and if there could be only one alpha leader in the household hierarchy, I wanted it to be me. This little three-day run would give me a head start.

A week later Jenny left for Orlando—a three-and-a-half-hour drive away. That evening after work, a Friday, I returned to the breeder's house to fetch the new addition to our lives. When Lori brought my new dog out from the back of the house, I gasped audibly. The tiny, fuzzy puppy we had picked out three weeks earlier had more than doubled in size. He came barreling at me and ran headfirst into my ankles, collapsing in a pile at my feet and rolling onto his back, paws in the air, in what I could only hope was a sign of supplication. Lori must have sensed my shock. "He's a growing boy, isn't he?" she said cheerily. "You should see him pack away the puppy chow!"

I leaned down, rubbed his belly, and said, "Ready to go home, Marley?" It was my first time using his new name for real, and it felt right.

In the car, I used beach towels to fashion a cozy nest for him on the passenger seat and set him down in it. But I was barely out of the driveway when he began squirming and wiggling his way out of the towels. He belly-crawled in my direction across the seat, whimpering as he advanced. At the center console, Marley met the first of the countless predicaments he would find himself in over the course of his life. There he was, hind legs hanging over the passenger side of the console and front legs hanging over the driver's side. In the middle, his stomach was firmly beached on the emergency brake. His little legs were going in all directions, clawing at the air. He wiggled and rocked and swayed, but he was grounded like a freighter on a sandbar. I reached over and ran my hand down his back, which only excited him more and brought on a new flurry of squiggling. His hind paws desperately sought purchase on the carpeted hump between the two seats. Slowly, he began working his hind quarters into the air, his butt rising up, up, up, tail furiously going, until the law of gravity finally kicked in. He slalomed headfirst down the other side of the console, somersaulting onto the floor at my feet and flipping onto his back. From there it was a quick, easy scramble up into my lap.

Man, was he happy—desperately happy. He quaked with joy as he burrowed his head into my stomach and nibbled the buttons of my shirt, his tail slapping the steering wheel like the needle on a metronome.

I quickly discovered I could affect the tempo of his wagging by simply touching him. When I had both hands on the wheel, the beat came at a steady three thumps per second. *Thump. Thump. Thump*. But all I needed to do was press one finger against the top of his head and the rhythm jumped from a waltz to a bossa nova. *Thump-thump-thump-thump-thump-thump!* Two fingers and it jumped up to a mambo. *Thump-thumpa-thump-thump-thumpa-thump!* And when I cupped my entire hand over his head and massaged my fingers into his scalp, the beat exploded into a machine-gun, rapid-fire samba. *Thumpthumpthumpthumpthumpthumpthumpthump!*

"Wow! You've got rhythm!" I told him. "You really are a reggae dog."

When we got home, I led him inside and unhooked his leash. He began sniffing and didn't stop until he had sniffed every square inch of the place. Then he sat back on his haunches and looked up at me with cocked head as if to say, *Great digs, but where are my brothers and sisters?*

The reality of his new life did not fully set in until bedtime. Before leaving to get him, I had set up his sleeping quarters in the one-car garage attached to the side of the house. We never parked there, using it more as a storage and utility room. The washer and dryer were out there, along with our ironing board. The room was dry and comfortable and had a rear door that led out into the fenced backyard. And with its concrete floor and walls, it was virtually indestructible. "Marley," I said cheerfully, leading him out there, "this is your room."

I had scattered chew toys around, laid newspapers down in the middle of the floor, filled a bowl with water, and made a bed out of a cardboard box lined with an old bedspread. "And here is where you'll be sleeping," I said, and lowered him into the box. He was used to such accommodations but had always shared them with his siblings. Now he paced the perimeter of the box and looked forlornly up at me. As a test, I stepped back into the house and closed the door. I stood and listened. At first nothing. Then a slight, barely audible whimper. And then full-fledged crying. It sounded like someone was in there torturing him.

I opened the door, and as soon as he saw me he stopped. I reached in and pet him for a couple of minutes, then left again. Standing on the other side of the door, I began to count. One, two, three . . . He made it seven seconds before the yips and cries began again. We repeated the exercise several times, all with the same result. I was tired and decided it was time for him to cry himself to sleep. I left the garage light on for him, closed the door, walked to the opposite side of the house, and crawled into bed. The concrete walls did little to muffle his pitiful cries. I lay there, trying to ignore them, figuring any minute now he would give up and go to sleep. The crying continued. Even after I wrapped my pillow around my head, I could still hear it. I thought of him out there alone for the first time in his life, in this strange environment without a single dog scent to be had anywhere. His mother was missing in action, and so were all his siblings. The poor little thing. How would I like it?

I hung on for another half hour before getting up and going to him. As soon as he spotted me, his face brightened and his tail began to beat the side of the box. It was as if he were saying, *Come on, hop in; there's plenty of room.*

Instead, I lifted the box with him in it and carried it into my bedroom, where I placed it on the floor tight against the side of the bed. I lay down on the very edge of the mattress, my arm dangling into the box. There, my hand resting on his side, feeling his rib cage rise and fall with his every breath, we both drifted off to sleep.

CHAPTER 4

Mr. Wiggles

For the next three days I threw myself with abandon into our new puppy. I lay on the floor with him and let him scamper all over me. I wrestled with him. I used an old hand towel to play tug-of-war with him—and was surprised at how strong he already was. He followed me everywhere—and tried to gnaw on anything he could get his teeth around. It took him just one day to discover the best thing about his new home: toilet paper. He disappeared into the bathroom and, five seconds later, came racing back out, the end of the toilet-paper roll clenched in his teeth, a paper ribbon unrolling behind him as he sprinted across the house. The place looked like it had been decorated for Halloween.

Every half hour or so I would lead him into the backyard to relieve himself. When he had accidents in the house, I scolded him. When he peed outside, I placed my cheek against his and praised him in my sweetest voice. And when he pooped outside, I carried on as though he had just delivered the winning Florida Lotto ticket.

When Jenny returned from Disney World, she threw herself into him with the same utter abandon. It was an amazing thing to behold. As the days unfolded I saw in my young wife a calm, gentle, nurturing side I had not known existed. She held him; she caressed him; she played with him; she fussed over him. She combed through every strand of his fur in search of fleas and ticks. She rose every couple of hours through the night—night after night—to take him outside for bathroom breaks. That more than anything was responsible for him becoming fully housebroken in just a few short weeks.

Mostly, she fed him.

Following the instructions on the bag, we gave Marley three large bowls of puppy chow a day. He wolfed down every morsel in a matter of seconds. What went in came out, of course, and soon our backyard was as inviting as a minefield. We didn't dare venture out into it without eyes sharply peeled. If Marley's appetite was huge, his droppings were huger still, giant mounds that looked virtually unchanged from what had earlier gone in the other end. Was he even digesting this stuff?

Apparently he was. Marley was growing at a furious pace. Like one of those amazing jungle vines that can cover a house in hours, he was expanding exponentially in all directions. Each day he was a little longer, a little wider, a little taller, a little heavier. He was twenty-one pounds when I brought him home and within weeks was up to fifty. His cute little puppy head that I so easily cradled in one hand as I drove him home that first night had rapidly morphed into something resembling the shape and heft of a blacksmith's anvil. His paws were enormous, his flanks already rippled with muscle, and his chest almost as broad as a bulldozer. Just as the books promised, his slip of a puppy tail was becoming as thick and powerful as an otter's.

What a tail it was. Every last object in our house that was at knee level or below was knocked asunder by Marley's wildly wagging weapon. He cleared coffee tables, scattered magazines, knocked framed photographs off shelves, sent beer bottles and wineglasses flying. He even cracked a pane in the French door. Gradually every item that was not bolted down migrated to higher ground safely above the sweep of his swinging mallet. Our friends with children would visit and marvel, "Your house is already baby-proofed!"

Marley didn't actually wag his tail. He more wagged his whole body, starting with the front shoulders and working backward. He was like the canine version of a Slinky. We swore there were no bones inside him, just one big, elastic muscle. Jenny began calling him Mr. Wiggles.

And at no time did he wiggle more than when he had something in his mouth. His reaction to any situation was the same: grab the nearest shoe or pillow or pencil—really, any item would do—and run with it. Some little voice in his head seemed to be whispering to him, "Go ahead! Pick it up! Drool all over it! Run!"

Some of the objects he grabbed were small enough to conceal, and this especially pleased him—he seemed to think he was getting away with something. But Marley would never have made it as a poker player. When he had something to hide, he could not mask his glee. He was always on the rambunctious side, but then there were those moments when he would explode into a manic sort of hyperdrive, as if some invisible prankster had just goosed him. His body would quiver, his head would bob from side to side, and his entire rear end would swing in a sort of spastic dance. We called it the Marley Mambo.

"All right, what have you got this time?" I'd say, and as I approached he would begin evasive action, waggling his way around the room, hips sashaying, head flailing up and down like a whinnying filly's, so overjoyed with his forbidden prize he could not contain himself. When I would finally get him cornered and pry open his jaws, I never came up empty-handed. Always there was something he had plucked out of the trash or off the floor or, as he got taller, right off the dining room table. Paper towels, wadded Kleenex, grocery receipts, wine corks, paper clips, chess pieces, bottle caps—it was like a salvage yard in there. One day I pried open his jaws and peered in to find my paycheck plastered to the roof of his mouth.

Within weeks, we had a hard time remembering what life had been like without our new boarder. Quickly, we fell into a routine. I started each morning, before the first cup of coffee, by taking him for a brisk walk down to the water and back. After breakfast and before my shower, I patrolled the backyard with a shovel, burying his land mines in the sand at the back of the lot. Jenny left for work before nine, and I seldom left the house before ten, first locking Marley out in the concrete bunker with a fresh bowl of water, a host of toys, and my cheery directive to "be a good boy, Marley." By twelve-thirty, Jenny was home on her lunch break, when she would give Marley his midday meal and throw him a ball in the backyard until he was tuckered out. In the early weeks, she also made a quick trip home in the middle of the afternoon to let him out. After dinner most evenings we walked together with him back down to the waterfront, where we would stroll along the Intracoastal as the yachts from Palm Beach idled by in the glow of the sunset.

Stroll is probably the wrong word. Marley strolled like a runaway locomotive strolls. He surged ahead, straining against his leash with everything he had, choking himself hoarse in the process. We yanked him back; he yanked us forward. We tugged; he pulled, coughing like a chain smoker from the collar strangling him. He veered left and right, darting to every mailbox and shrub, sniffing, panting, and peeing without fully stopping, usually getting more pee on himself than the intended target. He circled behind us, wrapping the leash around our ankles before lurching forward again, nearly tripping us. When someone approached with another dog, Marley would bolt at them joyously, rearing up on his hind legs when he reached the end of his leash, dying to make friends. "He sure seems to love life," one dog owner commented, and that about said it all.

He was still small enough that we could win these leash tug-of-wars, but with each week the balance of power was shifting. He was growing bigger and stronger. It was obvious that before long he would be more powerful than either of us. We knew we would need to rein him in and teach him to heel properly before he dragged us to humiliating deaths beneath the wheels of a passing car. Our friends who were veteran dog owners told us not to rush the obedience regimen. "It's too early," one of them advised. "Enjoy his puppyhood while you can. It'll be gone soon enough, and then you can get serious about training him."

That is what we did, which is not to say that we let him totally have his way. We set rules and tried to enforce them consistently. Beds and furniture were off-limits. Drinking from the toilet, sniffing crotches, and chewing chair legs were actionable offenses, though apparently worth suffering a scolding for. *No* became our favorite word. We worked with him on the basic commands—come, stay, sit, down— with limited success. Marley was young and wired, with the attention span of algae and the volatility of nitroglycerine. He was so excitable, any interaction at all would send him into a tizzy of bounce-off-the-walls, triple-espresso exuberance. We wouldn't realize it until years later, but he showed early signs of that condition that would later be coined to describe the behavior of thousands of hard-to-control, ants-in-their-pants schoolchildren. Our puppy had a textbook case of attention deficit hyperactivity disorder.

Still, for all his juvenile antics, Marley was serving an important role in our home and our relationship. Through his very helplessness, he was showing Jenny she could handle this maternal nurturing thing. He had been in her care for several weeks, and she hadn't killed him yet. Quite to the contrary, he was thriving. We joked that maybe we should start withholding food to stunt his growth and suppress his energy levels.

Jenny's transformation from coldhearted plant killer to

nurturing dog mom continued to amaze me. I think she amazed herself a little. She was a natural. One day Marley began gagging violently. Before I even fully registered that he was in trouble, Jenny was on her feet. She swooped in, pried his jaws open with one hand, and reached deep into his gullet with the other, pulling out a large, saliva-coated wad of cellophane. All in a day's work. Marley let out one last cough, banged his tail against the wall, and looked up at her with an expression that said, *Can we do it again?*

As we grew more comfortable with the new member of our family, we became more comfortable talking about expanding our family in other ways. Within weeks of bringing Marley home, we decided to stop using birth control. That's not to say we decided to get pregnant, which would have been way too bold a gesture for two people who had dedicated their lives to being as indecisive as possible. Rather, we backed into it, merely deciding to stop trying *not* to get pregnant. The logic was convoluted, we realized, but it somehow made us both feel better. No pressure. None at all. We weren't trying for a baby; we were just going to let whatever happened happen. Let nature take its course. *Que será, será* and all that.

Frankly, we were terrified. We had several sets of friends who had tried for months, years even, to conceive without luck and who had gradually taken their pitiful desperation public. At dinner parties they would talk obsessively about doctor's visits, sperm counts, and timed menstrual cycles, much to the discomfort of everyone else at the table. I mean, what were you supposed to say? "I think your sperm counts sound just fine!" It was almost too painful to bear. We were scared to death we would end up joining them.

Jenny had suffered several severe bouts of endometriosis before we were married and had undergone laparoscopic surgery to remove excess scar tissue from her fallopian tubes, none of which boded well for her fertility. Even more troubling was a little secret from our past. In those blindly passionate early days of our relationship, when desire had a stranglehold on anything resembling common sense, we had thrown caution into the corner with our clothes and had sex with reckless abandon, using no birth control whatsoever. Not just once but many times. It was incredibly dumb, and, looking back on it several years later, we should have been kissing the ground in gratitude for miraculously escaping an unwanted pregnancy. Instead, all either of us could think was, *What's wrong with us? No normal couple could possibly have done all that unprotected fornicating and gotten away with it.* We were both convinced conceiving was going to be no easy task.

So as our friends announced their plans to try to get pregnant, we remained silent. Jenny was simply going to stash her birth-control prescription away in the medicine cabinet and forget about it. If she ended up pregnant, fantastic. If she didn't, well, we weren't actually trying anyway, now, were we?

Winter in West Palm Beach is a glorious time of year, marked by crisp nights and warm, dry, sunny days. After the insufferably long, torpid summer, most of it spent in air-conditioning or hopping from one shade tree to the next in an attempt to dodge the blistering sun, winter was our time to celebrate the gentle side of the subtropics. We ate all our meals on the back porch, squeezed fresh orange juice from the fruit of the backyard tree each morning, tended a tiny herb garden and a few tomato plants along the side of the house, and picked saucer-sized hibiscus blooms to float in little bowls of water on the dining room table. At night we slept beneath open windows, the gardenia-scented air wafting in over us.

On one of those gorgeous days in late March, Jenny invited a friend from work to bring her basset hound, Buddy, over for a dog playdate. Buddy was a rescued pound dog with the saddest face I had ever seen. We let the two dogs loose in the backyard, and off they bounded. Old Buddy wasn't quite sure what to make of this hyperenergized yellow juvenile who raced and streaked and ran tight circles around him. But he took it in good humor, and the two of them romped and played together for more than an hour before they both collapsed in the shade of the mango tree, exhausted.

A few days later Marley started scratching and wouldn't stop. He was clawing so hard at himself, we were afraid he might draw blood. Jenny dropped to her knees and began one of her routine inspections, working her fingers through his coat, parting his fur as she went to see his skin below. After just a few seconds, she called out, "Damn it! Look at this." I peered over her shoulder at where she had parted Marley's fur just in time to see a small black dot dart back under cover. We laid him flat on the floor and began going through every inch of his fur. Marley was thrilled with the two-on-one attention and panted happily, his tail thumping the floor. Everywhere we looked we found them. Fleas! Swarms of them. They were between his toes and under his collar and burrowed inside his floppy ears. Even if they were slow enough to catch, which they were not, there were simply too many of them to even begin picking off.

We had heard about Florida's legendary flea and tick problems. With no hard freezes, not even any frosts, the bug populations were never knocked back, and they flourished in the warm, moist environment. This was a place where even the millionaires' mansions along the ocean in Palm Beach had cockroaches. Jenny was freaked out; her puppy was crawling with vermin. Of course, we blamed Buddy without having any solid proof. Jenny had images of not only the dog being infested but our entire home, too. She grabbed her car keys and ran out the door.

A half hour later she was back with a bag filled with enough chemicals to create our own Superfund site. There were flea baths and flea powders and flea sprays and flea foams and flea dips. There was a pesticide for the lawn, which the guy at the store told her we had to spray if we were to have any hope of bringing the little bastards to their knees. There was a special comb designed to remove insect eggs.

I reached into the bag and pulled out the receipt. "Jesus Christ, honey," I said. "We could have rented our own crop duster for this much."

My wife didn't care. She was back in assassin mode—this

time to protect her loved ones—and she meant business. She threw herself into the task with a vengeance. She scrubbed Marley in the laundry tub, using special soaps. She then mixed up the dip, which contained the same chemical, I noted, as the lawn insecticide, and poured it over him until every inch of him was saturated. As he was drying in the garage, smelling like a miniature Dow Chemical plant, Jenny vacuumed furiously—floors, walls, carpets, curtains, upholstery. And then she sprayed. And while she doused the inside with flea killer, I doused the outside with it. "You think we nailed the little buggers?" I asked when we were finally finished.

"I think we did," she said.

Our multipronged attack on the flea population of 345 Churchill Road was a roaring success. We checked Marley daily, peering between his toes, under his ears, beneath his tail, along his belly, and everywhere else we could reach. We could find no sign of a flea anywhere. We checked the carpets, the couches, the bottoms of the curtains, the grass—nothing. We had annihilated the enemy.

CHAPTER 5

The Test Strip

A few weeks later we were lying in bed reading when Jenny closed her book and said, "It's probably nothing."

"What's probably nothing," I said absently, not looking up from my book.

"My period's late."

She had my attention. "Your period? It is?" I turned to face her.

"That happens sometimes. But it's been over a week. And I've been feeling weird, too."

"Weird how?"

"Like I have a low-level stomach flu or something. I had one sip of wine at dinner the other night, and I thought I was going to throw up."

"That's not like you."

"Just the thought of alcohol makes me nauseous."

I wasn't going to mention it, but she also had been rather cranky lately.

"Do you think—" I began to ask.

"I don't know. Do you?"

"How am I supposed to know?"

"I almost didn't say anything," Jenny said. "Just in case—you know. I don't want to jinx us."

That's when I realized just how important this was to her— and to me, too. Somehow parenthood had snuck up on us; we were ready for a baby. We lay there side by side for a long while, saying nothing, looking straight ahead.

"We're never going to fall asleep," I finally said.

"The suspense is killing me," she admitted.

"Come on, get dressed," I said. "Let's go to the drugstore and get a home test kit."

We threw on shorts and T-shirts and opened the front door, Marley bounding out ahead of us, overjoyed at the prospect of a late-night car ride. He pranced on his hind legs by our tiny Toyota Tercel, hopping up and down, shaking, flinging saliva off his jowls, panting, absolutely beside himself with anticipation of the big moment when I would open the back door. "Geez, you'd think he was the father," I said. When I opened the door, he leaped into the backseat with such gusto that he sailed clear to the other side without touching down, not stopping until he cracked his head loudly, but apparently with no ill effect, against the far window.

The pharmacy was open till midnight, and I waited in the car with Marley while Jenny ran in. There are some things guys just are not meant to shop for, and home pregnancy tests come pretty close to the top of the list. The dog paced in the backseat, whining, his eyes locked on the front door of the pharmacy. As was his nature whenever he was excited, which was nearly every waking moment, he was panting, salivating heavily.

"Oh for God's sake, settle down," I told him. "What do you think she's going to do? Sneak out the back door on us?" He responded by shaking himself off in a great flurry, showering me in a spray of dog drool and loose hair. We had become used to Marley's car etiquette and always kept an emergency bath towel on the front seat, which I used to wipe down myself and the interior of the car. "Hang tight," I said. "I'm pretty sure she plans to return."

Five minutes later Jenny was back, a small bag in her hand. As we pulled out of the parking lot, Marley wedged his shoulders between the bucket seats of our tiny hatchback, balancing his front paws on the center console, his nose touching the rearview mirror. Every turn we made sent him crashing down, chest first, against the emergency brake. And after each spill, unfazed and happier than ever, he would teeter back up on his perch.

A few minutes later we were back home in the bathroom with the $8.99 kit spread out on the side of the sink. I read the directions aloud. "Okay," I said. "It says it's accurate ninety-nine percent of the time. First thing you have to do is pee in this cup." The next step was to dip a skinny plastic test strip into the urine and then into a small vial of a solution that came with the kit. "Wait five minutes," I said. "Then we put it in the second solution for fifteen minutes. If it turns blue, you're officially knocked up, baby!"

We timed off the first five minutes. Then Jenny dropped the strip into the second vial and said, "I can't stand here watching it."

We went out into the living room and made small talk, pretending we were waiting for something of no more significance than the tea kettle to boil. "So how about them Dolphins," I quipped. But my heart was pounding wildly, and a feeling of nervous dread was rising from my stomach. If the test came back positive, whoa, our lives were about to change forever. If it came back negative, Jenny would be crushed. It was beginning to dawn on me that I might be, too. An eternity later, the timer rang. "Here we go," I said. "Either way, you know I love you."

I went to the bathroom and fished the test strip out of the vial. No doubt about it, it was blue. As blue as the deepest ocean. A dark, rich, navy-blazer blue. A blue that could be confused with no other shade. "Congratulations, honey," I said.

"Oh my God" is all she could answer, and she threw herself into my arms.

As we stood there by the sink, arms around each other, eyes closed, I gradually became aware of a commotion at our feet. I looked down and there was Marley, wiggling, head bobbing, tail banging the linen-closet door so hard I thought he might dent it. When I reached down to pet him, he dodged away. Uh-oh. It was the Marley Mambo, and that could mean just one thing.

"What do you have this time?" I said, and began chasing him. He loped into the living room, weaving just out of my reach. When I finally cornered him and pried open his jaws, at first I saw nothing. Then far back on his tongue, on the brink of no return, ready to slip down the hatch, I spotted something. It was skinny and long and flat. And as blue as the deepest ocean. I reached in and pulled out our positive test strip. "Sorry to disappoint you, pal," I said, "but this is going in the scrapbook."

Jenny and I started laughing and kept laughing for a long time. We had great fun speculating on what was going through that big blocky head of his. *Hmmm, if I destroy the evidence, maybe they'll forget all about this unfortunate episode, and I won't have to share my castle with an interloper after all.*

Then Jenny grabbed Marley by the front paws, lifted him up on his hind legs and danced around the room with him. "You're going to be an uncle!" she sang. Marley responded in his trademark way—by lunging up and planting a big wet tongue squarely on her mouth.

The next day Jenny called me at work. Her voice was bubbling. She had just returned from the doctor, who had officially confirmed the results of our home test. "He says all systems are go," she said.

The night before, we had counted back on the calendar, trying to pinpoint the date of conception. She was worried that she had already been pregnant when we went on our hysterical flea-eradication spree a few weeks earlier. Exposing herself to all those pesticides couldn't be good, could it? She raised her concerns with the doctor, and he told her it was probably not an issue. Just don't use them anymore, he advised. He gave her a prescription for prenatal vitamins and told her he'd see her back in his office in three weeks for a sonogram, an electronic-imaging process that would give us our first glimpse of the tiny fetus growing inside Jenny's belly.

"He wants us to make sure we bring a videotape," she said, "so we can save our own copy for posterity."

On my desk calendar, I made a note of it.

CHAPTER 6

Matters of the Heart

The natives will tell you South Florida has four seasons. Subtle ones, they admit, but four distinct seasons nonetheless. Do not believe them. There are only two—the warm, dry season and the hot, wet one. It was about the time of this overnight return to tropical swelter when we awoke one day to realize our puppy was a puppy no more. As rapidly as winter had morphed into summer, it seemed, Marley had morphed into a gangly adolescent. At five months old, his body had filled out the baggy wrinkles in its oversized yellow fur coat. His enormous paws no longer looked so comically out of proportion. His needle-sharp baby teeth had given way to imposing fangs that could destroy a Frisbee—or a brand-new leather shoe—in a few quick chomps. The timbre of his bark had deepened to an intimidating boom. When he stood on his hindlegs, which he did often, tottering around like a dancing Russian circus bear, he could rest his front paws on my shoulders and look me straight in the eye.

The first time the veterinarian saw him, he let out a soft

whistle and said, "You're going to have a big boy on your hands."

And that we did. He had grown into a handsome specimen, and I felt obliged to point out to the doubting Miss Jenny that my formal name for him was not so far off the mark. Grogan's Majestic Marley of Churchill, besides residing on Churchill Road, was the very definition of majestic. When he stopped chasing his tail, anyway. Sometimes, after he ran every last ounce of nervous energy out of himself, he would lie on the Persian rug in the living room, basking in the sun slanting through the blinds. His head up, nose glistening, paws crossed before him, he reminded us of an Egyptian sphinx.

We were not the only ones to notice the transformation. We could tell from the wide berth strangers gave him and the way they recoiled when he bounded their way that they no longer viewed him as a harmless puppy. To them he had grown into something to be feared.

Our front door had a small oblong window at eye level, four inches wide by eight inches long. Marley lived for company, and whenever someone rang the bell, he would streak across the house, going into a full skid as he approached the foyer, careening across the wood floors, tossing up throw rugs as he slid and not stopping until he crashed into the door with a loud thud. He then would hop up on his hind legs, yelping wildly, his big head filling the tiny window to stare straight into the face of whoever was on the other side. For Marley, who considered himself the resident Welcome Wagon, it was a joyous overture. For door-to-door sales people, postal carriers, and anyone else who didn't know him, though, it was as if Cujo had just jumped out of the Stephen King novel and the only thing that stood between them and a merciless mauling was our wooden door. More than one stranger, after ringing the doorbell and seeing Marley's barking face peering out at them, beat a quick retreat to the middle of the driveway, where they stood waiting for one of us to answer.

This, we found, was not necessarily a bad thing.

Ours was what urban planners call a changing neighborhood. Built in the 1940s and '50s and initially populated by snowbirds and retirees, it began to take on a gritty edge as the original homeowners died off and were replaced by a motley group of renters and working-class families. By the time we moved in, the neighborhood was again in transition, this time being gentrified by gays, artists, and young professionals drawn to its location near the water and its funky, Deco-style architecture.

Our block served as a buffer between hard-bitten South Dixie Highway and the posh estate homes along the water. Dixie Highway was the original U.S. 1 that ran along Florida's eastern coast and served as the main route to Miami before the arrival of the interstate. It was five lanes of sun-baked pavement, two in each direction with a shared left-turn lane, and it was lined with a slightly decayed and unseemly assortment of thrift stores, gas stations, fruit stands, consignment shops, diners, and mom-and-pop motels from a bygone era.

On the four corners of South Dixie Highway and Churchill Road stood a liquor store, a twenty-four-hour convenience mart, an import shop with heavy bars on the window, and an open-air coin laundry where people hung out all night, often leaving bottles in brown bags behind. Our house was in the middle of the block, eight doors down from the action.

The neighborhood seemed safe to us, but there were telltales of its rough edge. Tools left out in the yard disappeared, and during a rare cold spell, someone stole every stick of firewood I had stacked along the side of the house. One Sunday we were eating breakfast at our favorite diner, sitting at the table we always sat at, right in the front window, when Jenny pointed to a bullet hole in the plate glass just above our heads and noted dryly, "That definitely wasn't there last time we were here."

One morning as I was pulling out of our block to drive to work, I spotted a man lying in the gutter, his hands and face bloody. I parked and ran up to him, thinking he had been hit by a car. But when I squatted down beside him, a strong stench of alcohol and urine hit me, and when he began to talk, it was clear he was inebriated. I called an ambulance and waited with him, but when the crew arrived he refused treatment. As the paramedics and I stood watching, he staggered away in the direction of the liquor store.

And there was the night a man with a slightly desperate air about him came to my door and told me he was visiting a house in the next block and had run out of gas for his car. Could I lend him five dollars? He'd pay me back first thing in the morning. *Sure you will, pal*, I thought. When I offered to call the police for him instead, he mumbled a lame excuse and disappeared.

Most unsettling of all was what we learned about the small

house kitty-corner from ours. A murder had taken place there just a few months before we moved in. And not just a run-of-the-mill murder, but a horribly gruesome one involving an invalid widow and a chain saw. The case had been all over the news, and before we moved in we were well familiar with its details—everything, that is, except the location. And now here we were living across the street from the crime scene.

The victim was a retired school teacher named Ruth Ann Nedermier, who had lived in the house alone and was one of the original settlers of the neighborhood. After hip-replacement surgery, she had hired a day nurse to help care for her, which was a fatal decision. The nurse, police later ascertained, had been stealing checks out of Mrs. Nedermier's checkbook and forging her signature.

The old woman had been frail but mentally sharp, and she confronted the nurse about the missing checks and the unexplained charges to her bank account. The panicked nurse bludgeoned the poor woman to death, then called her boyfriend, who arrived with a chain saw and helped her dismember the body in the bathtub. Together they packed the body parts in a large trunk, rinsed the woman's blood down the drain, and drove away.

For several days, Mrs. Nedermier's disappearance remained a mystery, our neighbors later told us. The mystery was solved when a man called the police to report a horrible stench coming from his garage. Officers discovered the trunk and its ghastly contents. When they asked the homeowner how it got there, he told them the truth: his daughter had asked if she could store it there for safekeeping.

Although the grisly murder of Mrs. Nedermier was the most-talked-about event in the history of our block, no one had mentioned a word about it to us as we prepared to buy the house. Not the real estate agent, not the owners, not the inspector, not the surveyor. Our first week in the house, the neighbors came over with cookies and a casserole and broke the news to us. As we lay in our bed at night, it was hard not to think that just a hundred feet from our bedroom window a defenseless widow had been sawn into pieces. It was an inside job, we told ourselves, something that would never happen to us. Yet we couldn't walk by the place or even look out our front window without thinking about what had happened there.

Somehow, having Marley aboard with us, and seeing how strangers eyed him so warily, gave us a sense of peace we might not have had otherwise. He was a big, loving dope of a dog whose defense strategy against intruders would surely have been to lick them to death. But the prowlers and predators out there didn't need to know that. To them he was big, he was powerful, and he was unpredictably crazy. And that is how we liked it.

Pregnancy suited Jenny well. She began rising at dawn to exercise and walk Marley. She prepared wholesome, healthy meals, loaded with fresh vegetables and fruits. She swore off caffeine and diet sodas and, of course, all alcohol, not even allowing me to stir a tablespoon of cooking sherry into the pot.

We had sworn to keep the pregnancy a secret until we

were confident the fetus was viable and beyond the risk of miscarriage, but on this front neither of us did well. We were so excited that we dribbled out our news to one confidant after another, swearing each to silence, until our secret was no longer a secret at all. First we told our parents, then our siblings, then our closest friends, then our office mates, then our neighbors. Jenny's stomach, at ten weeks, was just starting to round slightly. It was beginning to seem real. Why not share our joy with the world? By the time the day arrived for Jenny's examination and sonogram, we might as well have plastered it on a billboard: John and Jenny are expecting.

I took off work the morning of the doctor's appointment and, as instructed, brought a blank videotape so I could capture the first grainy images of our baby. The appointment was to be part checkup, part informational meeting. We would be assigned to a nurse-midwife who could answer all our questions, measure Jenny's stomach, listen for the baby's heartbeat, and, of course, show us its tiny form inside of her.

We arrived at 9:00 A.M., brimming with anticipation. The nurse-midwife, a gentle middle-aged woman with a British accent, led us into a small exam room and immediately asked: "Would you like to hear your baby's heartbeat?" Would we ever, we told her. We listened intently as she ran a sort of microphone hooked to a speaker over Jenny's abdomen. We sat in silence, smiles frozen on our faces, straining to hear the tiny heartbeat, but only static came through the speaker.

The nurse said that was not unusual. "It depends on how

the baby is lying. Sometimes you can't hear anything. It might still be a little early." She offered to go right to the sonogram. "Let's have a look at your baby," she said breezily.

"Our first glimpse of baby Grogie," Jenny said, beaming at me. The nurse-midwife led us into the sonogram room and had Jenny lie back on a table with a monitor screen beside it.

"I brought a tape," I said, waving it in front of her.

"Just hold on to it for now," the nurse said as she pulled up Jenny's shirt and began running an instrument the size and shape of a hockey puck over her stomach. We peered at the computer monitor at a gray mass without definition. "Hmm, this one doesn't seem to be picking anything up," she said in a completely neutral voice. "We'll try a vaginal sonogram. You get much more detail that way."

She left the room and returned moments later with another nurse, a tall bleached blonde with a monogram on her fingernail. Her name was Essie, and she asked Jenny to remove her panties, then inserted a latex-covered probe into her vagina. The nurse was right: the resolution was far superior to that of the other sonogram. She zoomed in on what looked like a tiny sac in the middle of the sea of gray and, with the click of a mouse, magnified it, then magnified it again. And again. But despite the great detail, the sac just looked like an empty, shapeless sock to us. Where were the little arms and legs the pregnancy books said would be formed by ten weeks? Where was the tiny head? Where was the beating heart? Jenny, her neck craned sideways to see the screen, was still brimming with anticipation and asked the nurses with a little nervous laugh, "Is there anything in there?"

I looked up to catch Essie's face, and I knew the answer was the one we did not want to hear. Suddenly I realized why she hadn't been saying anything as she kept clicking up the magnification. She answered Jenny in a controlled voice: "Not what you'd expect to see at ten weeks." I put my hand on Jenny's knee. We both continued staring at the blob on the screen, as though we could will it to life.

"Jenny, I think we have a problem here," Essie said. "Let me get Dr. Sherman."

As we waited in silence, I learned what people mean when they describe the swarm of locusts that descends just before they faint. I felt the blood rushing out of my head and heard buzzing in my ears. *If I don't sit down,* I thought, *I'm going to collapse.* How embarrassing would that be? My strong wife bearing the news stoically as her husband lay unconscious on the floor, the nurses trying to revive him with smelling salts. I half sat on the edge of the examining bench, holding Jenny's hand with one of mine and stroking her neck with the other. Tears welled in her eyes, but she didn't cry.

Dr. Sherman, a tall, distinguished-looking man with a gruff but affable demeanor, confirmed that the fetus was dead. "We'd be able to see a heartbeat, no question," he said. He gently told us what we already knew from the books we had been reading. That one in six pregnancies ends in miscarriage. That this was nature's way of sorting out the weak, the retarded, the grossly deformed. Apparently remembering Jenny's worry about the flea sprays, he told us it was nothing we did or did not do. He placed his hand on Jenny's cheek and leaned in close as if to kiss her. "I'm sorry," he said. "You can try again in a couple of months."

We both just sat there in silence. The blank videotape sitting on the bench beside us suddenly seemed like an incredible embarrassment, a sharp reminder of our blind, naïve optimism. I wanted to throw it away. I wanted to hide it. I asked the doctor: "Where do we go from here?"

"We have to remove the placenta," he said. "Years ago, you wouldn't have even known you had miscarried yet, and you would have waited until you started hemorrhaging."

He gave us the option of waiting over the weekend and returning on Monday for the procedure, which was the same as an abortion, with the fetus and placenta being vacuumed from the uterus. But Jenny wanted to get it behind her, and so did I. "The sooner the better," she said.

"Okay then," Dr. Sherman said. He gave her something to force her to dilate and was gone. Down the hall we could hear him enter another exam room and boisterously greet an expectant mother with jolly banter.

Alone in the room, Jenny and I fell heavily into each other's arms and stayed that way until a light knock came at the door. It was an older woman we had never seen before. She carried a sheaf of papers. "I'm sorry, sweetie," she said to Jenny. "I'm so sorry." And then she showed her where to sign the waiver acknowledging the risks of uterine suction.

When Dr. Sherman returned he was all business. He injected Jenny first with Valium and then Demerol, and the procedure was quick if not painless. He was finished before the drugs seemed to fully kick in. When it was over, she lay nearly unconscious as the sedatives took their full effect. "Just make sure she doesn't stop breathing," the doctor said, and he walked out of the room. I couldn't believe it. Wasn't it his job to make sure she didn't stop breathing? The waiver she signed never said "Patient could stop breathing at any time due to overdose of barbiturates." I did as I was told, talking to her in a loud voice, rubbing her arm, lightly slapping her cheek, saying things like, "Hey, Jenny! What's my name?" She was dead to the world.

After several minutes Essie stuck her head in to check on us. She caught one glimpse of Jenny's gray face and wheeled out of the room and back in again a moment later with a wet washcloth and smelling salts, which she held under Jenny's nose for what seemed forever before Jenny began to stir, and then only briefly. I kept talking to her in a loud voice, telling her to breathe deeply so I could feel it on my hand. Her skin was ashen; I found her pulse: sixty beats per minute. I nervously dabbed the wet cloth across her forehead, cheeks, and neck. Eventually, she came around, though she was still extremely groggy. "You had me worried," I said. She just looked blankly at me as if trying to ascertain why I might be worried. Then she drifted off again.

A half hour later the nurse helped dress her, and I walked her out of the office with these orders: for the next two weeks, no baths, no swimming, no douches, no tampons, no sex.

In the car, Jenny maintained a detached silence, pressing herself against the passenger door, gazing out the window. Her eyes were red but she would not cry. I searched for comforting words without success. Really, what could be said? We had lost our baby. Yes, I could tell her we could try again. I could tell her that many couples go through the same thing. But she didn't want to hear it, and I didn't want to say it. Someday we would be able to see it all in perspective. But not today.

I took the scenic route home, winding along Flagler Drive, which hugs West Palm Beach's waterfront from the north end of town, where the doctor's office was, to the south end, where we lived. The sun glinted off the water; the palm trees swayed gently beneath the cloudless blue sky. It was a day meant for joy, not for us. We drove home in silence.

When we arrived at the house, I helped Jenny inside and onto the couch, then went into the garage where Marley, as always, awaited our return with breathless anticipation. As soon as he saw me, he dove for his oversized rawhide bone and proudly paraded it around the room, his body wagging, tail whacking the washing machine like a mallet on a kettledrum. He begged me to try to snatch it from him.

"Not today, pal," I said, and let him out the back door into the yard. He took a long pee against the loquat tree and then came barreling back inside, took a deep drink from his bowl, water sloshing everywhere, and careened down the hall, searching for Jenny. It took me just a few seconds to lock the back door, mop up the water he had spilled, and follow him into the living room.

When I turned the corner, I stopped short. I would have bet a week's pay that what I was looking at couldn't possibly happen. Our rambunctious, wired dog stood with his shoulders between Jenny's knees, his big, blocky head resting quietly in her lap. His tail hung flat between his legs, the first time I could remember it not wagging whenever he was touching one of us. His eyes were turned up at her, and he whimpered softly. She stroked his head a few times and then, with no warning, buried her face in the thick fur of his neck and began sobbing. Hard, unrestrained, from-the-gut sobbing.

They stayed like that for a long time, Marley statue-still, Jenny clutching him to her like an oversized doll. I stood off to the side feeling like a voyeur intruding on this private moment, not quite knowing what to do with myself. And then, without lifting her face, she raised one arm up toward me, and I joined her on the couch and wrapped my arms around her. There the three of us stayed, locked in our embrace of shared grief.

CHAPTER 7

Master and Beast

✳

The next morning, a Saturday, I awoke at dawn to find Jenny lying on her side with her back to me, weeping softly. Marley was awake, too, his chin resting on the mattress, once again commiserating with his mistress. I got up and made coffee, squeezed fresh orange juice, brought in the newspaper, made toast. When Jenny came out in her robe several minutes later, her eyes were dry and she gave me a brave smile as if to say she was okay now.

After breakfast, we decided to get out of the house and walk Marley down to the water for a swim. A large concrete breakwater and mounds of boulders lined the shore in our neighborhood, making the water inaccessible. But if you walked a half dozen blocks to the south, the breakwater curved inland, exposing a small white sand beach littered with driftwood—a perfect place for a dog to frolic. When we reached the little beach, I wagged a stick in front of Marley's face and unleashed him. He stared at the stick as a starving man would stare at a loaf of bread, his eyes never leaving the prize. "Go get it!" I shouted, and hurled the stick as far out into the water as I could. He cleared the concrete wall in one spectacular leap, galloped down the beach and out into the shallow water, sending up plumes of spray around him. This is what Labrador retrievers were born to do. It was in their genes and in their job description.

No one is certain where Labrador retrievers originated, but this much is known for sure: it was not in Labrador. These muscular, short-haired water dogs first surfaced in the 1600s a few hundred miles to the south of Labrador, in Newfoundland. There, early diarists observed, the local fishermen took the dogs to sea with them in their dories, putting them to good use hauling in lines and nets and fetching fish that came off the hooks. The dogs' dense, oily coats made them impervious to the icy waters, and their swimming prowess, boundless energy, and ability to cradle fish gently in their jaws without damaging the flesh made them ideal work dogs for the tough North Atlantic conditions.

How the dogs came to be in Newfoundland is anyone's guess. They were not indigenous to the island, and there is no evidence that early Eskimos who first settled the area brought dogs with them. The best theory is that early ancestors of the retrievers were brought to Newfoundland by fishermen from Europe and Britain, many of whom jumped ship and settled on the coast, establishing communities. From there, what is now known as the Labrador retriever may have evolved through unintentional, willy-nilly cross-breeding. It likely shares common ancestry with the larger and shaggier Newfoundland breed.

However they came to be, the amazing retrievers soon were pressed into duty by island hunters to fetch game birds and waterfowl. In 1662, a native of St. John's, Newfoundland, named W. E. Cormack journeyed on foot across the island and noted the abundance of the local water dogs, which he found to be "admirably trained as retrievers in fowling and . . . otherwise useful." The British gentry eventually took notice and by the early nineteenth century were importing the dogs to England for use by sportsmen in pursuit of pheasant, grouse, and partridges.

According to the Labrador Retriever Club, a national hobbyist group formed in 1931 and dedicated to preserving the integrity of the breed, the name Labrador retriever came about quite inadvertently sometime in the 1830s when the apparently geographically challenged third earl of Malmesbury wrote to the sixth duke of Buccleuch to gush about his fine line of sporting retrievers. "We always call mine Labrador dogs," he wrote. From that point forward, the name stuck. The good earl noted that he went to great lengths to keep "the breed as pure as I could from the first." But others were less religious about genetics, freely crossing Labradors with other retrievers in hopes that their excellent qualities would transfer. The Labrador genes proved indomitable, and the Labrador retriever line remained distinct, winning recognition by the Kennel Club of England as a breed all its own on July 7, 1903.

B. W. Ziessow, an enthusiast and longtime breeder, wrote for the Labrador Retriever Club: "The American sportsmen adopted the breed from England and subsequently developed and trained the dog to fulfill the hunting needs of this country. Today, as in the past, the Labrador will eagerly enter ice cold water in Minnesota to retrieve a shot bird; he'll work all day hunting doves in the heat of the Southwest—his only reward is a pat for a job well done."

This was Marley's proud heritage, and it appeared he had inherited at least half of the instinct. He was a master at pursuing his prey. It was the concept of returning it that he did not seem to quite grasp. His general attitude seemed to be, *If you want the stick back that bad, YOU jump in the water for it.*

He came charging back up onto the beach with his prize in his teeth. "Bring it here!" I yelled, slapping my hands together. "C'mon, boy, give it to me!" He pranced over, his whole body wagging with excitement, and promptly shook water and sand all over me. Then to my surprise he dropped the stick at my feet. *Wow,* I thought. *How's that for service?* I looked back at Jenny, sitting on a bench beneath an Australian pine, and gave her a thumbs-up. But when I reached down to pick up the stick, Marley was ready. He dove in, grabbed it, and raced across the beach in crazy figure-eights. He swerved back, nearly colliding with me, taunting me to chase him. I made a few lunges at him, but it was clear he had both speed and agility on his side. "You're supposed to be a Labrador retriever!" I shouted. "Not a Labrador evader!"

But what I had that my dog didn't was an evolved brain that at least slightly exceeded my brawn. I grabbed a second stick and made a tremendous fuss over it. I held it over my head and tossed it from hand to hand. I swung it from side to side. I could see Marley's resolve softening. Suddenly, the stick in his mouth, just moments earlier the most prized possession he could imagine on earth, had lost its cachet. My stick drew him in like a temptress. He crept closer and closer until he was just inches in front of me. "Oh, a sucker is born every day, isn't he, Marley?" I cackled, rubbing the stick across his snout and watching as he went cross-eyed trying to keep it in his sights.

I could see the little cogs going in his head as he tried to figure out how he could grab the new stick without relinquishing the old one. His upper lip quivered as he tested the concept of making a quick two-for-one grab. Soon I had my free hand firmly around the end of the stick in his mouth. I tugged and he tugged back, growling. I pressed the second stick against his nostrils. "You know you want it," I whispered. And did he ever; the temptation was too much to bear. I could feel his grip loosening. And then he made his move. He opened his jaws to try to grab the second stick without losing the first. In a heartbeat, I whipped both sticks high above my head. He leaped in the air, barking and spinning, obviously at a loss as to how such a carefully laid battle strategy could have gone so badly awry. "This is why I am the master and you are the beast," I told him. And with that he shook more water and sand in my face.

I threw one of the sticks out into the water and he raced after it, yelping madly as he went. He returned a new, wiser opponent. This time he was cautious and refused to come anywhere near me. He stood about ten yards away, stick in mouth, eying the new object of his desire, which just happened to be the old object of his desire, his first stick, now perched high above my head. I could see the cogs moving again. He was thinking, *This time I'll just wait right here until he throws it, and then he'll have no sticks and I'll have both sticks.* "You think I'm really dumb, don't you, dog," I said. I heaved back and with a great, exaggerated groan hurled the stick with all my might. Sure enough, Marley roared into the water with his stick still locked in his teeth. The only thing was, I hadn't let go of mine. Do you think Marley figured that out? He swam halfway to Palm Beach before catching on that the stick was still in my hand.

"You're cruel!" Jenny yelled down from her bench, and I looked back to see she was laughing.

When Marley finally got back onshore, he plopped down in the sand, exhausted but not about to give up his stick. I showed him mine, reminding him how far superior it was to his, and ordered, "Drop it!" I cocked my arm back as if to throw, and the dummy bolted back to his feet and began heading for the water again. "Drop it!" I repeated when he returned. It took several tries, but finally he did just that. And the instant his stick hit the sand, I launched mine into the air for him. We did it over and over, and each time he seemed to understand the concept a little more clearly. Slowly the lesson was sinking into that thick skull of his. If he returned his stick to me, I would throw a new one for him. "It's like an office gift exchange," I told him. "You've got to give to get." He leaped up and smashed his sandy mouth against mine, which I took to be an acknowledgment of a lesson learned.

As Jenny and I walked home, the tuckered Marley for once did not strain against his leash. I beamed with pride at what we had accomplished. For weeks Jenny and I had been working to teach him some basic social skills and manners, but progress had been painfully slow. It was like we were living with a wild stallion—and trying to teach it to sip tea from fine porcelain. Some days I felt like Anne Sullivan to Marley's Helen Keller. I thought back to Saint Shaun and how quickly I, a mere ten-year-old boy, had been able to teach him all he needed to know to be a great dog. I wondered what I was doing wrong this time.

But our little fetching exercise offered a glimmer of hope. "You know," I said to Jenny, "I really think he's starting to get it."

She looked down at him, plodding along beside us. He was soaking wet and coated in sand, spittle foaming on his lips, his hard-won stick still clenched in his jaws. "I wouldn't be so sure of that," she said.

The next morning I again awoke before dawn to the sounds of Jenny softly sobbing beside me. "Hey," I said, and wrapped my arms around her. She nestled her face against my chest, and I could feel her tears soaking through my T-shirt.

"I'm fine," she said. "Really. I'm just—you know."

I did know. I was trying to be the brave soldier, but I felt it, too, the dull sense of loss and failure. It was odd. Less than forty-eight hours earlier we had been bubbling with anticipation over our new baby. And now it was as if there had never been a pregnancy at all. As if the whole episode was just a dream from which we were having trouble waking.

Later that day I took Marley with me in the car to pick up a few groceries and some things Jenny needed at the pharmacy. On the way back, I stopped at a florist shop and bought a giant bouquet of spring flowers arranged in a vase, hoping they would cheer her up. I strapped them into the seat belt in the backseat beside Marley so they wouldn't spill. As we passed the pet shop, I made the split-second decision that Marley deserved a pick-me-up, too. After all, he had done a better job than I at comforting the inconsolable woman in our lives. "Be a good boy!" I said. "I'll be right back." I ran into the store just long enough to buy an oversized rawhide chew for him.

When we got home a few minutes later, Jenny came out to meet us, and Marley tumbled out of the car to greet her. "We have a little surprise for you," I said. But when I reached in the backseat for the flowers, the surprise was on me. The bouquet was a mix of white daisies, yellow mums, assorted lilies, and bright red carnations. Now, however, the carnations were nowhere to be found. I looked more closely and found the decapitated stems that minutes earlier had held blossoms. Nothing else in the bouquet was disturbed. I glared at Marley and he was dancing around like he was auditioning for *Soul Train*. "Get over here!" I yelled, and when I finally caught him and pried open his jaws, I found the incontrovertible evidence of his guilt. Deep in his cavernous mouth, tucked up in one jowl like a wad of chewing tobacco, was a single red carnation. The others presumably were already down the hatch. I was ready to murder him.

I looked up at Jenny and tears were streaming down her cheeks. But this time, they were tears of laughter. She could not have been more amused had I flown in a mariachi band for a private serenade. There was nothing left for me to do but laugh, too.

"That dog," I muttered.

"I've never been crazy about carnations anyway," she said.

Marley was so thrilled to see everyone happy and laughing again that he jumped up on his hind legs and did a break dance for us.

The next morning, I awoke to bright sun dappling through the branches of the Brazilian pepper tree and across the bed. I glanced at the clock; it was nearly eight. I looked over at my wife sleeping peacefully, her chest rising and falling with long, slow breaths. I kissed her hair, draped an arm across her waist, and closed my eyes again.

CHAPTER 8

A Battle of Wills

When Marley was not quite six months old, we signed him up for obedience classes. God knew he needed it. Despite his stick-fetching breakthrough on the beach that day, he was proving himself a challenging student, dense, wild, constantly distracted, a victim of his boundless nervous energy. We were beginning to figure out that he wasn't like other dogs. As my father put it shortly after Marley attempted marital relations with his knee, "That dog's got a screw loose." We needed professional help.

Our veterinarian told us about a local dog-training club that offered basic obedience classes on Tuesday nights in the parking lot behind the armory. The teachers were unpaid volunteers from the club, serious amateurs who presumably had already taken their own dogs to the heights of advanced behavior modification. The course ran eight lessons and cost fifty dollars, which we thought was a bargain, especially considering that Marley could destroy fifty dollars' worth of shoes in thirty seconds. And the club all but guaranteed we'd be marching home after graduation with the next great Lassie. At registration we met the woman who would be teaching our class. She was a stern, no-nonsense dog trainer who subscribed to the theory that there are no incorrigible dogs, just weak-willed and hapless owners.

The first lesson seemed to prove her point. Before we were fully out of the car, Marley spotted the other dogs gathering with their owners across the tarmac. A party! He leaped over us and out of the car and was off in a tear, his leash dragging behind him. He darted from one dog to the next, sniffing private parts, dribbling pee, and flinging huge wads of spit through the air. For Marley it was a festival of smells—so many genitals, so little time—and he was seizing the moment, being careful to stay just ahead of me as I raced after him. Each time I was nearly upon him, he would scoot a few feet farther away. I finally got within striking distance and took a giant leap, landing hard with both feet on his leash. This brought him to a jolting halt so abrupt that for a moment I thought I might have broken his neck. He jerked backward, landed on his back, flipped around, and gazed up at me with the serene expression of a heroin addict who had just gotten his fix.

Meanwhile, the instructor was staring at us with a look that could not have been more withering had I decided to throw off my clothes and dance naked right there on the blacktop. "Take your place, please," she said curtly, and when she saw both Jenny and me tugging Marley into position, she added: "You are going to have to decide which of you is going to be trainer." I started to explain that we both wanted to participate so each of us could work with him at home, but she cut me off. "A dog," she said definitively, "can only answer to one master." I began to protest, but she silenced me with that glare of hers—I suppose the same glare she used to intimidate her dogs into submission—and I slinked off to the sidelines with my tail between my legs, leaving Master Jenny in command.

This was probably a mistake. Marley was already considerably stronger than Jenny and knew it. Miss Dominatrix was only a few sentences into her introduction on the importance of establishing dominance over our pets when Marley decided the standard poodle on the opposite side of the class deserved a closer look. He lunged off with Jenny in tow.

All the other dogs were sitting placidly beside their masters at tidy ten-foot intervals, awaiting further instructions. Jenny was fighting valiantly to plant her feet and bring Marley to a halt, but he lumbered on unimpeded, tugging her across the parking lot in pursuit of hot-poodle butt-sniffing action. My wife looked amazingly like a water-skier being towed behind a powerboat. Everyone stared. Some snickered. I covered my eyes.

Marley wasn't one for formal introductions. He crashed into the poodle and immediately crammed his nose between her legs. I imagined it was the canine male's way of asking, "So, do you come here often?"

After Marley had given the poodle a full gynecological examination, Jenny was able to drag him back into place. Miss Dominatrix announced calmly, "That, class, is an example of a dog that has been allowed to think he is the alpha male of his pack. Right now, he's in charge." As if to drive home the point, Marley attacked his tail, spinning wildly, his jaws snapping at thin air, and in the process he wrapped the leash around Jenny's ankles until she was fully immobilized. I winced for her, and gave thanks that it wasn't me out there.

The instructor began running the class through the sit and down commands. Jenny would firmly order, "Sit!" And Marley would jump up on her and put his paws on her shoulders. She would press his butt to the ground, and he would roll over for a belly rub. She would try to tug him into place, and he would grab the leash in his teeth, shaking his head from side to side as if he were wrestling a python. It was too painful to watch. At one point I opened my eyes to see Jenny lying on the pavement face down and Marley standing over her, panting happily. Later she told me she was trying to show him the down command.

As class ended and Jenny and Marley rejoined me, Miss Dominatrix intercepted us. "You really need to get control over that animal," she said with a sneer. *Well, thank you for that valuable advice. And to think we had signed up simply to provide comic relief for the rest of the class.* Neither of us breathed a word. We just retreated to the car in humiliation and drove home in silence, the only sound Marley's loud panting as he tried to come down from the high of his first structured classroom experience. Finally I said, "One thing you can say for him, he sure loves school."

The next week Marley and I were back, this time without Jenny. When I suggested to her that I was probably the closest thing to an alpha dog we were going to find in our home, she gladly relinquished her brief title as master and commander and vowed to never show her face in public again. Before leaving the house, I flipped Marley over on his back, towered over him, and growled in my most intimidating voice, "I'm the boss! You're not the boss! I'm the boss! Got it, Alpha Dog?" He thumped his tail on the floor and tried to gnaw on my wrists.

The night's lesson was walking on heel, one I was especially keen on mastering. I was tired of fighting Marley every step of every walk. He already had yanked Jenny off her feet once when he took off after a cat, leaving her with bloody knees. It was time he learned to trot placidly along by our sides. I wrestled him to our spot on the tarmac, yanking him back from every dog we passed along the way. Miss Dominatrix handed each of us a short length of chain with a steel ring welded to each end. These, she told us, were choker collars and would be our secret weapons for teaching our dogs to heel effortlessly at our sides. The choker chain was brilliantly simple in design. When the dog behaved and walked beside its master as it was supposed to, with slack in its lead, the chain hung limply around its neck. But if the dog lunged forward or veered off course, the chain tightened like a noose, choking the errant hound into gasping submission. It didn't take long, our instructor promised, before dogs learned to submit or die of asphyxia. *Wickedly delicious,* I thought.

I started to slip the choker chain over Marley's head, but he saw it coming and grabbed it in his teeth. I pried his jaw open to pull it out and tried again. He grabbed it again. All the other dogs had their chains on; everyone was waiting. I grabbed his muzzle with one hand and with the other tried to lasso the chain over his snout. He was pulling backward, trying to get his mouth open so he could attack the mysterious coiled silver snake again. I finally forced the chain over his head, and he dropped to the ground, thrashing and snapping, his paws in the air, his head jerking from side to side, until he managed to get the chain in his teeth again. I looked up at the teacher. "He likes it," I said.

As instructed, I got Marley to his feet and got the chain out of his mouth. Then, as instructed, I pushed his butt down into a sit position and stood beside him, my left leg brushing his right shoulder. On the count of three, I was to say, "Marley, heel!" and step off with my left—never my right—foot. If he began to wander off course, a series of minor corrections—sharp little tugs on the leash—would bring him back into line. "Class, on the count of three," Miss Dominatrix called out. Marley was quivering with excitement. The shiny foreign object around his neck had him in a complete lather. "One . . . two . . . three."

"Marley, heel!" I commanded. As soon as I took my first step, he took off like a fighter jet from an aircraft carrier. I yanked back hard on the leash and he made an awful coughing gasp as the chain tightened around his airway. He sprang back for an instant, but as soon as the chain loosened, the momentary choking was behind him, ancient history in that tiny compartment of his brain dedicated to life lessons learned. He lunged forward again. I yanked back and he gasped once more. We continued like this the entire length of the parking lot, Marley yanking ahead, me yanking back, each time with increasing vigor. He was coughing and panting; I was grunting and sweating.

"Rein that dog in!" Miss Dominatrix yelled. I tried to with all my might, but the lesson wasn't sinking in, and I considered that Marley just might strangle himself before he figured it out. Meanwhile, the other dogs were prancing along at their owners' sides, responding to minor corrections just as Miss Dominatrix said they would. "For God's sake, Marley," I whispered. "Our family pride is on the line."

The instructor had the class queue up and try it again. Once again, Marley lurched his way manically across the blacktop, eyes bulging, strangling himself as he went. At the other end, Miss Dominatrix held Marley and me up to the class as an example of how not to heel a dog. "Here," she said impatiently, holding out her hand. "Let me show you." I handed the leash to her, and she efficiently tugged Marley around into position, pulling up on the choker as she ordered him to sit. Sure enough, he sank back on his haunches, eagerly looking up at her. *Damn*.

With a smart yank of the lead, Miss Dominatrix set off with him. But almost instantly he barreled ahead as if he were pulling the lead sled in the Iditarod. The instructor corrected hard, pulling him off balance; he stumbled, wheezed, then lunged forward again. It looked like he was going to pull her arm out of its socket. I should have been embarrassed, but I felt an odd sort of satisfaction that often comes with vindication. She wasn't having any more success than I was. My classmates snickered, and I beamed with perverse pride. *See, my dog is awful for everyone, not just me!*

Now that I wasn't the one being made the fool, I had to admit, the scene was pretty hilarious. The two of them, having reached the end of the parking lot, turned and came lurching back toward us in fits and starts, Miss Dominatrix scowling with what clearly was apoplectic rage, Marley joyous beyond words. She yanked furiously at the leash, and Marley, frothing at the mouth, yanked back harder still, clearly enjoying this excellent new tug-of-war game his teacher had called on him to demonstrate. When he caught sight of me, he hit the gas. With a near-supernatural burst of adrenaline, he made a dash for me, forcing Miss Dominatrix to break into a sprint to keep from being pulled off her feet. Marley didn't stop until he slammed into me with his usual joie de vivre. Miss Dominatrix shot me a look that told me I had crossed some invisible line and there would be no crossing back. Marley had made a mockery of everything she preached about dogs and discipline; he had publicly humiliated her. She handed the leash back to me and, turning to the class as if this unfortunate little episode had never occurred, said, "Okay, class, on the count of three . . ."

When the lesson was over, she asked if I could stay after for a minute. I waited with Marley as she patiently fielded questions from other students in the class. When the last one had left, she turned to me and, in a newly conciliatory voice, said, "I think your dog is still a little young for structured obedience training."

"He's a handful, isn't he?" I said, feeling a new camaraderie with her now that we'd shared the same humiliating experience.

"He's simply not ready for this," she said. "He has some growing up to do."

It was beginning to dawn on me what she was getting at. "Are you trying to tell me—"

"He's a distraction to the other dogs."

"—that you're—"

"He's just too excitable."

"—kicking us out of class?"

"You can always bring him back in another six or eight months."

"So you're kicking us out?"

"I'll happily give you a full refund."

"You're kicking us out."

"Yes," she finally said. "I'm kicking you out."

Marley, as if on cue, lifted his leg and let loose a raging stream of urine, missing his beloved instructor's foot by mere centimeters.

Sometimes a man needs to get angry to get serious. Miss Dominatrix had made me angry. I owned a beautiful, pure-bred Labrador retriever, a proud member of the breed famous for its ability to guide the blind, rescue disaster victims, assist hunters, and pluck fish from roiling ocean swells, all with calm intelligence. How dare she write him off after just two lessons? So he was a bit on the spirited side; he was filled with nothing but good intentions. I was going to prove to that insufferable stuffed shirt that Grogan's Majestic Marley of Churchill was no quitter. We'd see her at Westminster.

First thing the next morning, I had Marley out in the backyard with me. "Nobody kicks the Grogan boys out of obedience school," I told him. "Untrainable? We'll see who's untrainable. Right?" He bounced up and down. "Can we do it, Marley?" He wiggled. "I can't hear you! Can we do it?" He yelped. "That's better. Now let's get to work."

We started with the sit command, which I had been practicing with him since he was a small puppy and which he already was quite good at. I towered over him, gave him my best alpha-dog scowl, and in a firm but calm voice ordered him to sit. He sat. I praised. We repeated the exercise several times. Next we moved to the down command, another one I had been practicing with him. He stared intently into my eyes, neck straining forward, anticipating my directive. I slowly raised my hand in the air and held it there as he waited for the word. With a sharp downward motion, I snapped my fingers, pointed at the ground and said, "Down!" Marley collapsed in a heap, hitting the ground with a thud. He could not possibly have gone down with more gusto had a mortar shell just exploded behind him. Jenny, sitting on the porch with her coffee, noticed it, too, and yelled out, "Incoming!"

After several rounds of hit-the-deck, I decided to move up to the next challenge: come on command. This was a tough one for Marley. The coming part was not the problem; it was waiting in place until we summoned him that he could not get. Our attention-deficit dog was so anxious to be plastered against us he could not sit still while we walked away from him.

I put him in the sit position facing me and fixed my eyes on his. As we stared at each other, I raised my palm, holding it out in front of me like a crossing guard. "Stay," I said, and took a step backward. He froze, staring anxiously, waiting for the slightest sign that he could join me. On my fourth step backward, he could take it no longer and broke free, racing up and tumbling against me. I admonished him and tried it again. And again and again. Each time he allowed me to get a little farther away before charging. Eventually, I stood fifty feet across the yard, my palm out toward him. I waited. He sat, locked in position, his entire body quaking with anticipation. I could see the nervous energy building in him; he was like a volcano ready to blow. But he held fast. I counted to ten. He did not budge. His eyes froze on me; his muscles bulged. *Okay, enough torture,* I thought. I dropped my hand and yelled, "Marley, come!"

As he catapulted forward, I squatted and clapped my hands to encourage him. I thought he might go racing willy-nilly across the yard, but he made a beeline for me. *Perfect!* I thought. "C'mon, boy!" I coached. "C'mon!" And come he did. He was barreling right at me. "Slow it down, boy," I said. He just kept coming. "Slow down!" He had this vacant, crazed look on his face, and in the instant before impact I realized the pilot had left the wheelhouse. It was a one-dog stampede. I had time for one final command. "STOP!" I screamed. *Blam!* He plowed into me without breaking stride and I pitched backward, slamming hard to the ground. When I opened my eyes a few seconds later, he was straddling me with all four paws, lying on my chest and desperately licking my face. *How did I do, boss?* Technically speaking, he had followed orders exactly. After all, I had failed to mention anything about stopping once he got to me.

"Mission accomplished," I said with a groan.

Jenny peered out the kitchen window at us and shouted, "I'm off to work. When you two are done making out, don't forget to close the windows. It's supposed to rain this afternoon." I gave Linebacker Dog a snack, then showered and headed off to work myself.

When I arrived home that night, Jenny was waiting for me at the front door, and I could tell she was upset. "Go look in the garage," she said.

I opened the door into the garage and the first thing I spotted was Marley, lying on his carpet, looking dejected. In that instant snapshot image, I could see that his snout and front paws were not right. They were dark brown, not their usual light yellow, caked in dried blood. Then my focus zoomed out and I sucked in my breath. The garage—our indestructible bunker—was a shambles. Throw rugs were shredded, paint was clawed off the concrete walls, and the ironing board was tipped over, its fabric cover hanging in ribbons. Worst of all, the doorway in which I stood looked like it had been attacked with a chipper-shredder. Bits of wood were sprayed in a ten-foot semicircle around the door, which was gouged halfway through to the other side. The bottom three feet of the doorjamb were missing entirely and nowhere to be found. Blood streaked the walls from where Marley had shredded his paws and muzzle. "Damn," I said, more in awe than anger. My mind flashed to poor Mrs. Nedermier and the chainsaw murder across the street. I felt like I was standing in the middle of a crime scene.

Jenny's voice came from behind me. "When I came home for lunch, everything was fine," she said. "But I could tell it was getting ready to rain." After she was back at work, an intense storm moved through, bringing with it sheets of rain, dazzling flashes of lightning, and thunder so powerful you could almost feel it thump against your chest.

When she arrived home a couple of hours later, Marley, standing amid the carnage of his desperate escape attempt, was in a complete, panic-stricken lather. He was so pathetic she couldn't bring herself to yell at him. Besides, the incident was over; he would have no idea what he was being punished for. Yet she was so heartsick about the wanton attack on our new house, the house we had worked so hard on, that she could not bear to deal with it or him. "Wait till your father gets home!" she had threatened, and closed the door on him.

Over dinner, we tried to put what we were now calling "the wilding" in perspective. All we could figure was that, alone and terrified as the storm descended on the neighborhood, Marley decided his best chance at survival was to begin digging his way into the house. He was probably listening to some ancient denning instinct handed down from his ancestor, the wolf. And he pursued his goal with a zealous efficiency I wouldn't have thought possible without the aid of heavy machinery.

When the dishes were done, Jenny and I went out into the garage where Marley, back to his old self, grabbed a chew toy and bounced around us, looking for a little tug-of-war action. I held him still while Jenny sponged the blood off his fur. Then he watched us, tail wagging, as we cleaned up his handiwork. We threw out the rugs and ironing-board cover, swept up the shredded remains of our door, mopped his blood off the walls, and made a list of materials we would need from the hardware store to repair the damage—the first of countless such repairs I would end up making over the course of his life. Marley seemed positively ebullient to have us out there, lending a hand with his remodeling efforts. "You don't have to look so happy about it," I scowled, and brought him inside for the night.

CHAPTER 9

The Stuff Males Are Made Of

❋

Every dog needs a good veterinarian, a trained professional who can keep it healthy and strong and immunized against disease. Every new dog owner needs one, too, mostly for the advice and reassurance and free counsel veterinarians find themselves spending inordinate amounts of their time dispensing. We had a few false starts finding a keeper. One was so elusive we only ever saw his high-school-aged helper; another was so old I was convinced he could no longer tell a Chihuahua from a cat. A third clearly was catering to Palm Beach heiresses and their palm-sized accessory dogs. Then we stumbled upon the doctor of our dreams. His name was Jay Butan—Dr. Jay to all who knew him—and he was young, smart, hip, and extraordinarily kind. Dr. Jay understood dogs like the best mechanics understand cars, intuitively. He clearly adored animals yet maintained a healthy sensibility about their role in the human world. In those early months, we kept him on speed dial and consulted him about the most inane concerns. When Marley began to develop rough scaly patches on his elbows, I feared he was developing some rare and, for all we knew, contagious skin ailment. Relax, Dr. Jay told me, those were just calluses from lying on the floor. One day Marley yawned wide and I spotted an odd purple discoloration on the back of his tongue. *Oh my God,* I thought. *He has cancer*. Kaposi's sarcoma of the mouth. Relax, Dr. Jay advised, it was just a birthmark.

Now, on this afternoon, Jenny and I stood in an exam room with him, discussing Marley's deepening neurosis over thunderstorms. We had hoped the chipper-shredder incident in the garage was an isolated aberration, but it turned out to be just the beginning of what would become a lifelong pattern of phobic, irrational behavior. Despite Labs' reputation as excellent gun dogs, we had ended up with one who was mortally terrified of anything louder than a popping champagne cork. Firecrackers, backfiring engines, and gunshots all terrified him. Thunder was a house of horrors all its own. Even the hint of a storm would throw Marley into a meltdown. If we were home, he would press against us, shaking and drooling uncontrollably, his eyes darting nervously, ears folded back, tail tucked between his legs. When he was alone, he turned destructive, gouging away at whatever stood between him and perceived safety. One day Jenny arrived home as clouds gathered to find a wild-eyed Marley standing on top of the washing machine, dancing a desperate jig, his nails clicking on the enamel top. How he got up there and why he felt the urge in the first place, we never determined. People could be certifiably nuts, and as best as we could figure, so could dogs.

Dr. Jay pressed a vial of small yellow pills into my hand

and said, "Don't hesitate to use these." They were sedatives that would, as he put it, "take the edge off Marley's anxiety." The hope, he said, was that, aided by the calming effects of the drug, Marley would be able to more rationally cope with storms and eventually realize they were nothing but a lot of harmless noise. Thunder anxiety was not unusual in dogs, he told us, especially in Florida, where huge boomers rolled across the peninsula nearly every afternoon during the torpid summer months. Marley nosed the vial in my hands, apparently eager to get started on a life of drug dependency.

Dr. Jay scruffed Marley's neck and began working his lips as though he had something important to say but wasn't quite sure how to say it. "And," he said, pausing, "you probably want to start thinking seriously about having him neutered."

"Neutered?" I repeated. "You mean, as in . . ." I looked down at the enormous set of testicles—comically huge orbs—swinging between Marley's hind legs.

Dr. Jay gazed down at them, too, and nodded. I must have winced, maybe even grabbed myself, because he quickly added: "It's painless, really, and he'll be a lot more comfortable." Dr. Jay knew all about the challenges Marley presented. He was our sounding board on all things Marley and knew about the disastrous obedience training, the numbskull antics, the destructiveness, the hyperactivity. And lately Marley, who was seven months old, had begun humping anything that moved, including our dinner guests. "It'll just remove all that nervous sexual energy and make him a happier, calmer dog," he said. He promised it wouldn't dampen Marley's sunny exuberance.

"God, I don't know," I said. "It just seems so . . . so final."

Jenny, on the other hand, was having no such compunctions. "Let's snip those suckers off!" she said.

"But what about siring a litter?" I asked. "What about carrying on his bloodline?" All those lucrative stud fees flashed before my eyes.

Again Dr. Jay seemed to be choosing his words carefully. "I think you need to be realistic about that," he said. "Marley's a great family pet, but I'm not sure he's got the credentials he would need to be in demand for stud." He was being as diplomatic as possible, but the expression on his face gave him away. It almost screamed out, *Good God, man! For the sake of future generations, we must contain this genetic mistake at all costs!*

I told him we would think about it, and with our new supply of mood-altering drugs in hand, we headed home.

It was at this same time, as we debated slicing away Marley's manhood, that Jenny was placing unprecedented demands on mine. Dr. Sherman had cleared her to try to get pregnant again. She accepted the challenge with the single-mindedness of an Olympic athlete. The days of simply putting away the birth control pills and letting whatever might happen happen were behind us. In the insemination wars, Jenny was going on the offensive. For that, she needed me, a key ally who controlled the flow of ammunition. Like most males, I had spent every waking moment from the age of fifteen trying to convince the opposite sex that I was a worthy mating partner. Finally, I had found someone who agreed. I should have been thrilled. For the first time in my life, a woman wanted me more than I wanted her. This was guy heaven. No more begging, no more groveling. Like the best stud dogs, I was at last in demand. I should have been ecstatic. But suddenly it all just seemed like work, and stressful work at that. It was not a rollicking good romp that Jenny craved from me; it was a baby. And that meant I had a job to perform. This was serious business. That most joyous of acts overnight became a clinical drill involving basal-temperature checks, menstrual calendars, and ovulation charts. I felt like I was in service to the queen.

It was all about as arousing as a tax audit. Jenny was used to me being game to go at the slightest hint of an invitation, and she assumed the old rules still applied. I would be, let's say, fixing the garbage disposal and she would walk in with her calendar in hand and say, "I had my last period on the seventeenth, which means"—and she would pause to count ahead from that date—"that we need to do it—NOW!"

The Grogan men have never handled pressure well, and I was no exception. It was only a matter of time before I suffered the ultimate male humiliation: performance failure. And once that happened, the game was over. My confidence was shot, my nerve gone. If it happened once, I knew it could happen again. Failure evolved into a self-fulfilling prophecy. The more I worried about performing my husbandly duty, the less I was able to relax and do what had always come naturally. I quashed all signs of physical affection lest I put ideas in Jenny's head. I began to live in mortal fear that my wife would, God forbid, ask me to rip her clothes off and have my way with her. I began thinking that perhaps a life of celibacy in a remote monastery wouldn't be such a bad future after all.

Jenny was not about to give up so easily. She was the hunter; I was the prey. One morning when I was working in my newspaper's West Palm Beach bureau, just ten minutes from home, Jenny called from work. Did I want to meet her at home for lunch? *You mean alone? Without a chaperone?*

"Or we could meet at a restaurant somewhere," I countered. A very crowded restaurant. Preferably with several of our coworkers along. And both mothers-in-law.

"Oh, c'mon," she said. "It'll be fun." Then her voice lowered to a whisper and she added, "Today's a good day. I . . . think . . . I'm . . . ovulating." A wave of dread washed over me. *Oh God, no. Not the O word.* The pressure was on. It was time to perform or perish. To, quite literally, rise or fall. *Please don't make me,* I wanted to plead into the phone. Instead I said as coolly as I could, "Sure. Does twelve-thirty work?"

When I opened the front door, Marley, as always, was there to greet me, but Jenny was nowhere to be found. I called out to her. "In the bathroom," she answered. "Out in a sec." I sorted through the mail, killing time, a general sense of doom hovering over me, the way I imagined it hovered over people waiting for their biopsy results. "Hey there, sailor," a voice behind me said, and when I turned around, Jenny was standing there in a little silky two-piece thing. Her flat stomach peeked out from below the top, which hung precariously from her shoulders by two impossibly thin straps. Her legs had never looked longer. "How do I look?" she said, holding her hands out at her sides. She looked incredible, that's how she looked. When it comes to sleep-wear, Jenny is squarely in the baggy T-shirt camp, and I could tell she felt silly in this seductive getup. But it was having the intended effect.

She scampered into the bedroom with me in pursuit. Soon we were on top of the sheets in each other's arms. I closed my eyes and could feel that old lost friend of mine stirring. The magic was returning. *You can do this, John.* I tried to conjure up the most impure thoughts I could. *This was going to work!* My fingers fumbled for those flimsy shoulder straps. *Roll with it, John. No pressure.* I could feel her breath now, hot and moist on my face. And heavy. Hot, moist, heavy breath. *Mmmm, sexy.*

But wait. What was that smell? Something on her breath. Something at once familiar and foreign, not exactly unplea-sant but not quite enticing, either. I knew that smell, but I couldn't place it. I hesitated. *What are you doing, you idiot? Forget the smell. Focus, man. Focus!* But that smell—I could not get it out of my head. *You're getting distracted, John. Don't get distracted.* What was it? *Stay the course!* My curiosity was getting the better of me. *Let it go, guy. Let it go!* I began sniffing the air. A food; yes, that was it. But what food? Not crackers. Not chips. Not tuna fish. I almost had it. It was . . . Milk-Bones?

Milk-Bones! That was it! She had Milk-Bone breath. *But why?* I wondered—and I actually heard a little voice ask the question in my head—*Why has Jenny been eating Milk-Bones?* And besides, I could feel her lips on my neck . . .

How could she be kissing my neck and breathing in my face all at once? It didn't make any—

Oh . . . my . . . God.

I opened my eyes. There, inches from my face, filling my entire frame of vision, loomed Marley's huge head. His chin rested on the mattress, and he was panting up a storm, drool soaking into the sheets. His eyes were half closed—and he looked entirely too in love. "Bad dog!" I shrieked, recoiling across the bed. "No! No! Go to bed!" I frantically ordered. "Go to bed! Go lie down!" But it was too late. The magic was gone. The monastery was back.

At ease, soldier.

The next morning I made an appointment to take Marley in to have his balls cut off. I figured if I wasn't going to have sex for the rest of my life, he wasn't either. Dr. Jay said we could drop Marley off before we went to work and pick him up on our way home. A week later, that's just what we did.

As Jenny and I got ready, Marley caromed happily off the walls, sensing an impending outing. For Marley, any trip was a good trip; it didn't matter where we were going or for how long. Take out the trash? *No problem!* Walk to the corner for a gallon of milk? *Count me in!* I began to feel pangs of guilt. The poor guy had no idea what lay in store for him. He trusted us to do the right thing, and here we were secretly plotting to emasculate him. Did betrayal get any more treacherous than this?

"Come here," I said, and wrestled him to the floor where I gave him a vigorous belly scratch. "It won't be so bad.

You'll see. Sex is highly overrated." Not even I, still re-
bounding from my bad run of luck the last couple of weeks,
believed that. Who was I fooling? Sex was great. Sex was
incredible. The poor dog was going to miss out on life's
single greatest pleasure. The poor bastard. I felt horrible.

And I felt even worse when I whistled for him and he
bounded out the door and into the car with utter blind faith
that I would not steer him wrong. He was revved up and
ready to go on whatever excellent adventure I saw fit. Jenny
drove and I sat in the passenger seat. As was his habit,
Marley balanced his front paws on the center console, his
nose touching the rearview mirror. Every time Jenny
touched the brakes, he went crashing into the windshield,
but Marley didn't care. He was riding shotgun with his two
best friends. Did life get any better than this?

I cracked my window, and Marley began listing to star-
board, leaning against me, trying to catch a whiff of the
outdoor smells. Soon he had squirmed his way fully onto my
lap and pressed his nose so firmly into the narrow crack of
the window that he snorted each time he tried to inhale. *Oh,
why not?* I thought. This was his last ride as a fully equipped
member of the male gender; the least I could do was give
him a little fresh air. I opened the window wide enough for
him to stick his snout out. He was enjoying the sensation so
much, I opened it farther, and soon his entire head was out
the window. His ears flapped behind him in the wind, and
his tongue hung out like he was drunk on the ether of the
city. God, was he happy.

As we drove down Dixie Highway, I told Jenny how bad I
felt about what we were about to put him through. She was

beginning to say something no doubt totally dismissive of my qualms when I noticed, more with curiosity than alarm, that Marley had hooked both of his front paws over the edge of the half-open window. And now his neck and upper shoulders were hanging out of the car, too. He just needed a pair of goggles and a silk scarf to look like one of those World War I flying aces.

"John, he's making me nervous," Jenny said.

"He's fine," I answered. "He just wants a little fresh—"

At that instant he slid his front legs out the window until his armpits were resting on the edge of the glass.

"John, grab him! Grab him!"

Before I could do anything, Marley was off my lap and scrambling out the window of our moving car. His butt was up in the air, his hind legs clawing for a foothold. He was making his break. As his body slithered past me, I lunged for him and managed to grab the end of his tail with my left hand. Jenny was braking hard in heavy traffic. Marley dangled fully outside the moving car, suspended upside down by his tail, which I had by the most tenuous of grips. My body was twisted around in a position that didn't allow me to get my other hand on him. Marley was frantically trotting along with his front paws on the pavement.

Jenny got the car stopped in the outside lane with cars lining up behind us, horns blaring. "Now what?" I yelled. I was stuck. I couldn't pull him back in the window. I couldn't open the door. I couldn't get my other arm out. And I didn't dare let go of him or he would surely dash in the path of one of the angry drivers swerving around us. I held on for dear life, my face, as it were, scrunched against the glass just inches from his giant flapping scrotum.

Jenny put the flashers on and ran around to my side, where she grabbed him and held him by the collar until I could get out and help her wrestle him back into the car. Our little drama had unfolded directly in front of a gas station, and as Jenny got the car back into gear I looked over to see that all the mechanics had come out to take in the show. I thought they were going to wet themselves, they were laughing so hard. "Thanks, guys!" I called out. "Glad we could brighten your morning."

When we got to the clinic, I walked Marley in on a tight leash just in case he tried any more smart moves. My guilt was gone, my resolve hardened. "You're not getting out of this one, Eunuch Boy," I told him. He was huffing and puffing, straining against his leash to sniff all the other animal smells. In the waiting area he was able to terrorize a couple of cats and tip over a stand filled with pamphlets. I turned him over to Dr. Jay's assistant and said, "Give him the works."

That night when I picked him up, Marley was a changed dog. He was sore from the surgery and moved gingerly. His eyes were bloodshot and droopy from the anesthesia, and he was still groggy. And where those magnificent crown jewels of his had swung so proudly, there was . . . nothing. Just a small, shriveled flap of skin. The irrepressible Marley bloodline had officially and forever come to an end.

CHAPTER 10

The Luck of the Irish

Our lives increasingly were being defined by work. Work at the newspapers. Work on the house. Work around the yard. Work trying to get pregnant. And, nearly a full-time vocation in itself, work raising Marley. In many ways, he was like a child, requiring the time and attention a child requires, and we were getting a taste of the responsibility that lay ahead of us if we ever did have a family. But only to a degree. Even as clueless as we were about parenting, we were pretty sure we couldn't lock the kids in the garage with a bowl of water when we went out for the day.

We hadn't even reached our second wedding anniversary and already we were feeling the grind of responsible, grown-up, married life. We needed to get away. We needed a vacation, just the two of us, far from the obligations of our daily lives. I surprised Jenny one evening with two tickets to Ireland. We would be gone for three weeks. There would be no itineraries, no guided tours, no must-see destinations. Only a rental car, a road map, and a guide to bed-and-breakfast inns along the way. Just having the tickets in hand lifted a yoke from our shoulders.

First we had a few duties to dole out, and at the top of the list was Marley. We quickly ruled out a boarding kennel. He was too young, too wired, too rambunctious to be cooped up in a pen twenty-three hours a day. As Dr. Jay had predicted, neutering had not diminished Marley's exuberance one bit. It did not affect his energy level or loony behavior, either. Except for the fact that he no longer showed an interest in mounting inanimate objects, he was the same crazed beast. He was way too wild—and too unpredictably destructive when panic set in—to pawn off at a friend's house. Or even at an enemy's house, for that matter. What we needed was a live-in dog-sitter. Obviously, not just anyone would do, especially given the challenges Marley presented. We needed someone who was responsible, trust-worthy, *very* patient, and strong enough to reel in seventy pounds of runaway Labrador retriever.

We made a list of every friend, neighbor, and coworker we could think of, then one by one crossed off names. Total party boy. *Scratch*. Too absentminded. *Scratch*. Averse to dog drool. *Scratch*. Too mousy to control a dachshund let alone a Lab. *Scratch*. Allergic. *Scratch*. Unwilling to pick up dog droppings. *Scratch*. Eventually, we were left with just one name. Kathy worked in my office and was single and unattached. She grew up in the rural Midwest, loved ani-mals, and longed to someday trade in her small apartment for a house with a yard. She was athletic and liked to walk. True, she was shy and a little on the meek side, which could make it hard for her to impose her will on alpha Marley, but otherwise she would be perfect. Best of all, she said yes.

The list of instructions I prepared for her couldn't have been more painstakingly detailed were we leaving a critically ill infant in her care. The Marley Memo ran six full pages single-spaced and read in part:

FEEDING: Marley eats three times a day, one two-cup measure at each meal. The measuring cup is inside the bag. Please feed him when you get up in the morning and when you get home from work. The neighbors will come in to feed him mid-afternoon. This totals six cups of food a day, but if he's acting famished please give him an extra cup or so. As you're aware, all that food has to go somewhere. See POOP PATROL below.

VITAMINS: Each morning, we give Marley one Pet Tab vitamin. The best way to give it to him is to simply drop it on the floor and pretend he's not supposed to have it. If he thinks it's forbidden, he will wolf it down. If for some reason that doesn't work, you can try disguising it in a snack.

WATER: In hot weather, it's important to keep plenty of fresh water on hand. We change the water next to his food bowl once a day and top it off if it's running low. A word of caution: Marley likes to submerge his snout in the water bowl and play submarine. This makes quite a mess. Also his jowls hold a surprising amount of water, which runs out as he walks away from the bowl. If you let him, he'll wipe his mouth on your clothes and the couches. One last thing: He usually shakes after taking a big drink, and his saliva will fly onto walls, lampshades, etc. We try to wipe this up before it dries, at which time it becomes almost impossible to remove.

FLEAS AND TICKS: If you notice these on him, you can spray him with the flea and tick sprays we have left. We've also left an insecticide that you can spray on the rugs, etc., if you think a problem is starting. Fleas are tiny and fast, and hard to catch, but they seldom bite humans, we've found, so I wouldn't be too concerned. Ticks are larger and slow and we do occasionally see these on him. If you spot one on him and have the stomach for it, just pick it off and either crush it in a tissue (you may need to use your fingernails; they're amazingly tough) or wash it down the sink or toilet (the best option if the tick is engorged with blood). You've probably read about ticks spreading Lyme disease to humans and all the long-term health problems that can cause, but several vets have assured us that there is very little danger of contracting Lyme disease here in Florida. Just to make sure, wash your hands well after removing a tick. The best way to pick a tick off Marley is to give him a toy to hold in his mouth to keep him occupied, and then pinch his skin together with one hand while you use your fingernails of the other hand as pincers to pull the tick off. Speaking of which, if he gets too smelly, and you're feeling brave, you can give him a bath in the kiddie pool we have in the backyard (for just that purpose), but wear a bathing suit. You'll get wet!

EARS: Marley tends to get a lot of wax buildup in his ears, which if left untreated can lead to infections. Once or twice while we're gone, please use cotton balls and the blue ear-cleaning solution to clean as much gunk out of his ears as you can. It's pretty nasty stuff so make sure you're wearing old clothes.

WALKS: Without his morning walk, Marley tends to get into mischief in the garage. For your own sanity, you may also want to give him a quick jaunt before bed, but that's optional. You will want to use the choker chain to walk him, but never leave it on him when he's unattended. He could strangle himself, and knowing Marley he probably would.

BASIC COMMANDS: Walking him is much easier if you can get him to heel. Always begin with him in a sitting position at your left, then give the command "Marley, heel!" and step off on your left foot. If he tries to lunge ahead, give him a sharp jerk on the leash. That usually works for us. (He's been to obedience school!) If he's off the leash, he usually is pretty good about coming to you with the command "Marley, come!" Note: It's best if you're standing and not crouched down when you call him.

THUNDERSTORMS: Marley tends to get a little freaked-out during storms or even light showers. We keep his sedatives (the yellow pills) in the cupboard with the vitamins. One pill thirty minutes before the storm arrives (you'll be a weather forecaster before you know it!) should do the trick. Getting Marley to swallow pills is a bit of an art form. He won't eat them like he does his vitamins, even if you drop them on the floor and pretend he shouldn't have them. The best technique is to straddle him and pry his jaws open with one hand. With the other, you push the pill as far down his throat as you can get it. It needs to be past the point of no return or he will cough it back up. Then stroke his throat until he swallows it. Obviously, you'll want to wash up afterward.

POOP PATROL: I have a shovel back under the mango tree that I use for picking up Marley's messes. Feel free to clean up after him as much or as little as you like, depending on how much you plan to walk around the backyard. Watch your step!

OFF-LIMITS: We do NOT allow Marley to:

* Get up on any piece of furniture.
* Chew on furniture, shoes, pillows, etc.
* Drink out of the toilet. (Best to keep lid down at all times, though beware: He's figured out how to flip it up with his nose.)
* Dig in the yard or uproot plants and flowers. He usually does this when he feels he's not getting enough attention.
* Go in any trash can. (You may have to keep it on top of the counter.)
* Jump on people, sniff crotches, or indulge in any other socially unacceptable behavior. We've especially been trying to cure him of arm chewing, which, as you can imagine, not a lot of people appreciate. He still has a way to go. Feel free to give him a swat on the rump and a stern "No!"

❄ Beg at the table.
❄ Push against the front screen door or the porch
   screens. (You'll see several have already been
   replaced.)

Thanks again for doing all this for us, Kathy. This is a
giant favor. I'm not quite sure how we could have
managed otherwise. Hope you and Marley become
good pals and you are as entertained by him as we are.

I brought the instructions in to Jenny and asked if there
was anything I had forgotten. She took several minutes to
read them and then looked up and said, "What are you
thinking? You can't show her this." She was waving them at
me. "You show her this and you can forget about Ireland.
She's the only person we could find willing to do this. If she
reads this, that's it. She'll start running and won't stop until
she hits Key West." Just in case I had missed it the first time
around, she repeated: "What on earth were you thinking?"

   "So you think it's too much?" I asked.
   But I've always believed in full disclosure, and show it to
her I did. Kathy did flinch noticeably a few times, especially
as we went over tick-removal techniques, but she kept any
misgivings to herself. Looking daunted and just a little green,
but far too kind to renege on a promise, she held fast. "Have
a great trip," she said. "We'll be fine."

Ireland was everything we dreamed it would be. Beautiful,
bucolic, lazy. The weather was gloriously clear and sunny

most days, leading the locals to fret darkly about the possibility of drought. As we had promised ourselves, we kept no schedules and set no itineraries. We simply wandered, bumping our way along the coast, stopping to stroll or shop or hike or quaff Guinness or simply gaze out at the ocean. We stopped the car to talk to farmers bringing in their hay and to photograph ourselves with sheep standing in the road. If we saw an interesting lane, we turned down it. It was impossible to get lost because we had no place we needed to be. All of our duties and obligations back home were just distant memories.

As evening approached each day, we would begin looking for a place to spend the night. Invariably, these were rooms in private homes run by sweet Irish widows who doted on us, served us tea, turned down our sheets, and always seemed to ask us the same question, "So, would you two be planning to start a family soon?" And then they would leave us in our room, flashing back knowing, oddly suggestive smiles as they closed the door behind them.

Jenny and I became convinced there was a national law in Ireland that required all guest beds to face a large, wall-mounted-likeness of either the pope or the Virgin Mary. Some places provided both. One even included an oversized set of rosary beads that dangled from the headboard. The Irish Celibate Traveler Law also dictated that all guest beds be extremely creaky, sounding a rousing alarm every time one of its occupants so much as rolled over.

It all conspired to create a setting that was about as conducive to amorous relations as a convent. We were in someone else's home—someone else's *very Catholic* home—with thin walls and a loud bed and statues of saints and virgins, and a nosy hostess who, for all we knew, was hovering on the other side of the door. It was the last place you would think to initiate sex. Which, of course, made me crave my wife in new and powerful ways.

We would turn off the lights and crawl into bed, the springs groaning under our weight, and immediately I would slip my hand beneath Jenny's top and onto her stomach.

"No way!" she would whisper.

"Why not?" I would whisper back.

"Are you nuts? Mrs. O'Flaherty is right on the other side of that wall."

"So what?"

"We can't!"

"Sure we can."

"She'll hear everything."

"We'll be quiet."

"Oh, *right*!"

"Promise. We'll barely move."

"Well, go put a T-shirt or something over the pope first," she would finally say, relenting. "I'm not doing anything with him staring at us."

Suddenly, sex seemed so . . . so . . . illicit. It was like I was in high school again, sneaking around under my mother's suspicious gaze. To risk sex in these surroundings was to risk shameful humiliation at the communal breakfast table the next morning. It was to risk Mrs. O'Flaherty's raised eyebrow as she served up eggs and fried tomatoes, asking with a leering grin, "So, was the bed comfortable for you?"

Ireland was a coast-to-coast No Sex Zone. And that was all the invitation I needed. We spent the trip bopping like bunnies.

Still, Jenny couldn't stop fretting about her big baby back home.

Every few days she would feed a fistful of coins into a pay phone and call home for a progress report from Kathy. I would stand outside the booth and listen to Jenny's end of the conversation.

"He did? . . . Seriously? . . . Right into traffic? . . . You weren't hurt, were you? . . . Thank God . . . I would have screamed, too . . . What? Your shoes? . . . Oh no! *And* your purse? . . . We'll certainly pay for repairs . . . Nothing left at all? . . . Of course, we insist on replacing them . . . And he what? . . . Wet cement, you say? What's the chance of that happening?''

And so it would go. Each call was a litany of transgressions, one worse than the next, many of which surprised even us, hardened survivors of the puppy wars. Marley was the incorrigible student and Kathy the hapless substitute teacher. He was having a field day.

When we arrived home, Marley raced outside to greet us. Kathy stood in the doorway, looking tired and strained. She had the faraway gaze of a shell-shocked soldier after a particularly unrelenting battle. Her bag was packed and sitting on the front porch, ready to go. She held her car key in her hand as if she could not wait to escape. We gave her gifts, thanked her profusely, and told her not to worry about the ripped-out screens and other damage. She excused herself politely and was gone.

As best as we could figure, Kathy had been unable to exert any authority at all over Marley, and even less control. With each victory, he grew bolder. He forgot all about heeling, dragging her behind him wherever he wished to go. He refused to come to her. He grabbed whatever suited him—shoes, purses, pillows—and would not let go. He stole food off her plate. He rifled through the garbage. He even tried taking over her bed. He had decided he was in charge while the parents were away, and he was not going to let some mild-mannered roommate pull rank and put the kibosh on his fun.

"Poor Kathy," Jenny said. "She looked kind of broken, don't you think?"

"Shattered is more like it."

"We probably shouldn't ask her to dog-sit for us again."

"No," I answered. "That probably wouldn't be a good idea."

Turning to Marley, I said, "The honeymoon's over, Chief. Starting tomorrow, you're back in training."

The next morning Jenny and I both started back to work. But first I slipped the choker chain around Marley's neck and took him for a walk. He immediately lunged forward, not even pretending to try to heel. "A little rusty, are we?" I asked, and heaved with all my might on his leash, knocking him off his paws. He righted himself, coughed, and looked up at me with a wounded expression as if to say, *You don't have to get rough about it. Kathy didn't mind me pulling.*

"Get used to it," I said, and placed him in a sit position. I adjusted the choke chain so it rode high on his neck, where experience had taught me it had the most effect. "Okay, let's try this again," I said. He looked at me with cool skepticism.

"Marley, heel!" I ordered, and stepped briskly off on my left foot with his leash so short my left hand was actually gripping the end of his choke chain. He lurched and I tugged sharply, tightening the stranglehold without mercy. "Taking advantage of a poor woman like that," I mumbled. "You ought to be ashamed of yourself." By the end of the walk, my grip on the leash so tight that my knuckles had turned white, I finally managed to convince him I wasn't fooling around. This was no game but rather a real-life lesson in actions and consequences. If he wanted to lurch, I would choke him. Every time, without exception. If he wanted to cooperate and walk by my side, I would loosen my grip and he would barely feel the chain around his neck. Lurch, choke; heel, breathe. It was simple enough for even Marley to grasp. Over and over and over again we repeated the sequence as we marched up and down the bike path. Lurch, choke; heel, breathe. Slowly it was dawning on him that I was the master and he was the pet, and that was the way it was going to stay. As we turned in to the driveway, my recalcitrant dog trotted along beside me, not perfectly but respectably. For the first time in his life he was actually heeling, or at least attempting a close proximity of it. I would take it as a victory. "Oh, yes," I sang joyously. "The boss is back."

Several days later Jenny called me at the office. She had just been to see Dr. Sherman. "Luck of the Irish," she said. "Here we go again."

CHAPTER 11

The Things He Ate

❄

This pregnancy was different. Our miscarriage had taught us some important lessons, and this time we had no intention of repeating our mistakes. Most important, we kept our news the most closely guarded secret since D-day. Except for Jenny's doctors and nurses, no one, not even our parents, was brought into our confidence. When we had friends over, Jenny sipped grape juice from a wineglass so as not to raise suspicions. In addition to the secrecy, we were simply more measured in our excitement, even when we were alone. We began sentences with conditional clauses, such as "If everything works out . . ." and "Assuming all goes well." It was as though we could jinx the pregnancy simply by gushing about it. We didn't dare let our joy out of check lest it turn and bite us.

We locked away all the chemical cleaners and pesticides. We weren't going down that road again. Jenny became a convert to the natural cleaning powers of vinegar, which was up to even the ultimate challenge of dissolving Marley's dried saliva off the walls. We found that boric acid, a white powder lethal to bugs and harmless to humans, worked pretty well at keeping Marley and his bedding flea-free. And if he needed an occasional flea dip, we would leave it to professionals.

Jenny rose at dawn each morning and took Marley for a brisk walk along the water. I would just be waking up when they returned, smelling of briny ocean air. My wife was the picture of robust health in all ways but one. She spent most days, all day long, on the verge of throwing up. But she wasn't complaining; she greeted each wave of nausea with what can only be described as gleeful acceptance, for it was a sign that the tiny experiment inside her was chugging along just fine.

Indeed it was. This time around, Essie took my videotape and recorded the first faint, grainy images of our baby. We could hear the heart beating, see its four tiny chambers pulsing. We could trace the outline of the head and count all four limbs. Dr. Sherman popped his head into the sonogram room to pronounce everything perfect, and then looked at Jenny and said in that booming voice of his, "What are you crying for, kid? You're supposed to be happy." Essie whacked him with her clipboard and scolded, "You go away and leave her alone," then rolled her eyes at Jenny as if to say, "Men! They are so clueless."

When it came to dealing with pregnant wives, clueless would describe me. I gave Jenny her space, sympathized with her in her nausea and pain, and tried not to grimace noticeably when she insisted on reading her *What to Expect When You're Expecting* book aloud to me. I complimented her figure as her belly swelled, saying things like "You look great. Really. You look like a svelte little shoplifter who just slipped a basketball under her shirt." I even tried my best to indulge her increasingly bizarre and irrational behavior. I was soon on a first-name basis with the overnight clerk at the twenty-four-hour market as I stopped in at all hours for ice cream or apples or celery or chewing gum in flavors I never knew existed. "Are you sure this is clove?" I would ask him. "She says it has to be clove."

One night when Jenny was about five months pregnant she got it in her head that we needed baby socks. Well, sure we did, I agreed, and of course we would lay in a full complement before the baby arrived. But she didn't mean we would need them eventually; she meant we needed them right now. "We won't have anything to put on the baby's feet when we come home from the hospital," she said in a quavering voice.

Never mind that the due date was still four months away. Never mind that by then the outside temperature would be a frosty ninety-six degrees. Never mind that even a clueless guy like me knew a baby would be bundled head to toe in a receiving blanket when released from the maternity ward.

"Honey, c'mon," I said. "Be reasonable. It's eight o'clock on Sunday night. Where am I supposed to find baby socks?"

"We need socks," she repeated.

"We have weeks to get socks," I countered. "Months to get socks."

"I just see those little tiny toes," she whimpered.

It was no use. I drove around grumbling until I found a Kmart that was open and picked out a festive selection of socks that were so ridiculously minuscule they looked like matching thumb warmers. When I got home and poured them out of the bag, Jenny was finally satisfied. At last we had socks. And thank God we had managed to grab up the last few available pair before the national supply ran dry, which could have happened at any moment without warning. Our baby's fragile little digits were now safe. We could go to bed and sleep in peace.

As the pregnancy progressed, so did Marley's training. I worked with him every day, and now I was able to entertain our friends by yelling, "Incoming!" and watching him crash to the floor, all four limbs splayed. He came consistently on command (unless there was something riveting his attention, such as another dog, cat, squirrel, butterfly, mailman, or floating weed seed); he sat consistently (unless he felt strongly like standing); and heeled reliably (unless there was something so tempting it was worth strangling himself over—see dogs, cats, squirrels, etc., above). He was coming along, but that's not to say he was mellowing into a calm, well-behaved dog. If I towered over him and barked stern orders, he would obey, sometimes even eagerly. But his default setting was stuck on eternal incorrigibility.

He also had an insatiable appetite for mangoes, which fell by the dozens in the backyard. Each weighed a pound or more and was so sweet it could make your teeth ache. Marley would stretch out in the grass, anchor a ripe mango between his front paws, and go about surgically removing every speck of flesh from the skin. He would hold the large pits in his mouth like lozenges, and when he finally spit them out they looked like they had been cleaned in an acid bath. Some days he would be out there for hours, noshing away in a fruit-and-fiber frenzy.

As with anyone who eats too much fruit, his constitution began to change. Soon our backyard was littered with large piles of loose, festively colored dog droppings. The one advantage to this was that you would have to be legally blind to accidentally step in a heap of his poop, which in mango season took on the radiant fluorescence of orange traffic cones.

He ate other things as well. And these, too, did pass. I saw the evidence each morning as I shoveled up his piles. Here a toy plastic soldier, there a rubber band. In one load a mangled soda-bottle top. In another the gnawed cap to a ballpoint pen. "So that's where my comb went!" I exclaimed one morning.

He ate bath towels, sponges, socks, used Kleenex. Handi Wipes were a particular favorite, and when they eventually came out the other end, they looked like little blue flags marking each fluorescent orange mountain.

Not everything went down easily, and Marley vomited with the ease and regularity of a hard-core bulimic. We would hear him let out a loud *gaaaaack!* in the next room, and by the time we rushed in, there would be another household item, sitting in a puddle of half-digested mangoes and dog chow. Being considerate, Marley never puked on the hardwood floors or even the kitchen linoleum if he could help it. He always aimed for the Persian rug.

✽

Jenny and I had the foolish notion that it would be nice to
have a dog we could trust to be alone in the house for short
periods. Locking him in the bunker every time we stepped
out was becoming tedious, and as Jenny said, "What's the
point of having a dog if he can't greet you at the door when
you get home?" We knew full well we didn't dare leave him
in the house unaccompanied if there was any possibility of a
rainstorm. Even with his doggie downers, he still proved
himself capable of digging quite energetically for China.
When the weather was clear, though, we didn't want to
have to lock him in the garage every time we stepped out for
a few minutes.

We began leaving him briefly while we ran to the store or
dropped by a neighbor's house. Sometimes he did just fine
and we would return to find the house unscathed. On these
days, we would spot his black nose pushed through the
miniblinds as he stared out the living room window waiting
for us. Other days he didn't do quite so well, and we usually
knew trouble awaited us before we even opened the door
because he was not at the window but off hiding somewhere.

In Jenny's sixth month of pregnancy, we returned after
being away for less than an hour to find Marley under the
bed—at his size, he really had to work to get under there—
looking like he'd just murdered the mailman. Guilt radiated
off him. The house seemed fine, but we knew he was hiding
some dark secret, and we walked from room to room, trying
to ascertain just what he had done wrong. Then I noticed
that the foam cover to one of the stereo speakers was
missing. We looked everywhere for it. Gone without a trace.

Marley just might have gotten away with it had I not found incontrovertible evidence of his guilt when I went on poop patrol the next morning. Remnants of the speaker cover surfaced for days.

During our next outing, Marley surgically removed the woofer cone from the same speaker. The speaker wasn't knocked over or in any way amiss; the paper cone was simply gone, as if someone had sliced it out with a razor blade. Eventually he got around to doing the same to the other speaker. Another time, we came home to find that our four-legged footstool was now three-legged, and there was no sign whatsoever—not a single splinter—of the missing limb.

We swore it could never snow in South Florida, but one day we opened the front door to find a full blizzard in the living room. The air was filled with soft white fluff floating down. Through the near whiteout conditions we spotted Marley in front of the fireplace, half buried in a snowdrift, violently shaking a large feather pillow from side to side as though he had just bagged an ostrich.

For the most part we were philosophical about the damage. In every dog owner's life a few cherished family heirlooms must fall. Only once was I ready to slice him open to retrieve what was rightfully mine.

For her birthday I bought Jenny an eighteen-karat gold necklace, a delicate chain with a tiny clasp, and she immediately put it on. But a few hours later she pressed her hand to her throat and screamed, "My necklace! It's gone." The clasp must have given out or never been fully secured.

"Don't panic," I told her. "We haven't left the house. It's

got to be right here somewhere." We began scouring the house, room by room. As we searched, I gradually became aware that Marley was more rambunctious than usual. I straightened up and looked at him. He was squirming like a centipede. When he noticed I had him in my sights, he began evasive action. *Oh, no,* I thought—the Marley Mambo. It could mean only one thing.

"What's that," Jenny asked, panic rising in her voice, "hanging out of his mouth?"

It was thin and delicate. And gold. "Oh, shit!" I said.

"No sudden moves," she ordered, her voice dropping to a whisper. We both froze.

"Okay, boy, it's all right," I coaxed like a hostage negotiator on a SWAT team. "We're not mad at you. Come on now. We just want the necklace back." Instinctively, Jenny and I began to circle him from opposite directions, moving with glacial slowness. It was as if he were wired with high explosives and one false move could set him off.

"Easy, Marley," Jenny said in her calmest voice. "Easy now. Drop the necklace and no one gets hurt."

Marley eyed us suspiciously, his head darting back and forth between us. We had him cornered, but he knew he had something we wanted. I could see him weighing his options, a ransom demand, perhaps. *Leave two hundred unmarked Milk-Bones in a plain paper bag or you'll never see your precious little necklace again.*

"Drop it, Marley," I whispered, taking another small step forward. His whole body began to wag. I crept forward by degrees. Almost imperceptibly, Jenny closed in on his flank. We were within striking distance. We glanced at each other and knew, without speaking, what to do. We had been through the Property Recovery Drill countless times before. She would lunge for the hindquarters, pinning his back legs to prevent escape. I would lunge for the head, prying open his jaws and nabbing the contraband. With any luck, we'd be in and out in a matter of seconds. That was the plan, and Marley saw it coming.

We were less than two feet away from him. I nodded to Jenny and silently mouthed, "On three." But before we could make our move, he threw his head back and made a loud smacking sound. The tail end of the chain, which had been dangling out of his mouth, disappeared. "He's eating it!" Jenny screamed. Together we dove at him, Jenny tackling him by the hind legs as I gripped him in a headlock. I forced his jaws open and pushed my whole hand into his mouth and down his throat. I probed every flap and crevice and came up empty. "It's too late," I said. "He swallowed it." Jenny began slapping him on the back, yelling, "Cough it up, damn it!" But it was no use. The best she got out of him was a loud, satisfied burp.

Marley may have won the battle, but we knew it was just a matter of time before we won the war. Nature's call was on our side. Sooner or later, what went in had to come out. As disgusting as the thought was, I knew if I poked through his excrement long enough, I would find it. Had it been, say, a silver chain, or a gold-plated chain, something of any less value, my queasiness might have won out. But this chain was solid gold and had set me back a decent chunk of pay. Grossed out or not, I was going in.

And so I prepared Marley his favorite laxative—a giant

bowl of dead-ripe sliced mangoes—and settled in for the long wait. For three days I followed him around every time I let him out, eagerly waiting to swoop in with my shovel. Instead of tossing his piles over the fence, I carefully placed each on a wide board in the grass and poked it with a tree branch while I sprayed with a garden hose, gradually washing the digested material away into the grass and leaving behind any foreign objects. I felt like a gold miner working a sluice and coming up with a treasure trove of swallowed junk, from shoelaces to guitar picks. But no necklace. Where the hell was it? Shouldn't it have come out by now? I began wondering if I had missed it, accidentally washing it into the grass, where it would remain lost forever. But how could I miss a twenty-inch gold chain? Jenny was following my recovery operation from the porch with keen interest and even came up with a new nickname for me. "Hey, Scat Man Doo, any luck yet?" she called out.

On the fourth day, my perseverance paid off. I scooped up Marley's latest deposit, repeating what had become my daily refrain—"I can't believe I'm doing this"—and began poking and spraying. As the poop melted away, I searched for any sign of the necklace. Nothing. I was about to give up when I spotted something odd: a small brown lump, about the size of a lima bean. It wasn't even close to being large enough to be the missing jewelry, yet clearly it did not seem to belong there. I pinned it down with my probing branch, which I had officially christened the Shit Stick, and gave the object a strong blast from the hose nozzle. As the water washed it clean, I got a glimmer of something exceptionally bright and shiny. Eureka! I had struck gold.

The necklace was impossibly compressed, many times smaller than I would have guessed possible. It was as though some unknown alien power, a black hole perhaps, had sucked it into a mysterious dimension of space and time before spitting it out again. And, actually, that wasn't too far from the truth. The strong stream of water began to loosen the hard wad, and gradually the lump of gold unraveled back to its original shape, untangled and unmangled. Good as new. No, actually better than new. I took it inside to show Jenny, who was ecstatic to have it back, despite its dubious passage. We both marveled at how blindingly bright it was now—far more dazzling than when it had gone in. Marley's stomach acids had done an amazing job. It was the most brilliant gold I had ever seen. "Man," I said with a whistle. "We should open a jewelry-cleaning business."

"We could make a killing with the dowagers in Palm Beach," Jenny agreed.

"Yes, ladies," I parroted in my best slick-salesman voice, "our secret patented process is not available at any store! The proprietary Marley Method will restore your treasured valuables to a blinding brilliance you never thought possible."

"It's got possibilities, Grogan," Jenny said, and went off to disinfect her recovered birthday present. She wore that gold chain for years, and every time I looked at it I had the same vivid flashback to my brief and ultimately successful career in gold speculation. Scat Man Doo and his trusty Shit Stick had gone where no man had ever gone before. And none should ever go again.

CHAPTER 12

Welcome to the Indigent Ward

❖

You don't give birth to your first child every day, and so, when St. Mary's Hospital in West Palm Beach offered us the option of paying extra for a luxury birthing suite, we jumped at the chance. The suites looked like upper-end hotel rooms, spacious, bright, and well appointed with wood-grained furniture, floral wallpaper, curtains, a whirlpool bath, and, just for Dad, a comfy couch that folded out into a bed. Instead of standard-issue hospital food, "guests" were offered a choice of gourmet dinners. You could even order a bottle of champagne, though this was mostly for the fathers to chug on their own, as breast-feeding mothers were discouraged from having more than a celebratory sip.

"Man, it's just like being on vacation!" I exclaimed, bouncing on the Dad Couch as we took a tour several weeks before Jenny's due date.

The suites catered to the yuppie set and were a big source of profits for the hospital, bringing in hard cash from couples with money to blow above the standard insurance allotment for deliveries. A bit of an indulgence, we agreed, but why not?

When Jenny's big day came and we arrived at the hospital, overnight bag in hand, we were told there was a little problem.

"A problem?" I asked.

"It must be a good day for having babies," the receptionist said cheerfully. "All the birthing suites are already taken."

Taken? This was the most important day of our lives. What about the comfy couch and romantic dinner for two and champagne toast? "Now, wait a second," I complained. "We made our reservation weeks ago."

"I'm sorry," the woman said with a noticeable lack of sympathy. "We don't exactly have a lot of control over when mothers go into labor."

She made a valid point. It wasn't like she could hurry someone along. She directed us to another floor, where we would be issued a standard hospital room. But when we arrived in the maternity ward, the nurse at the counter had more bad news. "Would you believe every last room is filled?" she said. No, we couldn't. Jenny seemed to take it in stride, but I was getting testy now. "What do you suggest, the parking lot?" I snapped.

The nurse smiled calmly at me, apparently well familiar with the antics of nervous fathers-to-be, and said, "Don't you worry. We'll find a spot for you."

After a flurry of phone calls, she sent us down a long hallway and through a set of double doors, where we found ourselves in a mirror image of the maternity ward we had just left except for one obvious difference—the patients were definitely not the buttoned-down, disposable-income yuppies we had gone through Lamaze class with. We could hear the nurses talking in Spanish to patients, and standing in the hallway outside the rooms, brown-skinned men holding straw hats in rugged hands waited nervously.

Palm Beach County is known as a playground for the obscenely rich, but what is less widely known is that it also is home to huge farms that stretch across drained Everglades swamp for miles west of town. Thousands of migrant workers, mostly from Mexico and Central America, migrate into South Florida each growing season to pick the peppers, tomatoes, lettuce, and celery that supply much of the East Coast's winter vegetable needs. It seems we had discovered where the migrant workers came to have their babies. Periodically, a woman's anguished scream would pierce the air, followed by awful moans and calls of *"Mi madre!"* The place sounded like a house of horrors. Jenny was white as a ghost.

The nurse led us into a small cubicle containing one bed, one chair, and a bank of electronic monitors and handed Jenny a gown to change into. "Welcome to the indigent ward!" Dr. Sherman said brightly when he breezed in a few minutes later. "Don't be fooled by the bare-bones rooms," he said. They were outfitted with some of the most sophisticated medical equipment in the hospital, and the nurses were some of the best trained. Because poor women often lacked access to prenatal care, theirs were some of the highest-risk pregnancies. We were in good hands, he assured us as he broke Jenny's water. Then, as quickly as he had appeared, he was gone.

Indeed, as the morning progressed and Jenny fought her way through ferocious contractions, we discovered we were in very good hands. The nurses were seasoned professionals who exuded confidence and warmth, attentively hovering over her, checking the baby's heartbeat and coaching Jenny along. I stood helplessly by, trying my best to be supportive, but it wasn't working. At one point Jenny snarled at me through gritted teeth, "If you ask me one more time how I'm doing, I'm going to RIP YOUR FACE OFF!" I must have looked wounded because one of the nurses walked around to my side of the bed, squeezed my shoulders sympathetically, and said, "Welcome to childbirth, Dad. It's all part of the experience."

I began slipping out of the room to join the other men waiting in the hallway. Each of us leaned against the wall beside our respective doors as our wives screamed and moaned away. I felt a little ridiculous, dressed in my polo shirt, khakis, and Top-Siders, but the farmworkers didn't seem to hold it against me. Soon we were smiling and nodding knowingly to one another. They couldn't speak English and I couldn't speak Spanish, but that didn't matter. We were in this together.

Or almost together. I learned that day that in America pain relief is a luxury, not a necessity. For those who could afford it—or whose insurance covered it, as ours did—the hospital provided epidurals, which delivered pain-blocking oblivion directly into the central nervous system. About four hours into Jenny's labor, an anesthesiologist arrived and slipped a long needle through the skin along her spine and attached it to an intravenous drip. Within minutes, Jenny was numb from the waist down and resting comfortably. The Mexican women nearby were not so lucky. They were left to tough it out the old-fashioned way, and their shrieks continued to puncture the air.

The hours passed. Jenny pushed. I coached. As night fell I stepped out into the hall bearing a tiny swaddled football. I lifted my newborn son above my head for my new friends to see and called out, *"Es el niño!"* The other dads flashed big smiles and held up their thumbs in the international sign of approval. Unlike our heated struggle to name our dog, we would easily and almost instantly settle on a name for our firstborn son. He would be named Patrick for the first of my line of Grogans to arrive in the United States from County Limerick, Ireland. A nurse came into our cubicle and told us a birthing suite was now available. It seemed rather beside the point to change rooms now, but she helped Jenny into a wheelchair, placed our son in her arms, and whisked us away. The gourmet dinner wasn't all it was cracked up to be.

During the weeks leading up to her due date, Jenny and I had had long strategy talks about how best to acclimate Marley to the new arrival who would instantly knock him off his until-now undisputed perch as Most Favored Dependent. We wanted to let him down gently. We had heard stories of dogs becoming terribly jealous of infants and acting out in unacceptable ways—everything from urinating on prized possessions to knocking over bassinets to outright attacks— that usually resulted in a one-way ticket to the pound. As we converted the spare bedroom into a nursery, we gave Marley full access to the crib and bedding and all the various accoutrements of infancy. He sniffed and drooled and licked until his curiosity was satisfied. In the thirty-six hours that Jenny remained hospitalized recuperating after the birth, I made frequent trips home to visit Marley, armed with receiving blankets and anything else that carried the baby's scent. On one of my visits, I even brought home a tiny used disposable diaper, which Marley sniffed with such vigor I feared he might suck it up his nostril, requiring more costly medical intervention.

When I finally brought mother and child home, Marley was oblivious. Jenny placed baby Patrick, asleep in his car carrier, in the middle of our bed and then joined me in greeting Marley out in the garage, where we had an uproarious reunion. When Marley had settled down from frantically wild to merely desperately happy, we brought him into the house with us. Our plan was to just go about our business, not pointing the baby out to him. We would hover nearby and let him gradually discover the presence of the newcomer on his own.

Marley followed Jenny into the bedroom, jamming his nose deep into her overnight bag as she unpacked. He clearly had no idea there was a living thing sitting on our bed. Then Patrick stirred and let out a small, birdlike chirp. Marley's ears pulled up and he froze. *Where did that come from?* Patrick chirped again, and Marley lifted one paw in the air, pointing like a bird dog. My God, he was *pointing* at our baby boy like a hunting dog would point at . . . *prey*. In that instant, I thought of the feather pillow he had attacked with such ferocity. He wasn't so dense as to mistake a baby for a pheasant, was he?

Then he lunged. It was not a ferocious "kill the enemy" lunge; there were no bared teeth or growls. But it wasn't a "welcome to the neighborhood, little buddy" lunge, either. His chest hit the mattress with such force that the entire bed jolted across the floor. Patrick was wide awake now, eyes wide. Marley recoiled and lunged again, this time bringing his mouth within inches of our newborn's toes. Jenny dove for the baby and I dove for the dog, pulling him back by the collar with both hands. Marley was beside himself, straining to get at this new creature that somehow had snuck into our inner sanctum. He reared on his hind legs and I pulled back on his collar, feeling like the Lone Ranger with Silver. "Well, that went well," I said.

Jenny unbuckled Patrick from his car seat; I pinned Marley between my legs and held him tightly by the collar with both fists. Even Jenny could see Marley meant no harm. He was panting with that dopey grin of his; his eyes were bright and his tail was wagging. As I held tight, she gradually came closer, allowing Marley to sniff first the baby's toes, then his feet and calves and thighs. The poor kid was only a day and a half old, and he was already under attack by a Shop-Vac. When Marley reached the diaper, he seemed to enter an altered state of consciousness, a sort of Pampers-induced trance. He had reached the holy land. The dog looked positively euphoric.

"One false move, Marley, and you're toast," Jenny warned, and she meant it. If he had shown even the slightest aggression toward the baby, that would have been it. But he never did. We soon learned our problem was not keeping Marley from hurting our precious baby boy. Our problem was keeping him out of the diaper pail.

As the days turned into weeks and the weeks into months, Marley came to accept Patrick as his new best friend. One night early on, as I was turning off the lights to go to bed, I couldn't find Marley anywhere. Finally I thought to look in the nursery, and there he was, stretched out on the floor beside Patrick's crib, the two of them snoring away in stereophonic fraternal bliss. Marley, our wild crashing bronco, was different around Patrick. He seemed to understand that this was a fragile, defenseless little human, and he moved gingerly whenever he was near him, licking his face and ears delicately. As Patrick began crawling, Marley would lie quietly on the floor and let the baby scale him like a mountain, tugging on his ears, poking his eyes, and pulling out little fistfuls of fur. None of it fazed him. Marley just sat like a statue. He was a gentle giant around Patrick, and he accepted his second-fiddle status with bonhomie and good-natured resignation.

Not everyone approved of the blind faith we placed in our dog. They saw a wild, unpredictable, and powerful beast—he was approaching a hundred pounds by now—and thought us foolhardy to trust him around a defenseless infant. My mother was firmly in this camp and not shy about letting us know it. It pained her to watch Marley lick her grandson. "Do you know where that tongue has been?" she would ask rhetorically. She warned us darkly that we should never leave a dog and a baby alone in the same room. The ancient predatory instinct could surface without warning. If it were up to her, a concrete wall would separate Marley and Patrick at all times.

One day while she was visiting from Michigan, she let out a shriek from the living room. "John, quick!" she screamed. "The dog's biting the baby!" I raced out of the bedroom, half dressed, only to find Patrick swinging happily in his wind-up swing, Marley lying beneath him. Indeed, the dog was snapping at the baby, but it was not as my panicky mother had feared. Marley had positioned himself directly in Patrick's flight path with his head right where Patrick's bottom, strapped in a fabric sling, stopped at the peak of each arc before swinging back in the opposite direction. Each time Patrick's diapered butt came within striking distance, Marley would snap playfully at it, goosing him in the process. Patrick squealed with delight. "Aw, Ma, that's nothing," I said. "Marley just has a thing for his diapers."

Jenny and I settled into a routine. At nighttime she would get up with Patrick every few hours to nurse him, and I would take the 6:00 A.M. feeding so she could sleep in. Half asleep, I would pluck him from his crib, change his diaper, and make a bottle of formula for him. Then the payoff: I would sit on the back porch with his tiny, warm body nestled against my stomach as he sucked on the bottle. Sometimes I would let my face rest against the top of his head and doze off as he ate lustily. Sometimes I would listen to National Public Radio and watch the dawn sky turn from purple to pink to blue. When he was fed and I had gotten a good burp out of him, I would get us both dressed, whistle for Marley, and take a morning walk along the water. We invested in a jogging stroller with three large bicycle tires that allowed it to go pretty much anywhere, including through sand and over curbs. The three of us must have made quite a sight each morning, Marley out in front leading the charge like a mush dog, me in the rear holding us back for dear life, and Patrick in the middle, gleefully waving his arms in the air like a traffic cop. By the time we arrived home, Jenny would be up and have coffee on. We would strap Patrick into his high chair and sprinkle Cheerios on the tray for him, which Marley would snitch the instant we turned away, laying his head sideways on the tray and using his tongue to scoop them into his mouth. *Stealing food from a baby*, we thought; *how low will he stoop?* But Patrick seemed immensely amused by the whole routine, and pretty soon he learned how to push his Cheerios over the side so he could watch Marley scramble around, eating them off the floor. He also discovered that if he dropped Cheerios into his lap, Marley would poke his head up under the tray and jab Patrick in the stomach as he went for the errant cereal, sending him into peals of laughter.

Parenthood, we found, suited us well. We settled into its rhythms, celebrated its simple joys, and grinned our way through its frustrations, knowing even the bad days soon enough would be cherished memories. We had everything we could ask for. We had our precious baby. We had our numbskull dog. We had our little house by the water. Of course, we also had each other. That November, my newspaper promoted me to columnist, a coveted position that gave me my own space on the section front three times a week to spout off about whatever I wanted. Life was good. When Patrick was nine months old, Jenny wondered aloud when we might want to start thinking about having another baby.

"Oh, gee, I don't know," I said. We always knew we wanted more than one, but I hadn't really thought about a time frame. Repeating everything we had just gone through seemed like something best not rushed into. "I guess we could just go back off birth control again and see what happens," I suggested.

"Ah," Jenny said knowingly. "The old *Que será, será* school of family planning."

"Hey, don't knock it," I said. "It worked before."

So that is what we did. We figured if we conceived anytime in the next year, the timing would be about right. As Jenny did the math, she said, "Let's say six months to get pregnant and then nine more months to deliver. That would put two full years between them."

It sounded good to me. Two years was a long way off. Two years was next to an eternity. Two years was almost not real. Now that I had proved myself capable of the manly duty of insemination, the pressure was off. No worries, no stress. Whatever would be would be.

A week later, Jenny was knocked up.

CHAPTER 13

A Scream in the Night

�֍

With another baby growing inside her, Jenny's odd, late-night food cravings returned. One night it was root beer, the next grapefruit. "Do we have any Snickers bars?" she asked once a little before midnight. It looked like I was in for another jaunt down to the all-night convenience store. I whistled for Marley, hooked him to his leash, and set off for the corner. In the parking lot, a young woman with teased blond hair, bright lavender lips, and some of the highest heels I had ever seen engaged us. "Oh, he's so cute!" she gushed. "Hi, puppy. What's your name, cutie?" Marley, of course, was more than happy to strike up a friendship, and I pulled him tight against me so he wouldn't slobber on her purple miniskirt and white tank top. "You just want to kiss me, poochie, don't you?" she said, and made smooching noises with her lips.

As we chatted, I wondered what this attractive woman was doing out in a parking lot along Dixie Highway alone at this hour. She did not appear to have a car. She did not appear to be on her way into or out of the store. She was just there, a parking-lot ambassador cheerfully greeting strangers and their dogs as they approached as though she were our neighborhood's answer to the Wal-Mart greeters. Why was she so immensely friendly? Beautiful women were never friendly, at least not to strange men in parking lots at midnight. A car pulled up, and an older man rolled down his window. "Are you Heather?" he asked. She shot me a bemused smile as if to say, *You do what you have to do to pay the rent*. "Gotta run," she said, hopping into the car. "Bye, puppy."

"Don't fall too in love, Marley," I said as they drove off. "You can't afford her."

A few weeks later, at ten o'clock on a Sunday morning, I walked Marley to the same store to buy a *Miami Herald,* and again we were approached, this time by two young women, teenagers really, who both looked strung out and nervous. Unlike the first woman we had met, they were not terribly attractive and had taken no efforts to make themselves more so. They both looked desperate for their next hit off a crack pipe. "Harold?" one of them asked me. "Nope," I said, but what I was thinking was, *Do you really think some guy would show up for anonymous sex and bring his Labrador retriever along?* How twisted did these two think I was? As I pulled a newspaper out of the box in front of the store, a car arrived—Harold, I presumed—and the girls drove off with him.

I wasn't the only one witnessing the burgeoning prostitution trade along Dixie Highway. On a visit, my older sister, dressed as modestly as a nun, went for a midday walk and was propositioned twice by would-be johns trolling by in cars. Another guest arrived at our house to report that a woman had just exposed her breasts to him as he drove past, not that he particularly minded.

In response to complaints from residents, the mayor promised to publicly embarrass men arrested for soliciting, and the police began running stings, positioning undercover women officers on the corner and waiting for would-be customers to take the bait.

The decoy cops were the homeliest hookers I had ever seen— think J. Edgar Hoover in drag—but that didn't stop men from seeking their services. One bust went down on the curb directly in front of our house—with a television news crew in tow.

If it had been just the hookers and their customers, we could have made our separate peace, but the criminal activity didn't stop there. Our neighborhood seemed to grow dicier each day. On one of our walks along the water, Jenny, suffering a particularly debilitating bout of pregnancy-related nausea, decided to head home alone while I continued on with Patrick and Marley. As she walked along a side street, she heard a car idling behind her. Her first thought was that it was a neighbor pulling up to say hello or someone needing directions. When she turned to look into the car, the driver sat fully exposed and masturbating. After he got the expected response, he sped in reverse down the street so as to hide his license tag.

When Patrick was not quite a year old, murder again came to our block. Like Mrs. Nedermier, the victim was an elderly woman who lived alone. Hers was the first house as you turned onto Churchill Road off Dixie Highway, directly behind the all-night, open-air Laundromat, and I only knew her to wave to as I passed. Unlike Mrs. Nedermier's murder, this crime did not afford us the tidy self-denial of an inside job. The victim was chosen at random, and the attacker was a stranger who snuck into her house while she was in the backyard hanging her laundry on a Saturday afternoon. When she returned, he bound her wrists with telephone cord and shoved her beneath a mattress as he ransacked the house for money. He fled with his plunder as my frail neighbor slowly suffocated beneath the weight of the mattress. Police quickly arrested a drifter who had been seen hanging around the coin laundry; when they emptied his pockets they found his total haul had been sixteen dollars and change. The price of a human life.

The crime swirling around us made us grateful for Marley's bigger-than-life presence in our house. So what if he was an avowed pacifist whose most aggressive attack strategy was known as the Slobber Offensive? Who cared if his immediate response to the arrival of any stranger was to grab a tennis ball in the hope of having someone new to play catch with? The intruders didn't need to know that. When strangers came to our door, we no longer locked Marley away before answering. We stopped assuring them how harmless he was. Instead we now let drop vaguely ominous warnings, such as "He's getting so unpredictable lately," and "I don't know how many more of his lunges this screen door can take."

We had a baby now and another on the way. We were no longer so cheerfully cavalier about personal safety. Jenny and I often speculated about just what, if anything, Marley would do if someone ever tried to hurt the baby or us. I tended to think he would merely grow frantic, yapping and panting. Jenny placed more faith in him. She was convinced his special loyalty to us, especially to his new Cheerios pusher, Patrick, would translate in a crisis to a fierce primal protectiveness that would rise up from deep within him. "No way," I said. "He'd ram his nose into the bad guy's crotch and call it a day." Either way, we agreed, he scared the hell out of people. That was just fine with us. His presence made the difference between us feeling vulnerable or secure in our own home. Even as we continued to debate his effectiveness as a protector, we slept easily in bed knowing he was beside us. Then one night he settled the dispute once and for all.

It was October and the weather still had not turned. The night was sweltering, and we had the air-conditioning on and windows shut. After the eleven o'clock news I let Marley out to pee, checked Patrick in his crib, turned off the lights, and crawled into bed beside Jenny, already fast asleep. Marley, as he always did, collapsed in a heap on the floor beside me, releasing an exaggerated sigh. I was just drifting off when I heard it—a shrill, sustained, piercing noise. I was instantly wide awake, and Marley was, too. He stood frozen beside the bed in the dark, ears cocked. It came again, penetrating the sealed windows, rising above the hum of the air conditioner. A scream. A woman's scream, loud and unmistakable. My first thought was teenagers clowning around in the street, not an unusual occurrence. But this was not a happy, stop-tickling-me scream. There was desperation in it, real terror, and it was dawning on me that someone was in terrible trouble.

"Come on, boy," I whispered, slipping out of bed.

"Don't go out there." Jenny's voice came from beside me in the dark. I hadn't realized she was awake and listening.

"Call the police," I told her. "I'll be careful."

Holding Marley by the end of his choker chain, I stepped out onto the front porch in my boxer shorts just in time to glimpse a figure sprinting down the street toward the water. The scream came again, from the opposite direction. Outside, without the walls and glass to buffet it, the woman's voice filled the night air with an amazing, piercing velocity, the likes of which I had heard only in horror movies. Other porch lights were flicking on. The two young men who shared a rental house across the street from me burst outside, wearing nothing but cutoffs, and ran toward the screams. I followed cautiously at a distance, Marley tight by my side. I saw them run up on a lawn a few houses away and then, seconds later, come dashing back toward me.

"Go to the girl!" one of them shouted, pointing. "She's been stabbed."

"We're going after him!" the other yelled, and they sprinted off barefoot down the street in the direction the figure had fled. My neighbor Barry, a fearless single woman who had bought and rehabilitated a rundown bungalow next to the Nedermier house, jumped into her car and joined the chase.

I let go of Marley's collar and ran toward the scream. Three doors down I found my seventeen-year-old neighbor standing alone in her driveway, bent over, sobbing in jagged raspy gasps. She clasped her ribs, and beneath her hands I could see a circle of blood spreading across her blouse. She was a thin, pretty girl with sand-colored hair that fell over her shoulders. She lived in the house with her divorced mother, a pleasant woman who worked as a night nurse. I had chatted a few times with the mother, but I only knew her daughter to wave to. I didn't even know her name.

"He said not to scream or he'd stab me," she said, sobbing; her words gushed out in heaving, hyperventilated gulps. "But I screamed. I screamed, and he stabbed me." As if I might not believe her, she lifted her shirt to show me the puckered wound that had punctured her rib cage. "I was sitting in my car with the radio on. He just came out of nowhere." I put my hand on her arm to calm her, and as I did I saw her knees buckling. She collapsed into my arms, her legs folding fawnlike beneath her. I eased her down to the pavement and sat cradling her. Her words came softer, calmer now, and she fought to keep her eyes open. "He told me not to scream," she kept saying. "He put his hand on my mouth and told me not to scream."

"You did the right thing," I said. "You scared him away."

It occurred to me that she was going into shock, and I had not the first idea what to do about it. *Come on, ambulance. Where are you?* I comforted her in the only way I knew how, as I would comfort my own child, stroking her hair, holding my palm against her cheek, wiping her tears away. As she grew weaker, I kept telling her to hang on, help was on the way. "You're going to be okay," I said, but I wasn't sure I believed it. Her skin was ashen. We sat alone on the pavement like that for what seemed hours but was in actuality, the police report later showed, about three minutes. Only gradually did I think to check on what had become of Marley. When I looked up, there he stood, ten feet from us, facing the street, in a determined, bull-like crouch I had never seen before. It was a fighter's stance. His muscles bulged at the neck; his jaw was clenched; the fur between his shoulder blades bristled. He was intensely focused on the street and appeared poised to lunge. I realized in that instant that Jenny had been right. If the armed assailant returned, he would have to get past my dog first. At that moment I knew—I absolutely knew without doubt—that Marley would fight him to the death before he would let him at us. I was emotional anyway as I held this young girl, wondering if she was dying in my arms. The sight of Marley so uncharacteristically guarding us like that, so majestically fierce, brought tears to my eyes. Man's best friend? Damn straight he was.

"I've got you," I told the girl, but what I meant to say, what I should have said, was that *we* had her. Marley and me. "The police are coming," I said. "Hold on. Please, just hold on."

Before she closed her eyes, she whispered, "My name is Lisa."

"I'm John," I said. It seemed ridiculous, introducing ourselves in these circumstances as though we were at a neighborhood potluck. I almost laughed at the absurdity of it. Instead, I tucked a strand of her hair behind her ear and said, "You're safe now, Lisa."

Like an archangel sent from heaven, a police officer came charging up the sidewalk. I whistled to Marley and called,

"It's okay, boy. He's okay." And it was as if, with that whistle, I had broken some kind of trance. My goofy, good-natured pal was back, trotting in circles, panting, trying to sniff us. Whatever ancient instinct had welled up from the recesses of his ancestral psyche was back in its bottle again. Then more officers swarmed around us, and soon an ambulance crew arrived with a stretcher and wads of sterile gauze. I stepped out of the way, told the police what I could, and walked home, Marley loping ahead of me.

Jenny met me at the door and together we stood in the front window watching the drama unfold on the street. Our neighborhood looked like the set from a police television drama. Red strobe lights splashed through the windows. A police helicopter hovered overhead, shining its spotlight down on backyards and alleys. Cops set up roadblocks and combed the neighborhood on foot. Their efforts would be in vain; a suspect was never apprehended and a motive never determined. My neighbors who gave chase later told me they had not even caught a glimpse of him. Jenny and I eventually returned to bed, where we both lay awake for a long time.

"You would have been proud of Marley," I told her. "It was so strange. Somehow he knew how serious this was. He just knew. He felt the danger, and he was like a completely different dog."

"I told you so," she said. And she had.

As the helicopter thumped the air above us, Jenny rolled onto her side and, before drifting off, said, "Just another ho-hum night in the neighborhood." I reached down and felt in the dark for Marley, lying beside me.

"You did all right tonight, big guy," I whispered, scratching his ears. "You earned your dog chow." My hand on his back, I drifted off to sleep.

It said something about South Florida's numbness to crime that the stabbing of a teenage girl as she sat in her car in front of her home would merit just six sentences in the morning newspaper. The *Sun-Sentinel*'s account of the crime ran in the briefs column on page 3B beneath the headline "Man Attacks Girl."

The story made no mention of me or Marley or the guys across the street who set out half naked after the assailant. It didn't mention Barry, who gave chase in her car. Or all the neighbors up and down the block who turned on porch lights and dialed 911. In South Florida's seamy world of violent crime, our neighborhood's drama was just a minor hiccup. No deaths, no hostages, no big deal.

The knife had punctured Lisa's lung, and she spent five days in the hospital and several weeks recuperating at home. Her mother kept the neighbors apprised of her recovery, but the girl remained inside and out of sight. I worried about the emotional wounds the attack might leave. Would she ever again be comfortable leaving the safety of her home? Our lives had come together for just three minutes, but I felt invested in her as a brother might be in a kid sister. I wanted to respect her privacy, but I also wanted to see her, to prove to myself she was going to be all right.

Then as I washed the cars in the driveway on a Saturday, Marley chained up beside me, I looked up and there she stood. Prettier than I had remembered. Tanned, strong, athletic—looking whole again. She smiled and asked, "Remember me?"

"Let's see," I said, feigning puzzlement. "You look vaguely familiar. Weren't you the one in front of me at the Tom Petty concert who wouldn't sit down?"

She laughed, and I asked, "So how are you doing, Lisa?"

"I'm good," she said. "Just about back to normal."

"You look great," I told her. "A little better than the last time I saw you."

"Yeah, well," she said, and looked down at her feet. "What a night."

"What a night," I repeated.

That was all we said about it. She told me about the hospital, the doctors, the detective who interviewed her, the endless fruit baskets, the boredom of sitting at home as she healed. But she steered clear of the attack, and so did I. Some things were best left behind.

Lisa stayed a long time that afternoon, following me around the yard as I did chores, playing with Marley, making small talk. I sensed there was something she wanted to say but could not bring herself to. She was seventeen; I didn't expect her to find the words. Our lives had collided without plan or warning, two strangers thrown together by a burst of inexplicable violence. There had been no time for the usual proprieties that exist between neighbors; no time to establish boundaries. In a heartbeat, there we were, intimately locked together in crisis, a dad in boxer shorts and a teenage girl in a blood-soaked blouse, clinging to each other and to hope. There was a closeness there now. How could there

not be? There was also awkwardness, a slight embarrassment, for in that moment we had caught each other with
our guards down. Words were not necessary. I knew she
was grateful that I had come to her; I knew she appreciated
my efforts to comfort her, however lame. She knew I cared
deeply and was in her corner. We had shared something that
night on the pavement— one of those brief, fleeting moments of clarity that define all the others in a life—that
neither of us would soon forget.

"I'm glad you stopped by," I said.

"I'm glad I did, too," Lisa answered.

By the time she left, I had a good feeling about this girl.
She was strong. She was tough. She would move forward.
And indeed I found out years later, when I learned she had
built a career for herself as a television broadcaster, that she
had.

CHAPTER 14

An Early Arrival

❋

"John."

Through the fog of sleep, I gradually registered my name being called. "John. John, wake up." It was Jenny; she was shaking me. "John, I think the baby might be coming."

I propped myself up on an elbow and rubbed my eyes. Jenny was lying on her side, knees pulled to her chest. "The baby what?"

"I'm having bad cramps," she said. "I've been lying here timing them. We need to call Dr. Sherman."

I was wide awake now. *The baby was coming?* I was wild with anticipation for the birth of our second child—another boy, we already knew from the sonogram. The timing, though, was wrong, terribly wrong. Jenny was twenty-one weeks into the pregnancy, barely halfway through the forty-week gestation period. Among her motherhood books was a collection of high-definition in vitro photographs showing a fetus at each week of development. Just days earlier we had sat with the book, studying the photos taken at twenty-one weeks and marveling at how our baby was coming along. At twenty-one weeks a fetus can fit in the palm of a hand. It weighs less than a pound. Its eyes are fused shut, its fingers like fragile little twigs, its lungs not yet developed enough to distill oxygen from air. At twenty-one weeks, a baby is barely viable. The chance of surviving outside the womb is small, and the chance of surviving without serious, long-term health problems smaller yet. There's a reason nature keeps babies in the womb for nine long months. At twenty-one weeks, the odds are exceptionally long.

"It's probably nothing," I said. But I could feel my heart pounding as I speed-dialed the ob-gyn answering service. Two minutes later Dr. Sherman called back, sounding groggy himself. "It might just be gas," he said, "but we better have a look." He told me to get Jenny to the hospital immediately. I raced around the house, throwing items into an overnight bag for her, making baby bottles, packing the diaper bag. Jenny called her friend and coworker Sandy, another new mom who lived a few blocks away, and asked if we could drop Patrick off. Marley was up now, too, stretching, yawning, shaking. *Late-night road trip!* "Sorry, Mar," I told him as I led him out to the garage, grave disappointment on his face. "You've got to hold down the fort." I scooped Patrick out of his crib, buckled him into his car seat without waking him, and into the night we went.

At St. Mary's neonatal intensive care unit, the nurses quickly went to work. They got Jenny into a hospital gown and hooked her to a monitor that measured contractions and the baby's heartbeat. Sure enough, Jenny was having a contraction every six minutes. This was definitely not gas. "Your baby wants to come out," one of the nurses said. "We're going to do everything we can to make sure he doesn't just yet."

Over the phone Dr. Sherman asked them to check whether she was dilating. A nurse inserted a gloved finger and reported that Jenny was dilated one centimeter. Even I knew this was not good. At ten centimeters the cervix is fully dilated, the point at which, in a normal delivery, the mother begins to push. With each painful cramp, Jenny's body was pushing her one step closer to the point of no return.

Dr. Sherman ordered an intravenous saline drip and an injection of the labor inhibitor Brethine. The contractions leveled out, but less than two hours later they were back again with a fury, requiring a second shot, then a third.

For the next twelve days Jenny remained hospitalized, poked and prodded by a parade of perinatalogists and tethered to monitors and intravenous drips. I took vacation time and played single parent to Patrick, doing my best to hold everything together— the laundry, the feedings, meals, bills, housework, the yard. Oh, yes, and that other living creature in our home. Poor Marley's status dropped precipitously from second fiddle to not even in the orchestra. Even as I ignored him, he kept up his end of the relationship, never letting me out of his sight. He faithfully followed me as I careened through the house with Patrick in one arm, vacuuming or toting laundry or fixing a meal with the other. I would stop in the kitchen to toss a few dirty plates into the dishwasher, and Marley would plod in after me, circle around a half dozen times trying to pinpoint the exact perfect location, and then drop to the floor. No sooner had he settled in than I would dart to the laundry room to move the clothes from the washing machine to the dryer. He would follow after me, circle around, paw at the throw rugs until they were arranged to his liking, and plop down again, only to have me head for the living room to pick up the newspapers. So it would go. If he was lucky, I would pause in my mad dash to give him a quick pat.

One night after I finally got Patrick to sleep, I fell back on the couch, exhausted. Marley pranced over and dropped his rope tug toy in my lap and looked up at me with those giant brown eyes of his. "Aw, Marley," I said. "I'm beat." He put his snout under the rope toy and flicked it up in the air, waiting for me to try to grab it, ready to beat me to the draw. "Sorry, pal," I said. "Not tonight." He crinkled his brow and cocked his head. Suddenly, his comfortable daily routine was in tatters. His mistress was mysteriously absent, his master no fun, and nothing the same. He let out a little whine, and I could see he was trying to figure it out. *Why doesn't John want to play anymore? What happened to the morning walks? Why no more wrestling on the floor? And where exactly is Jenny, anyway? She hasn't run off with that Dalmatian in the next block, has she?*

Life wasn't completely bleak for Marley. On the bright side, I had quickly reverted to my premarriage (read: slovenly) lifestyle. By the power vested in me as the only adult in the house, I suspended the Married Couple Domesticity Act and proclaimed the once banished Bachelor Rules to be the law of the land. While Jenny was in the hospital, shirts

would be worn twice, even three times, barring obvious
mustard stains, between washes; milk could be drunk
directly from the carton, and toilet seats would remain in
the upright position unless being sat on. Much to Marley's
delight, I instituted a 24/7 open-door policy for the bathroom. After all, it was just us guys. This gave Marley yet a
new opportunity for closeness in a confined space. From
there, it only made sense to let him start drinking from the
bathtub tap. Jenny would have been appalled, but the way I
saw it, it sure beat the toilet. Now that the Seat-Up Policy
was firmly in place (and thus, by definition, the Lid-Up
Policy, too), I needed to offer Marley a viable alternative
to that attractive porcelain pool of water just begging him to
play submarine with his snout.

I got into the habit of turning the bathtub faucet on at a
trickle while I was in the bathroom so Marley could lap up
some cool, fresh water. The dog could not have been more
thrilled had I built him an exact replica of Splash Mountain.
He would twist his head up under the faucet and lap away,
tail banging the sink behind him. His thirst had no bounds,
and I became convinced he had been a camel in an earlier
life. I soon realized I had created a bathtub monster; pretty
soon Marley began going into the bathroom alone without
me and standing there, staring forlornly at the faucet, licking
at it for any lingering drop, flicking the drain knob with his
nose until I couldn't stand it any longer and would come in
and turn it on for him. Suddenly the water in his bowl was
somehow beneath him.

The next step on our descent into barbarity came when I
was showering. Marley figured out he could shove his head

past the shower curtain and get not just a trickle but a whole waterfall. I'd be lathering up and without warning his big tawny head would pop in and he'd begin lapping at the shower spray. "Just don't tell Mom," I said.

I tried to fool Jenny into thinking I had everything effortlessly under control. "Oh, we're totally fine," I told her, and then, turning to Patrick, I would add, "aren't we, partner?" To which he would give his standard reply: "Dada!" and then, pointing at the ceiling fan: "Fannnnn!" She knew better. One day when I arrived with Patrick for our daily visit, she stared at us in disbelief and asked, "What in God's name did you do to him?"

"What do you mean, what did I do to him?" I replied. "He's great. You're great, aren't you?"

"Dada! Fannnn!"

"His outfit," she said. "How on earth—"

Only then did I see. Something was amiss with Patrick's snap-on one-piece, or "onesie" as we manly dads like to call it. His chubby thighs, I now realized, were squeezed into the armholes, which were so tight they must have been cutting off his circulation. The collared neck hung between his legs like an udder. Up top, Patrick's head stuck out through the unsnapped crotch, and his arms were lost somewhere in the billowing pant legs. It was quite a look.

"You goof," she said. "You've got it on him upside down."

"That's your opinion," I said.

But the game was up. Jenny began working the phone from her hospital bed, and a couple of days later my sweet, dear aunt Anita, a retired nurse who had come to America from Ireland as a teenager and now lived across the state from us, magically appeared, suitcase in hand, and cheerfully went about restoring order. The Bachelor Rules were history.

When her doctors finally let Jenny come home, it was with the strictest of orders. If she wanted to deliver a healthy baby, she was to remain in bed, as still as possible. The only time she was allowed on her feet was to go to the bathroom. She could take one quick shower a day, then back into bed. No cooking, no changing diapers, no walking out for the mail, no lifting anything heavier than a toothbrush—and that meant her baby, a stipulation that nearly killed her. Complete bed rest, no cheating. Jenny's doctors had successfully shut down the early labor; their goal now was to keep it shut down for the next twelve weeks minimum. By then the baby would be thirty-five weeks along, still a little puny but fully developed and able to meet the outside world on its own terms. That meant keeping Jenny as still as a glacier. Aunt Anita, bless her charitable soul, settled in for the long haul. Marley was tickled to have a new playmate. Pretty soon he had Aunt Anita trained, too, to turn on the bathtub faucet for him.

A hospital technician came to our home and inserted a catheter into Jenny's thigh; this she attached to a small battery-powered pump that strapped to Jenny's leg and delivered a continuous trickle of labor-inhibiting drugs into her bloodstream. As if that weren't enough, she rigged Jenny with a monitoring system that looked like a torture device—

an oversized suction cup attached to a tangle of wires that hooked into the telephone. The suction cup attached to Jenny's belly with an elastic band and registered the baby's heartbeat and any contractions, sending them via phone line three times a day to a nurse who watched for the first hint of trouble. I ran down to the bookstore and returned with a small fortune in reading materials, which Jenny devoured in the first three days. She was trying to keep her spirits up, but the boredom, the tedium, the hourly uncertainty about the health of her unborn child, were conspiring to drag her down. Worst of all, she was a mother with a fifteen-month-old son whom she was not allowed to lift, to run to, to feed when he was hungry, to bathe when he was dirty, to scoop up and kiss when he was sad. I would drop him on top of her on the bed, where he would pull her hair and stick his fingers into her mouth. He'd point to the whirling paddles above the bed, and say, "Mama! Fannnnn!" It made her smile, but it wasn't the same. She was slowly going stir-crazy.

Her constant companion through it all, of course, was Marley. He set up camp on the floor beside her, surrounding himself with a wide assortment of chew toys and rawhide bones just in case Jenny changed her mind and decided to jump out of bed and engage in a little spur-of-the-moment tug-of-war. There he held vigil, day and night. I would come home from work and find Aunt Anita in the kitchen cooking dinner, Patrick in his bouncy seat beside her. Then I would walk into the bedroom to find Marley standing beside the bed, chin on the mattress, tail wagging, nose nuzzled into Jenny's neck as she read or snoozed or merely stared at the ceiling, her arm draped over his back. I marked off each day on the calendar to help her track her progress, but it only served as a reminder of how slowly each minute, each hour, passed. Some people are content to spend their lives in idle recline; Jenny was not one of them. She was born to bustle, and the forced idleness dragged her down by imperceptible degrees, a little more each day. She was like a sailor caught in the doldrums, waiting with increasing desperation for the faintest hint of a breeze to fill the sails and let the journey continue. I tried to be encouraging, saying things like "A year from now we're going to look back on this and laugh," but I could tell part of her was slipping from me. Some days her eyes were very far away.

When Jenny had a full month of bed rest still to go, Aunt Anita packed her suitcase and kissed us good-bye. She had stayed as long as she could, in fact extending her visit several times, but she had a husband at home who she only half jokingly fretted was quite possibly turning feral as he survived alone on TV dinners and ESPN. Once again, we were on our own.

I did my best to keep the ship afloat, rising at dawn to bathe and dress Patrick, feed him oatmeal and puréed carrots, and take him and Marley for at least a short walk. Then I would drop Patrick at Sandy's house for the day while I worked, picking him up again in the evening. I would come home on my lunch hour to make Jenny her lunch, bring her the mail—the highlight of her day—throw sticks to Marley, and straighten up the house, which was slowly taking on a patina of neglect. The grass went uncut, the laundry unwashed, and the screen on the back porch remained unrepaired after Marley crashed through it, cartoon-style, in pursuit of a squirrel. For weeks the shredded screen flapped in the breeze, becoming a de facto doggie door that allowed Marley to come and go as he pleased between the backyard and house during the long hours home alone with the bedridden Jenny. "I'm going to fix it," I promised her. "It's on the list." But I could see dismay in her eyes. It took all of her self-control not to jump out of bed and whip her home back into shape. I grocery-shopped after Patrick was asleep for the night, sometimes walking the aisles at midnight. We survived on carry-outs, Cheerios, and pots of pasta. The journal I had faithfully kept for years abruptly went silent.

There was simply no time and less energy. In the last brief entry, I wrote only: "Life is a little overwhelming right now."

Then one day, as we approached Jenny's thirty-fifth week of pregnancy, the hospital technician arrived at our door and said, "Congratulations, girl, you've made it. You're free again." She unhooked the medicine pump, removed the catheter, packed up the fetal monitor, and went over the doctor's written orders. Jenny was free to return to her regular lifestyle. No restrictions. No more medications. We could even have sex again. The baby was fully viable now. Labor would come when it would come. "Have fun," she said. "You deserve it."

Jenny tossed Patrick over her head, romped with Marley in the backyard, tore into the housework. That night we celebrated by going out for Indian food and catching a show at a local comedy club. The next day the three of us continued the festivities by having lunch at a Greek restaurant. Before the gyros ever made it to our table, however, Jenny was in full-blown labor. The cramps had begun the night before as she ate curried lamb, but she had ignored them. She wasn't going to let a few contractions interrupt her hard-earned night on the town. Now each contraction nearly doubled her over. We raced home, where Sandy was on standby to take Patrick and keep an eye on Marley. Jenny waited in the car, puffing her way through the pain with sharp, shallow breaths as I grabbed her overnight bag. By the time we got to the hospital and checked into a room, Jenny was dilated to seven centimeters. Less than an hour later, I held our new son in my arms. Jenny counted his fingers and toes. His eyes were open and alert, his cheeks blushed.

"You did it," Dr. Sherman declared. "He's perfect."

Conor Richard Grogan, five pounds and thirteen ounces, was born October 10, 1993. I was so happy I barely gave a second thought to the cruel irony that for this pregnancy we had rated one of the luxury suites but had hardly a moment to enjoy it. If the delivery had been any quicker, Jenny would have given birth in the parking lot of the Texaco station. I hadn't even had time to stretch out on the Dad Couch.

Considering what we had been through to bring him safely into this world, we thought the birth of our son was big news—but not so big that the local news media would turn out for it. Below our window, though, a crush of television news trucks gathered in the parking lot, their satellite dishes poking into the sky. I could see reporters with microphones doing their stand-ups in front of the cameras. "Hey, honey," I said, "the paparazzi have turned out for you."

A nurse, who was in the room attending to the baby, said, "Can you believe it? Donald Trump is right down the hall."

"Donald Trump?" Jenny asked. "I didn't know he was pregnant."

The real estate tycoon had caused quite a stir when he moved to Palm Beach several years earlier, setting up house in the sprawling former mansion of Marjorie Merriweather Post, the late cereal heiress. The estate was named Mar-a-Lago, meaning "Sea to Lake," and as the name implied, the property stretched for seventeen acres from the Atlantic Ocean to the Intracoastal Waterway and included a nine-hole golf course. From the foot of our street we could look across the water and see the fifty-eight-bedroom mansion's Moorish-influenced spires rising above the palm trees. The Trumps and the Grogans were practically neighbors.

I flicked on the TV and learned that The Donald and girlfriend Marla Maples were the proud parents of a girl, appropriately named Tiffany, who was born not long after Jenny delivered Conor. "We'll have to invite them over for a playdate," Jenny said.

We watched from the window as the television crews swarmed in to catch the Trumps leaving the hospital with their new baby to return to their estate. Marla smiled demurely as she held her newborn for the cameras to capture; Donald waved and gave a jaunty wink. "I feel great!'' he told the cameras. Then they were off in a chauffeured limousine.

The next morning when our turn came to leave for home, a pleasant retiree who volunteered at the hospital guided Jenny and baby Conor through the lobby in a wheelchair and out the automatic doors into the sunshine. There were no camera crews, no satellite trucks, no sound bites, no live reports. It was just us and our senior volunteer. Not that anyone was asking, but I felt great, too. Donald Trump was not the only one bursting with pride over his progeny.

The volunteer waited with Jenny and the baby while I pulled the car up to the curb. Before buckling my newborn son into his car seat, I lifted him high above my head for the whole world to see, had anyone been looking, and said, ''Conor Grogan, you are every bit as special as Tiffany Trump, and don't you ever forget it.''

CHAPTER 15

A Postpartum Ultimatum

These should have been the happiest days of our lives, and in many ways they were. We had two sons now, a toddler and a newborn, just seventeen months apart. The joy they brought us was profound. Yet the darkness that had descended over Jenny while she was on forced bed rest persisted. Some weeks she was fine, cheerfully tackling the challenges of being responsible for two lives completely dependent on her for every need. Other weeks, without warning, she would turn glum and defeated, locked in a blue fog that sometimes would not lift for days. We were both exhausted and sleep deprived. Patrick was still waking us at least once in the night, and Conor was up several more times, crying to be nursed or changed. Seldom did we get more than two hours of uninterrupted sleep at a stretch. Some nights we were like zombies, moving silently past each other with glazed eyes, Jenny to one baby and I to the other. We were up at midnight and at two and at three-thirty and again at five. Then the sun would rise and with it another day, bringing renewed hope and a bone-aching weariness as we began the cycle over again. From down the hall would come Patrick's sweet, cheery, wide-awake voice—"Mama! Dada! Fannnn!"—and as much as we tried to will it otherwise, we knew sleep, what there had been of it, was behind us for another day. I began making the coffee stronger and showing up at work with shirts wrinkled and baby spit-up on my ties. One morning in my newsroom, I caught the young, attractive editorial assistant staring intently at me. Flattered, I smiled at her. *Hey, I might be a dad twice over now, but the women still notice me.* Then she said, "Do you know you have a Barney sticker in your hair?"

Complicating the sleep-deprived chaos that was our lives, our new baby had us terribly worried. Already underweight, Conor was unable to keep nourishment down. Jenny was on a single-minded quest to nurse him to robust health, and he seemed equally intent on foiling her. She would offer him her breast, and he would oblige her, suckling hungrily. Then, in one quick heave, he would throw it all up. She would nurse him again; he would eat ravenously, then empty his stomach yet again. Projectile vomiting became an hourly occurrence in our lives. Over and over the routine repeated itself, each time Jenny becoming more frantic. The doctors diagnosed reflux and referred us to a specialist, who sedated our baby boy and snaked a scope down his throat to scrutinize his insides. Conor eventually would outgrow the condition and catch up on his weight, but for four long months we were consumed with worry over him. Jenny was a basket case of fear and stress and frustration, all exacerbated by lack of sleep, as she nursed him nearly nonstop and then watched helpless as he tossed her milk back at her. "I feel so inadequate," she

would say. "Moms are supposed to be able to give their babies everything they need." Her fuse was as short as I had seen it, and the smallest infractions—a cupboard door left open, crumbs on the counter—would set her off.

The good news was that Jenny never once took out her anxiety on either baby. In fact, she nurtured both of them with almost obsessive care and patience. She poured every ounce of herself into them. The bad news was that she directed her frustration and anger at me and even more at Marley. She had lost all patience with him. He was squarely in her crosshairs and could do no right. Each transgression—and there continued to be many—pushed Jenny a little closer to the edge. Oblivious, Marley stayed the course with his antics and misdeeds and boundless ebullience. I bought a flowering shrub and planted it in the garden to commemorate Conor's birth; Marley pulled it out by the roots the same day and chewed it into mulch. I finally got around to replacing the ripped porch screen, and Marley, by now quite accustomed to his self-made doggie door, promptly dove through it again. He escaped one day and when he finally returned, he had a pair of women's panties in his teeth. I didn't want to know.

Despite the prescription tranquilizers, which Jenny was feeding him with increasing frequency, more for her sake than for his, Marley's thunder phobia grew more intense and irrational each day. By now a soft shower would send him into a panic. If we were home, he would merely glom on to us and salivate nervously all over our clothes. If we weren't home, he sought safety in the same warped way, by digging and gouging through doors and plaster and linoleum. The more I repaired, the more he destroyed. I could not keep up with him. I should have been furious, but Jenny was angry enough for both of us. Instead, I started covering for him. If I found a chewed shoe or book or pillow, I hid the evidence before she could find it. When he crashed through our small home, the bull in our china closet, I followed behind him, straightening throw rugs, righting coffee tables, and wiping up the spittle he flung on the walls. Before Jenny discovered them, I would race to vacuum up the wood chips in the garage where he had gouged the door once again. I stayed up late into the night patching and sanding so by morning when Jenny awoke the latest damage would be covered over. "For God's sake, Marley, do you have a death wish?" I said to him one night as he stood at my side, tail wagging, licking my ear as I knelt and repaired the most recent destruction. "You've got to stop this."

It was into this volatile environment that I walked one evening. I opened the front door to find Jenny beating Marley with her fists. She was crying uncontrollably and flailing wildly at him, more like she was pounding a kettledrum than imposing a beating, landing glancing blows on his back and shoulders and neck. "Why? Why do you do this?" she screamed at him. "Why do you wreck everything?" In that instant I saw what he had done. The couch cushion was gouged open, the fabric shredded and the stuffing pulled out. Marley stood with head down and legs splayed as though leaning into a hurricane. He didn't try to flee or dodge the blows; he just stood there and took each one without whimper or complaint.

"Hey! Hey! Hey!" I shouted, grabbing her wrists. "Come on. Stop. Stop!" She was sobbing and gasping for breath. "Stop," I repeated.

I stepped between her and Marley and shoved my face directly in front of hers. It was like a stranger was staring back at me. I did not recognize the look in her eyes. "Get him out of here," she said, her voice flat and tinged with a quiet burn. "Get him out of here now."

"Okay, I'll take him out," I said, "but you settle down."

"Get him out of here and keep him out of here," she said in an unsettling monotone.

I opened the front door and he bounded outside, and when I turned back to grab his leash off the table, Jenny said, "I mean it. I want him gone. I want him out of here for good."

"Come on," I said. "You don't mean that."

"I mean it," she said. "I'm done with that dog. You find him a new home, or I will."

She couldn't mean it. She loved this dog. She adored him despite his laundry list of shortcomings. She was upset; she was stressed to the breaking point. She would reconsider. For the moment I thought it was best to give her time to cool down. I walked out the door without another word. In the front yard, Marley raced around, jumping into the air and snapping his jaws, trying to bite the leash out of my hand. He was his old jolly self, apparently no worse for the pummeling. I knew she hadn't hurt him. In all honesty, I routinely whacked him much harder when I played rough with him, and he loved it, always bounding back for more. As was a hallmark of his breed, he was immune to pain, an unstoppable machine of muscle and sinew. Once when I was in the driveway washing the car, he jammed his head into the bucket of soapy water and galloped blindly off across the front lawns with the bucket firmly stuck over his head, not stopping until he crashed full force into a concrete wall. It didn't seem to faze him. But slap him lightly on the rump with an open palm in anger, or even just speak to him with a stern voice, and he acted deeply wounded. For the big dense oaf that he was, Marley had an incredibly sensitive streak. Jenny hadn't hurt him physically, not even close, but she had crushed his feelings, at least for the moment. Jenny was everything to him, one of his two best pals in the whole world, and she had just turned on him. She was his mistress and he her faithful companion. If she saw fit to strike him, he saw fit to suck it up and take it. As far as dogs went, he was not good at much; but he was unquestionably loyal. It was my job now to repair the damage and make things right again.

Out in the street, I hooked him to his leash and ordered, "Sit!" He sat. I pulled the choker chain up high on his throat in preparation for our walk. Before I stepped off I ran my hand over his head and massaged his neck. He flipped his nose in the air and looked up at me, his tongue hanging halfway down his neck. The incident with Jenny appeared to be behind him; now I hoped it would be behind her, as well. "What am I going to do with you, you big dope?" I asked him. He leaped straight up, as though outfitted with springs, and smashed his tongue against my lips.

Marley and I walked for miles that evening, and when I finally opened the front door, he was exhausted and ready to collapse quietly in the corner. Jenny was feeding Patrick a jar of baby food as she cradled Conor in her lap. She was calm and appeared back to her old self. I unleashed Marley and he took a huge drink, lapping lustily at the water, sloshing little tidal waves over the side of his bowl. I toweled up the floor and stole a glance in

Jenny's direction; she appeared unperturbed. Maybe the horrible moment had passed. Maybe she had reconsidered. Maybe she felt sheepish about her outburst and was searching for the words to apologize. As I walked past her, Marley close at my heels, she said in a calm, quiet voice without looking at me, "I'm dead serious. I want him out of here."

Over the next several days she repeated the ultimatum enough times that I finally accepted that this was not an idle threat. She wasn't just blowing off steam, and the issue was not going away. I was sick about it. As pathetic as it sounds, Marley had become my male-bonding soul mate, my near-constant companion, my friend. He was the undisciplined, recalcitrant, nonconformist, politically incorrect free spirit I had always wanted to be, had I been brave enough, and I took vicarious joy in his unbridled verve. No matter how complicated life became, he reminded me of its simple joys. No matter how many demands were placed on me, he never let me forget that willful disobedience is sometimes worth the price. In a world full of bosses, he was his own master. The thought of giving him up seared my soul. But I had two children to worry about now and a wife whom we needed. Our household was being held together by the most tenuous of threads. If losing Marley made the difference between meltdown and stability, how could I not honor Jenny's wishes?

I began putting out feelers, discreetly asking friends and coworkers if they might be interested in taking on a lovable and lively two-year-old Labrador retriever. Through word of mouth, I learned of a neighbor who adored dogs and couldn't refuse a canine in need. Even he said no. Unfortunately, Marley's reputation preceded him.

Each morning I opened the newspaper to the classifieds as if I might find some miracle ad: "Seeking wildly energetic, out-of-control Labrador retriever with multiple phobias. Destructive qualities a plus. Will pay top dollar." What I found instead was a booming trade in young adult dogs that, for whatever reason, had not worked out. Many were purebreds that their owners had spent several hundred dollars for just months earlier. Now they were being offered for a pittance or even for free. An alarming number of the unwanted dogs were male Labs.

The ads were in almost every day, and were at once heartbreaking and hilarious. From my insider's vantage point, I recognized the attempts to gloss over the real reasons these dogs were back on the market. The ads were full of sunny euphemisms for the types of behavior I knew all too well. "Lively . . . loves people . . . needs big yard . . . needs room to run . . . energetic . . . spirited . . . powerful . . . one of a kind." It all added up to the same thing: a dog its master could not control. A dog that had become a liability. A dog its owner had given up on.

Part of me laughed knowingly; the ads were comical in their deception. When I read "fiercely loyal" I knew the seller really meant "known to bite." "Constant companion" meant "suffers separation anxiety," and "good watchdog" translated to "incessant barker." And when I saw "best offer," I knew too well that the desperate owner really was asking, "How much do I need to pay you to take this thing off my hands?" Part of me ached with sadness. I was not a

quitter; I did not believe Jenny was a quitter, either. We
were not the kind of people who pawned off our problems
in the classifieds. Marley was undeniably a handful. He was
nothing like the stately dogs both of us had grown up with.
He had a host of bad habits and behaviors. Guilty as charged.
He also had come a great distance from the spastic puppy
we had brought home two years earlier. In his own flawed
way, he was trying. Part of our journey as his owners was to
mold him to our needs, but part also was to accept him for
what he was. Not just to accept him, but to celebrate him
and his indomitable canine spirit. We had brought into our
home a living, breathing being, not a fashion accessory to
prop in the corner. For better or worse, he was our dog. He
was a part of our family, and, for all his flaws, he had
returned our affection one hundredfold. Devotion such as
his could not be bought for any price.

I was not ready to give up on him.

Even as I continued to make halfhearted inquiries about
finding Marley a new home, I began working with him in
earnest. My own private Mission: Impossible was to reha-
bilitate this dog and prove to Jenny he was worthy. Interrupted sleep be damned, I began rising at dawn, buckling
Patrick into the jogging stroller, and heading down to the
water to put Marley through the paces. Sit. Stay. Down.
Heel. Over and over we practiced. There was a desperation
to my mission, and Marley seemed to sense it. The stakes
were different now; this was for real. In case he didn't fully
understand that, I spelled it out for him more than once
without mincing words: "We're not screwing around here,
Marley. This is it. Let's go." And I would put him through the

commands again, with my helper Patrick clapping and calling to his big yellow friend, "Waddy! Hee-O!"

By the time I reenrolled Marley in obedience school, he was a different dog from the juvenile delinquent I had first shown up with. Yes, still as wild as a boar, but this time he knew I was the boss and he was the underling. This time there would be no lunges toward other dogs (or at least not many), no out-of-control surges across the tarmac, no crashing into strangers' crotches. Through eight weekly sessions, I marched him through the commands on a tight leash, and he was happy—make that overjoyed—to cooperate. At our final meeting, the trainer—a relaxed woman who was the antithesis of Miss Dominatrix—called us forward. "Okay," she said, "show us what you've got."

I ordered Marley into a sit position, and he dropped neatly to his haunches. I raised the choker chain high around his throat and with a crisp tug of the lead ordered him to heel. We trotted across the parking lot and back, Marley at my side, his shoulder brushing my calf, just as the book said it should. I ordered him to sit again, and I stood directly in front of him and pointed my finger at his forehead. "Stay," I said calmly, and with the other hand I dropped his leash. I stepped backward several paces. His big brown eyes fixed on me, waiting for any small sign from me to release him, but he remained anchored. I walked in a 360-degree circle around him. He quivered with excitement and tried to rotate his head, Linda Blair–style, to watch me, but he did not budge. When I was back in front of him, just for kicks, I snapped my fingers and yelled, "Incoming!" He hit the deck like he was storming Iwo Jima. The teacher burst out laughing, a good sign. I turned my back on him and walked thirty feet away. I could feel his eyes burning into my back, but he held fast. He was quaking violently by the time I turned around to face him. The volcano was getting ready to blow. Then, spreading my feet into a wide boxer's stance in anticipation of what was coming, I said, "Marley . . ." I let his name hang in the air for a few seconds. "Come!" He shot at me with everything he had, and I braced for impact. At the last instant I deftly sidestepped him with a bullfighter's grace, and he blasted past me, then circled back and goosed me from behind with his nose.

"Good boy, Marley," I gushed, dropping to my knees. "Good, good, good boy! You a good boy!" He danced around me like we had just conquered Mount Everest together.

At the end of the evening, the instructor called us up and handed us our diploma. Marley had passed basic obedience training, ranking seventh in the class. So what if it was a class of eight and the eighth dog was a psychopathic pit bull that seemed intent on taking a human life at the first opportunity? I would take it. Marley, my incorrigible, untrainable, undisciplined dog, had passed. I was so proud I could have cried, and in fact I actually might have had Marley not leapt up and promptly eaten his diploma.

On the way home, I sang "We Are the Champions" at the top of my lungs. Marley, sensing my joy and pride, stuck his tongue in my ear. For once, I didn't even mind.

There was still one piece of unfinished business between Marley and me. I needed to break him of his worst habit of all: jumping on people. It didn't matter if it was a friend or a stranger, a child or an adult, the meter reader or the UPS driver. Marley greeted them the same way—by charging at them full speed, sliding across the floor, leaping up, and planting his two front paws on the person's chest or shoulders as he licked their face. What had been cute when he was a cuddly puppy had turned obnoxious, even terrifying for some recipients of his uninvited advances. He had knocked over children, startled guests, dirtied our friends' dress shirts and blouses, and nearly taken down my frail mother. No one appreciated it. I had tried without success to break him of jumping up, using standard dog-obedience techniques. The message was not getting through. Then a veteran dog owner I respected said, "You want to break him of that, give him a swift knee in the chest next time he jumps up on you."

"I don't want to hurt him," I said.

"You won't hurt him. A few good jabs with your knee, and I guarantee you he'll be done jumping."

It was tough-love time. Marley had to reform or relocate. The next night when I arrived home from work, I stepped in the front door and yelled, "I'm home!" As usual, Marley came barreling across the wood floors to greet me. He slid the last ten feet as though on ice, then lifted off to smash his paws into my chest and slurp at my face. Just as his paws made contact with me, I gave one swift pump of my knee, connecting in the soft spot just below his rib cage. He gasped slightly and slid down to the floor, looking up at me with a wounded expression, trying to figure out what had gotten into me. He had been jumping on me his whole life; what was with the sudden sneak attack?

The next night I repeated the punishment. He leapt, I

kneed, he dropped to the floor, coughing. I felt a little cruel, but if I were going to save him from the classifieds, I knew I had to drive home the point. "Sorry, guy," I said, leaning down so he could lick me with all four paws on the ground. "It's for your own good."

The third night when I walked in, he came charging around the corner, going into his typical high-speed skid as he approached. This time, however, he altered the routine. Instead of leaping, he kept his paws on the ground and crashed headfirst into my knees, nearly knocking me over. I'd take that as a victory. "You did it, Marley! You did it! Good boy! You didn't jump up." And I got on my knees so he could slobber me without risking a sucker punch. I was impressed. Marley had bent to the power of persuasion.

The problem was not exactly solved, however. He may have been cured of jumping on me, but he was not cured of jumping on anyone else. The dog was smart enough to figure out that only I posed a threat, and he could still jump on the rest of the human race with impunity. I needed to widen my offensive, and to do that I recruited a good friend of mine from work, a reporter named Jim Tolpin. Jim was a mild-mannered, bookish sort, balding, bespectacled, and of slight build. If there was anyone Marley thought he could jump up on without consequence, it was Jim. At the office one day I laid out the plan. He was to come to the house after work, ring the doorbell, and then walk in. When Marley jumped up to kiss him, he was to give him all he had. "Don't be shy about it," I coached. "Subtlety is lost on Marley."

That night Jim rang the bell and walked in the door. Sure enough, Marley took the bait and raced at him, ears flying back. When Marley left the ground to leap up on him, Jim took my advice to heart. Apparently worried he would be too timid, he dealt a withering blow with his knee to Marley's solar plexus, knocking the wind out of him. The thud was audible across the room. Marley let out a loud moan, went bug-eyed, and sprawled on the floor.

"Jesus, Jim," I said. "Have you been studying kung fu?"

"You told me to make him feel it," he answered.

He had. Marley got to his feet, caught his breath, and greeted Jim the way a dog should—on all four paws. If he could have talked, I swear he would have cried uncle. Marley never again jumped up on anyone, at least not in my presence, and no one ever kneed him in the chest or anywhere else again.

One morning, not long after Marley abandoned his jumping habit, I woke up and my wife was back. My Jenny, the woman I loved who had disappeared into that unyielding blue fog, had returned to me. As suddenly as the postpartum depression had swept over her, it swept away again. It was as if she had been exorcised of her demons. They were gone. Blessedly gone. She was strong, she was upbeat, she was not only coping as a young mother of two, but thriving. Marley was back in her good graces, safely on solid ground. With a baby in each arm, she leaned to kiss him. She threw him sticks and made him gravy from hamburger drippings. She danced him around the room when a good song came on the stereo. Sometimes at night when he was calm, I would find her lying on the floor with him, her head resting on his neck. Jenny was back. Thank God, she was back.

CHAPTER 16

The Audition

✳

Some things in life are just too bizarre to be anything but true, so when Jenny called me at the office to tell me Marley was getting a film audition, I knew she couldn't be making it up. Still, I was in disbelief. "A what?" I asked.

"A film audition."

"Like for a movie?"

"Yes, like for a movie, dumbo," she said. "A feature-length movie."

"Marley? A feature-length movie?"

We went on like this for some time as I tried to reconcile the image of our lug-head chewer of ironing boards with the image of a proud successor to Rin Tin Tin leaping across the silver screen, pulling helpless children from burning buildings.

"Our Marley?" I asked one more time, just to be sure.

It was true. A week earlier, Jenny's supervisor at the *Palm Beach Post* called and said she had a friend who needed to ask a favor of us. The friend was a local photographer named

Colleen McGarr who had been hired by a New York City film-production company called the Shooting Gallery to help with a movie they planned to make in Lake Worth, the town just south of us. Colleen's job was to find a "quintessential South Florida household" and photograph it top to bottom—the bookshelves, the refrigerator magnets, the closets, you name it—to help the directors bring realism to the film.

"The whole set crew is gay," Jenny's boss told her. "They're trying to figure out how married couples with kids live around here."

"Sort of like an anthropological case study," Jenny said.

"Exactly."

"Sure," Jenny agreed, "as long as I don't have to clean first."

Colleen came over and started photographing, not just our possessions but us, too. The way we dressed, the way we wore our hair, the way we slouched on the couch. She photographed toothbrushes on the sink. She photographed the babies in their cribs. She photographed the quintessentially heterosexual couple's eunuch dog, too. Or at least what she could catch of him on film. As she observed, "He's a bit of a blur."

Marley could not have been more thrilled to participate. Ever since babies had invaded, Marley took his affection where he could find it. Colleen could have jabbed him with a cattle prod; as long as he was getting some attention, he was okay with it. Colleen, being a lover of large animals and not intimidated by saliva showers, gave him plenty, dropping to her knees to wrestle with him.

As Colleen clicked away, I couldn't help thinking of the

possibilities. Not only were we supplying raw anthropological data to the filmmakers, we were essentially being given our own personal casting call. I had heard that most of the secondary actors and all of the extras for this film would be hired locally. What if the director spotted a natural star amid the kitchen magnets and poster art? Stranger things had happened.

I could just picture the director, who in my fantasy looked a lot like Steven Spielberg, bent over a large table scattered with hundreds of photographs. He flips impatiently through them, muttering, "Garbage! Garbage! This just won't do." Then he freezes over a single snapshot. In it a rugged yet sensitive, quintessentially heterosexual male goes about his family-man business. The director stubs his finger heavily into the photo and shouts to his assistants, "Get me this man! I must have him for my film!" When they finally track me down, I at first humbly demur before finally agreeing to take the starring role. After all, the show must go on.

Colleen thanked us for opening our home to her and left. She gave us no reason to believe she or anyone else associated with the movie would be calling back. Our duty was now fulfilled. But a few days later when Jenny called me at work to say, "I just got off the phone with Colleen McGarr, and you are NOT going to believe it," I had no doubt whatsoever that I had just been discovered. My heart leapt. "Go on," I said.

"She says the director wants Marley to try out."

"Marley?" I asked, certain I had misheard. She didn't seem to notice the dismay in my voice.

"Apparently, he's looking for a big, dumb, loopy dog to play the role of the family pet, and Marley caught his eye."

"Loopy?" I asked.

"That's what Colleen says he wants. Big, dumb, and loopy."

Well, he had certainly come to the right place. "Did Colleen mention if he said anything about me?" I asked.

"No," Jenny said. "Why would he?"

Colleen picked Marley up the next day. Knowing the importance of a good entrance, he came racing through the living room to greet her at full bore, pausing only long enough to grab the nearest pillow in his teeth because you never knew when a busy film director might need a quick nap, and if he did, Marley wanted to be ready.

When he hit the wood floor, he flew into a full skid, which did not stop until he hit the coffee table, went airborne, crashed into a chair, landed on his back, rolled, righted himself, and collided head-on with Colleen's legs. At least he didn't jump up, I noted.

"Are you sure you don't want us to sedate him?" Jenny asked.

The director would want to see him in his unbridled, unmedicated state, Colleen insisted, and off she went with our desperately happy dog beside her in her red pickup truck.

Two hours later Colleen and Company were back and the verdict was in: Marley had passed the audition. "Oh, shut up!" Jenny shrieked. "No way!" Our elation was not dampened a bit when Colleen told us Marley was the only one up for the part. Nor when she broke the news that his would be the only nonpaying role in the movie.

I asked her how the audition went.

"I got Marley in the car and it was like driving in a Jacuzzi," she said. "He was slobbering on everything. By the time I got him there, I was drenched." When they arrived at production headquarters at the GulfStream Hotel, a faded tourist landmark from an earlier era overlooking the Intracoastal Waterway, Marley immediately impressed the crew by jumping out of the truck and tearing around the parking lot in random patterns as if expecting the aerial bombing to commence at any moment. "He was just berserk," she recounted, "completely mental."

"Yeah, he gets a little excited," I said.

At one point, she said, Marley grabbed the checkbook out of a crew member's hand and raced away, running a series of tight figure-eights to nowhere, apparently determined this was one way to guarantee a paycheck.

"We call him our Labrador evader," Jenny apologized with the kind of smile only a proud mother can give.

Marley eventually calmed down enough to convince everyone he could do the part, which was basically to just play himself. The movie was called *The Last Home Run,* a baseball fantasy in which a seventy-nine-year-old nursing home resident becomes a twelve-year-old for five days to live his dream of playing Little League ball. Marley was cast as the hyperactive family dog of the Little League coach, played by retired major-league catcher Gary Carter.

"They really want him to be in their movie?" I asked, still incredulous.

"Everyone loved him," Colleen said. "He's perfect."

In the days leading up to shooting, we noticed a certain

subtle change in Marley's bearing. A strange calm had come over him. It was as if passing the audition had given him new confidence. He was almost regal. "Maybe he just needed someone to believe in him," I told Jenny.

If anyone believed, it was her, Stage Mom Extraordinaire. As the first day of filming approached, she bathed him. She brushed him. She clipped his nails and swabbed out his ears.

On the morning shooting was to begin, I walked out of the bedroom to find Jenny and Marley tangled together as if locked in mortal combat, bouncing across the room. She was straddling him with her knees tightly hugging his ribs and one hand grasping the end of his choker chain as he bucked and lurched. It was like having a rodeo right in my own living room. "What in God's name are you doing?" I asked.

"What's it look like?" she shot back. "Brushing his teeth!"

Sure enough, she had a toothbrush in the other hand and was doing her best to scrub his big white ivories as Marley, frothing prodigiously at the mouth, did his best to eat the toothbrush. He looked positively rabid.

"Are you using toothpaste?" I asked, which of course begged the bigger question, "And how exactly do you propose getting him to spit it out?"

"Baking soda," she answered.

"Thank God," I said. "So it's *not* rabies?"

An hour later we left for the GulfStream Hotel, the boys in their car seats and Marley between them, panting away with uncharacteristically fresh breath. Our instructions were to arrive by 9:00 A.M., but a block away, traffic came to a standstill. Up ahead the road was barricaded and a police

officer was diverting traffic away from the hotel. The filming
had been covered at length in the newspapers—the biggest
event to hit sleepy Lake Worth since *Body Heat* was filmed
there fifteen years earlier—and a crowd of spectators had
turned out to gawk. The police were keeping everyone
away. We inched forward in traffic, and when we finally got
up to the officer I leaned out the window and said, "We
need to get through."

"No one gets through," he said. "Keep moving. Let's go."

"We're with the cast," I said.

He eyed us skeptically, a couple in a minivan with
two toddlers and family pet in tow. "I said move it!" he
barked.

"Our dog is in the film," I said.

Suddenly he looked at me with new respect. "You have
the dog?" he asked. The dog was on his checklist.

"I have the dog," I said. "Marley the dog."

"Playing himself," Jenny chimed in.

He turned around and blew his whistle with great fanfare.
"He's got the dog!" he shouted to a cop a half block down.
"Marley the Dog!"

And that cop in turn yelled to someone else, "He's got the
dog! Marley the Dog's here!"

"Let 'em through!" a third officer shouted from the
distance.

"Let 'em through!" the second cop echoed.

The officer moved the barricade and waved us through.

"Right this way," he said politely. I felt like royalty. As we
rolled past him he said once again, as if he couldn't quite
believe it, "He's got the dog."

In the parking lot outside the hotel, the film crew was ready for action. Cables crisscrossed the pavement; camera tripods and microphone booms were set up. Lights hung from scaffolding. Trailers held racks of costumes. Two large tables of food and drinks were set up in the shade for cast and crew. Important-looking people in sunglasses bustled about. Director Bob Gosse greeted us and gave us a quick rundown of the scene to come. It was simple enough. A minivan pulls up to the curb, Marley's make-believe owner, played by the actress Liza Harris, is at the wheel. Her daughter, played by a cute teenager named Danielle from the local performing-arts school, and son, another local budding actor not older than nine, are in the back with their family dog, played by Marley. The daughter opens the sliding door and hops out; her brother follows with Marley on a leash. They walk off camera. End of scene.

"Easy enough," I told the director. "He should be able to handle that, no problem." I pulled Marley off to the side to wait for his cue to get into the van.

"Okay, people, listen up," Gosse told the crew. "The dog's a little nutty, all right? But unless he completely hijacks the scene, we're going to keep rolling." He explained his thinking: Marley was the real thing—a typical family dog— and the goal was to capture him behaving as a typical family dog would behave on a typical family outing. No acting or coaching; pure cinema verité. "Just let him do his thing," he coached, "and work around him."

When everyone was set to go, I loaded Marley into the van and handed his nylon leash to the little boy, who looked terrified of him. "He's friendly," I told him. "He'll just want to lick you. See?" I stuck my wrist into Marley's mouth to demonstrate.

Take one: The van pulls to the curb. The instant the daughter slides open the side door, a yellow streak shoots out like a giant fur ball being fired from a cannon and blurs past the cameras trailing a red leash.

"Cut!"

I chased Marley down in the parking lot and hauled him back.

"Okay, folks, we're going to try that again," Gosse said. Then to the boy he coached gently, "The dog's pretty wild. Try to hold on tighter this time."

Take two. The van pulls to the curb. The door slides open. The daughter is just beginning to exit when Marley huffs into view and leaps out past her, this time dragging the white-knuckled and white-faced boy behind him.

"Cut!"

Take three. The van pulls up. The door slides open. The daughter exits. The boy exits, holding the leash. As he steps away from the van the leash pulls taut, stretching back inside, but no dog follows. The boy begins to tug, heave, and pull. He leans into it and gives it everything he has. Not a budge. Long, painfully empty seconds pass. The boy grimaces and looks back at the camera.

"Cut!"

I peered into the van to find Marley bent over licking himself where no male was ever meant to lick. He looked up at me as if to say, *Can't you see I'm busy?*

Take four: I load Marley into the back of the van with the boy and shut the door. Before Gosse calls "Action!" he breaks for a few minutes to confer with his assistants. Finally, the scene rolls. The van pulls to the curb. The door slides open. The daughter steps out. The boy steps out, but with a bewildered look on his face. He peers directly into the camera and holds up his hand. Dangling from it is half the leash, its end jagged and wet with saliva.

"Cut! Cut! Cut!"

The boy explained that as he waited in the van, Marley began gnawing on the leash and wouldn't stop. The crew and cast were staring at the severed leash in disbelief, a mix of awe and horror on their faces as though they had just witnessed some great and mysterious force of nature. I, on the other hand, was not surprised in the least. Marley had sent more leashes and ropes to their graves than I could count; he even managed to chew his way through a rubber-coated steel cable that was advertised "as used in the airline industry." Shortly after Conor was born, Jenny came home with a new product, a doggie travel harness that allowed her to buckle Marley into a car seat belt so he couldn't wander around the moving vehicle. In the first ninety seconds using the new device, he managed to chew through not only the heavy harness itself but the shoulder strap of our brand-new minivan.

"Okay, everybody, let's take a break!" Gosse called out. Turning to me, he asked—in an amazingly calm voice— "How quickly can you find a new leash?" He didn't have to tell me how much each lost minute cost him as his union-scale actors and crew sat idle.

"There's a pet store a half mile from here," I said. "I can be back in fifteen minutes."

"And this time get something he can't chew through," he said.

I returned with a heavy chain leash that looked like something a lion trainer might use, and the filming continued, take after failed take. Each scene was worse than the one before. At one point, Danielle the teenage actress let out a desperate shriek mid-scene and screamed with true horror in her voice, "Oh my God! His thing is out!"

"Cut!"

In another scene, Marley was panting so loudly at Danielle's feet as she spoke on the telephone to her love interest that the sound engineer flipped off his headphones in disgust and complained loudly, "I can't hear a word she's saying. All I hear is heavy breathing. It sounds like a porn flick."

"Cut!"

So went day 1 of shooting. Marley was a disaster, unmitigated and without redemption. Part of me was defensive—*Well, what did they expect for free? Benji?*—and part was mortified. I self-consciously stole glances at the cast and crew and could see it plainly on their faces: *Where did this animal come from, and how can we send him back?* At the end of the day one of the assistants, clipboard in hand, told us the shooting lineup was still undecided for the next morning. "Don't bother coming in tomorrow," he said. "We'll call if we need Marley." And to ensure there was no confusion, he repeated: "So unless you hear from us, don't show up. Got it?" Yeah, I got it, loud and clear. Gosse had sent his underling to do the dirty work. Marley's fledgling acting career was over. Not that I could blame them.

With the possible exception of that scene in *The Ten Commandments* where Charlton Heston parts the Red Sea, Marley had presented the biggest logistical nightmare in the history of cinema. He had caused who knows how many thousands of dollars in needless delays and wasted film. He had slimed countless costumes, raided the snack table, and nearly toppled a thirty-thousand-dollar camera. They were cutting their losses, writing us out. It was the old "Don't call us, we'll call you" routine.

"Marley," I said when we got home, "your big chance and you really blew it."

The next morning I was still fretting over our dashed dreams of stardom when the phone rang. It was the assistant, telling us to get Marley to the hotel as soon as possible. "You mean you want him back?" I asked.

"Right away," he said. "Bob wants him in the next scene."

I arrived thirty minutes later, not quite believing they had invited us back. Gosse was ebullient. He had watched the raw footage from the day before and couldn't have been happier. "The dog was hysterical!" he gushed. "Just hilarious. Pure madcap genius!" I could feel myself standing taller, chest puffing out.

"We always knew he was a natural," Jenny said.

Shooting continued around Lake Worth for several more days, and Marley continued to rise to the occasion. We hovered in the wings with the other stage parents and hangers-on, chatting, socializing, and then falling abruptly silent whenever the stagehand yelled, "Ready on set!" When the word "Cut!" rang out, the party continued. Jenny even managed to get Gary Carter and Dave Winfield, the Baseball Hall of Fame all-star who was making a cameo in the movie, to sign baseballs for each of the boys.

Marley was lapping up stardom. The crew, especially the women, fawned over him. The weather was brutally hot, and one assistant was assigned the exclusive duty of following Marley around with a bowl and a bottle of spring water, pouring him drinks at will. Everyone, it seemed, was feeding him snacks off the buffet table. I left him with the crew for a couple of hours while I checked in at work, and when I returned I found him sprawled out like King Tut, paws in the air, accepting a leisurely belly rub from the strikingly gorgeous makeup artist. "He's such a lover!" she cooed.

Stardom was starting to go to my head, too. I began introducing myself as "Marley the Dog's handler" and dropping lines such as "For his next movie, we're hoping for a barking part." During one break in the shooting, I walked into the hotel lobby to use the pay phone. Marley was off his leash and sniffing around the furniture several feet away. A concierge, apparently mistaking my star for a stray, intercepted him and tried to hustle him out a side door. "Go home!" he scolded. "Shoo!"

"Excuse me?" I said, cupping my hand over the mouthpiece of the phone and leveling the concierge with my most withering stare. "Do you have any idea who you're talking to?"

We remained on the set for four straight days, and by the time we were told Marley's scenes were all completed and his services no longer needed, Jenny and I both felt we were part of the Shooting Gallery family. Granted, the only unpaid members of the family, but members nonetheless. "We love you guys!" Jenny blurted out to all within earshot as we herded Marley into the minivan. "Can't wait to see the final cut!"

But wait we did. One of the producers told us to give them eight months and then call and they'd mail us an advance copy. After eight months when I called, however, a front-desk person put me on hold and returned several minutes later to say, "Why don't you try in another couple months?" I waited and tried, waited and tried, but each time was put off. I started feeling like a stalker, and I could imagine the receptionist, hand cupped over the phone, whispering to Gosse at the editing table, "It's that crazy dog guy again. What do you want me to tell him this time?"

Eventually I stopped calling, resigned that we would never see *The Last Home Run,* convinced that no one ever would, that the project had been abandoned on the editing-room floor on account of the overwhelming challenges of trying to edit that damn dog out of every scene. It would be two full years later before I would finally get my chance to see Marley's acting skills.

I was in Blockbuster when on a whim I asked the clerk if he knew anything about a movie called *The Last Home Run*. Not only did he know about it; he had it in stock. In fact, as luck would have it, not a single copy was checked out.

Only later would I learn the whole sad story. Unable to attract a national distributor, the Shooting Gallery had no choice but to relegate Marley's movie debut to that most ignoble of celluloid fates. *The Last Home Run* had gone straight to video. I didn't care. I raced home with a copy and yelled to Jenny and the kids to gather round the VCR. All told, Marley was on-screen for less than two minutes, but I had to say they were two of the livelier minutes in the film. We laughed! We cried! We cheered!

"Waddy, that you!" Conor screamed.

"We're famous!" Patrick yelled.

Marley, never one to get hung up on pretenses, seemed unimpressed. He yawned and crawled beneath the coffee table. By the time the end credits rolled, he was sound asleep. We waited with breath held as the names of all the actors of the two-legged variety had scrolled by. For a minute, I thought our dog was not going to merit a credit. But then there it was, listed in big letters across the screen for all to see: "Marley the Dog . . . As Himself."

CHAPTER 17

In the Land of Bocahontas

❖

One month after filming ended for *The Last Home Run*, we said good-bye to West Palm Beach and all the memories it held. There had been two more murders within a block of our home, but in the end it was clutter, not crime, that drove us from our little bungalow on Churchill Road. With two children and all the accoutrements that went with them, we were packed, quite literally, to the rafters. The house had taken on the pallid sheen of a Toys "R" Us factory outlet. Marley was ninety-seven pounds, and he could not turn around without knocking something over. Ours was a two-bedroom house, and we foolishly thought the boys could share the second room. But when they kept waking each other up, doubling our nocturnal adventures, we moved Conor out to a narrow space between the kitchen and the garage. Officially, it was my "home office," where I played guitar and paid bills. To anyone who saw it, though, there was really no sugarcoating it: We had moved our baby out into the breezeway. It sounded horrible. A breezeway was just a half step up from a garage, which, in turn, was nearly synonymous with a barn. And what kind of parents would raise their boy in a barn? A breezeway had a certain unsecured sound to it: a place open to the wind—and anything else that might blow in. Dirt, allergens, stinging insects, bats, criminals, perverts. A breezeway was where you would expect to find the garbage cans and wet tennis shoes. And in fact it was the place where we kept Marley's food and water bowls, even after Conor took up residence there, not because it was a space fit only for an animal but simply because that's where Marley had come to expect them.

Our breezeway-cum-nursery sounded Dickensian, but it really wasn't that bad; it was almost charming. Originally, it was built as a covered, open-air pass-through between the house and garage, and the previous owners had closed it in years earlier. Before declaring it a nursery, I replaced the old leaky jalousies with modern, tight-fitting windows. I hung new blinds and applied a fresh coat of paint. Jenny covered the floor with soft rugs, hung cheerful drawings, and dangled whimsical mobiles from the ceiling. Still, how did it look? Our son was sleeping in the breezeway while the dog had full run of the master bedroom.

Besides, Jenny was now working half-time for the *Post*'s feature section, and mostly from home, as she attempted to juggle children and career. It only made sense for us to relocate closer to my office. We agreed it was time to move.

Life is full of little ironies, and one of them was the fact that, after months of searching, we settled on a house in the one South Florida city I took the greatest glee in publicly ridiculing. That place was Boca Raton, which, translated from the Spanish, means literally "Mouth of the Rat." And what a mouth it was.

Boca Raton was a wealthy Republican bastion largely populated with recent arrivals from New Jersey and New York. Most of the money in town was new money, and most of those who had it didn't know how to enjoy it without making fools of themselves. Boca Raton was a land of luxury sedans, red sports cars, pink stucco mansions crammed onto postage-stamp lots, and balkanized walled developments with guards at the gates. The men favored linen pants and Italian loafers sans socks and spent inordinate amounts of time making important-sounding cellphone calls to one another. The women were tanned to the consistency of the Gucci leather bags they favored, their burnished skin set off by hair dyed alarming shades of silver and platinum.

The city crawled with plastic surgeons, and they had the biggest homes and most radiant smiles of all. For Boca's well-preserved women, breast implants were a virtual requirement of residency. The younger women all had magnificent boob jobs; the older women all had magnificent boob jobs *and* face-lifts. Butt sculpting, nose jobs, tummy tucks, and tattooed mascara rounded out the cosmetic lineup, giving the city's female population the odd appearance of being foot soldiers in an army of anatomically correct inflatable dolls. As I once sang in a song I wrote for a press skit, "Liposuction and silicone, a girl's best friends in Boca Raton."

In my column I had been poking fun at the Boca lifestyle, starting with the name itself. Residents of Boca Raton never actually called their city Boca Raton. They simply referred to it by the familiar "Boca." And they did not pronounce it as the dictionary said they should, with a long *O, BO-kuh*. Rather they gave it a soft, nasal, Jersey-tinged inflection. It was *BOHW-kuh!* as in, "Oh, the manicured shrubbery is *bew-tee-ful* here in *BOHW-kuh!*"

The Disney movie *Pocahontas* was in the theaters then, and I launched a running spoof on the Indian-princess theme, which I titled "Bocahontas." My gold-draped protagonist was an indigenous suburban princess who drove a pink BMW, her rock-hard, surgically enhanced breasts jutting into the steering wheel, allowing her to drive hands-free, talking on her cell phone and teasing her frosted hair in the rearview mirror as she raced to the tanning salon. Bocahontas lived in a pastel designer wigwam, worked out each morning at the tribal gym—but only if she could find parking within ten feet of the front door—and spent her afternoons stalking wild furs, trusty AmEx card in hand, at the ceremonial hunting grounds known as Town Center Mall.

"Bury my Visa at Mizner Park," Bocahontas intones solemnly in one of my columns, a reference to the city's toniest shopping strip. In another, she adjusts her buckskin Wonderbra and campaigns to make cosmetic surgery tax-deductible.

My characterization was cruel. It was uncharitable. It was only slightly exaggerated. Boca's real-life Bocahontases were the biggest fans of those columns, trying to figure out which of them had inspired my fictional heroine. (I'll never tell.) I was frequently invited to speak before social and community groups and invariably someone would stand up and ask,

"Why do you hate *BOHW-kuh* so much?" It wasn't that I hated Boca, I told them; it was just that I loved high farce. No place on earth delivered it quite like the pretty-in-pink Mouth of the Rat.

So it only made sense that when Jenny and I finally settled on a house, it was located at ground zero of the Boca experience, midway between the waterfront estates of east Boca Raton and the snooty gated communities of west Boca Raton (which, I relished pointing out to the very zip-code-conscious residents, fell outside the city limits in unincorporated Palm Beach County). Our new neighborhood was in one of the few middle-class sections in the city, and its residents liked to joke with a certain reverse snobbery that they were on the wrong side of both sets of tracks. Sure enough, there were two sets of railroad tracks, one defining the eastern boundary of the neighborhood and one the western. At night you could lie in bed and listen to the freight trains moving through on their way to and from Miami.

"Are you crazy?" I said to Jenny. "We can't move to Boca! I'll be run out of town on a rail. They'll serve my head up on a bed of organic mesclun greens."

"Oh, come on," she said. "You're exaggerating again."

My paper, the *Sun-Sentinel,* was the dominant newspaper in Boca Raton, far outpacing the *Miami Herald,* the *Palm Beach Post,* or even the local *Boca Raton News* in circulation. My work was widely read in the city and its western developments, and because my photograph appeared above my column, I was frequently recognized. I didn't think I was exaggerating. "They'll skin me alive and hang my carcass in front of Tiffany's," I said.

But we had been looking for months, and this was the first house that met all our criteria. It was the right size at the right price and in the right place, strategically located between the two offices where I split my time. The public schools were about as good as public schools got in South Florida, and for all its superficialities, Boca Raton had an excellent park system, including some of the most pristine ocean beaches in the Miami–Palm Beach metropolitan area. With more than a little trepidation, I agreed to go forward with the purchase. I felt like a not-so-secret agent infiltrating the enemy's encampment. The barbarian was about to slip inside the gate, an unapologetic Boca-basher crashing the Boca garden party. Who could blame them for not wanting me?

When we first arrived, I slinked around town self-consciously, convinced all eyes were on me. My ears burned, imagining people were whispering as I passed. After I wrote a column welcoming myself to the neighborhood (and eating a fair amount of crow in the process), I received a number of letters saying things like "You trash our city and now you want to live here? What a shameless hypocrite!" I had to admit, they made a point. An ardent city booster I knew from work couldn't wait to confront me. "So," he said gleefully, "you decided tacky Boca isn't such a bad place after all, huh? The parks and the tax rate and the schools and beaches and zoning, all that's not so bad when it comes time to buy a house, is it?" All I could do was roll over and cry uncle.

I soon discovered, however, that most of my neighbors here on the wrong side of both sets of tracks were sympathetic to my written assaults on what one of them called "the gauche and vulgar among us." Pretty soon I felt right at home.

Our house was a 1970s-vintage four-bedroom ranch with twice the square footage of our first home and none of the charm. The place had potential, though, and gradually we put our mark on it. We ripped up the wall-to-wall shag carpeting and installed oak floors in the living room and Italian tile everywhere else. We replaced the ugly sliding glass doors with varnished French doors, and I slowly turned the bereft front yard into a tropical garden teeming with gingers and heliconias and passion vines that butterflies and passersby alike stopped to drink in.

The two best features of our new home had nothing to do with the house itself. Visible from our living room window was a small city park filled with playground equipment beneath towering pines. The children adored it. And in the backyard, right off the new French doors, was an in-ground swimming pool. We hadn't wanted a pool, worrying about the risk to our two toddlers, and Jenny made our Realtor blanch when she suggested filling it in. Our first act on the day we moved in was to surround the pool with a four-foot-high fence worthy of a maximum-security prison. The boys—Patrick had just turned three and Conor eighteen months when we arrived—took to the water like a pair of dolphins. The park became an extension of our backyard and the pool an extension of the mild season we so cherished. A swimming pool in Florida, we soon learned, made the difference between barely enduring the withering summer months and actually enjoying them.

No one loved the backyard pool more than our water dog, that proud descendant of fishermen's retrievers plying the ocean swells off the coast of Newfoundland. If the pool gate was open, Marley would charge for the water, getting a running start from the family room, going airborne out the open French doors and, with one bounce off the brick patio, landing in the pool on his belly with a giant flop that sent a geyser into the air and waves over the edge. Swimming with Marley was a potentially life-threatening adventure, a little like swimming with an ocean liner. He would come at you full speed ahead, his paws flailing out in front of him. You'd expect him to veer away at the last minute, but he would simply crash into you and try to climb aboard. If you were over your head, he pushed you beneath the surface. "What do I look like, a dock?" I would say, and cradle him in my arms to let him catch his breath, his front paws still paddling away on autopilot as he licked the water off my face.

One thing our new house did not have was a Marley-proof bunker. At our old house, the concrete one-car garage was pretty much indestructible, and it had two windows, which kept it tolerably comfortable even in the dead of summer. Our Boca house had a two-car garage, but it was unsuitable for housing Marley or any other life-form that could not survive temperatures above 150 degrees. The garage had no windows and was stiflingly hot. Besides, it was finished in drywall, not concrete, which Marley had already proved himself quite adept at pulverizing. His thunder-induced panic attacks were only getting worse, despite the tranquilizers.

The first time we left him alone in our new house, we shut him in the laundry room, just off the kitchen, with a blanket and a big bowl of water. When we returned a few hours later, he had scratched up the door. The damage was minor, but we had just mortgaged our lives for the next thirty years to buy this house, and we knew it didn't bode well. "Maybe he's just getting used to his new surroundings," I offered.

"There's not even a cloud in the sky," Jenny observed skeptically. "What's going to happen the first time a storm hits?"

The next time we left him alone, we found out. As thunderheads rolled in, we cut our outing short and hurried home, but it was too late. Jenny was a few steps ahead of me, and when she opened the laundry-room door she stopped short and uttered, "Oh my God." She said it the way you would if you had just discovered a body hanging from the chandelier. Again: "Oh . . . My . . . God." I peeked in over her shoulder, and it was uglier than I had feared. Marley was standing there, panting frantically, his paws and mouth bleeding. Loose fur was everywhere, as though the thunder had scared the hair right out of his coat. The damage was worse than anything he had done before, and that was saying a lot. An entire wall was gouged open, obliterated clear down to the studs. Plaster and wood chips and bent nails were everywhere. Electric wiring lay exposed. Blood smeared the floor and the walls. It looked, literally, like the scene of a shotgun homicide.

"Oh my God," Jenny said a third time.

"Oh my God," I repeated. It was all either of us could say.

After several seconds of just standing there mute, staring at the carnage, I finally said, "Okay, we can handle this. It's all fixable." Jenny shot me her look; she had seen my repairs. "I'll call a drywall guy and have it professionally repaired," I said. "I won't even try to do this one myself." I slipped Marley one of his tranquilizers and worried silently that this latest destructive jag might just throw Jenny back into the funk she had sunk into after Conor's birth. Those blues, however, seemed to be long behind her. She was surprisingly philosophical about it.

"A few hundred bucks and we'll be good as new," she chirped.

"That's what I'm thinking, too," I said. "I'll give a few extra speeches to bring in some cash. That'll pay for it."

Within a few minutes, Marley was beginning to mellow. His eyelids grew heavy and his eyes deeply bloodshot, as they always did when he was doped up. He looked like he belonged at a Grateful Dead concert. I hated to see him this way, I always hated it, and always resisted sedating him. But the pills helped him move past the terror, past the deadly threat that existed only in his mind. If he were human, I would call him certifiably psychotic. He was delusional, paranoid, convinced a dark, evil force was coming from the heavens to take him. He curled up on the rug in front of the kitchen sink and let out a deep sigh. I knelt beside him and stroked his blood-caked fur. "Geez, dog," I said. "What are we going to do with you?" Without lifting his head, he looked up at me with those bloodshot stoner eyes of his, the saddest, most mournful, eyes I have ever seen, and just gazed at me. It was as if he were trying to tell me something,

something important he needed me to understand. "I know," I said. "I know you can't help it."

The next day Jenny and I took the boys with us to the pet store and bought a giant cage. They came in all different sizes, and when I described Marley to the clerk he led us to the largest of them all. It was enormous, big enough for a lion to stand up and turn around in. Made out of heavy steel grating, it had two bolt-action barrel locks to hold the door securely shut and a heavy steel pan for a floor. This was our answer, our own portable Alcatraz. Conor and Patrick both crawled inside and I slid the bolts shut, locking them in for a moment. "What do you guys think?" I asked. "Will this hold our Superdog?"

Conor teetered at the cage door, his fingers through the bars like a veteran inmate, and said, "Me in jail."

"Waddy's going to be our prisoner!" Patrick chimed in, delighted at the prospect.

Back home, we set up the crate next to the washing machine. Portable Alcatraz took up nearly half the laundry room. "Come here, Marley!" I called when it was fully assembled. I tossed a Milk-Bone in and he happily pranced in after it. I closed and bolted the door behind him, and he stood there chewing his treat, unfazed by the new life experience he was about to enter, the one known in mental-health circles as "involuntary commitment."

"This is going to be your new home when we're away," I said cheerfully. Marley stood there panting contentedly, not a trace of concern on his face, and then he lay down and let out a sigh. "A good sign," I said to Jenny. "A very good sign."

That evening we decided to give the maximum-security

dog-containment unit a test run. This time I didn't even need a Milk-Bone to lure Marley in. I simply opened the gate, gave a whistle, and in he walked, tail banging the metal sides. "Be a good boy, Marley," I said. As we loaded the boys into the minivan to go out to dinner, Jenny said, "You know something?"

"What?" I asked.

"This is the first time since we got him that I don't have a pit in my stomach leaving Marley alone in the house," she said. "I never even realized how much it put me on edge until now."

"I know what you mean," I said. "It was always a guessing game: 'What will our dog destroy this time?'"

"Like, 'How much will this little night out at the movies cost us?'"

"It was like Russian roulette."

"I think that crate is going to be the best money we ever spent," she said.

"We should have done this a long time ago," I agreed. "You can't put a price on peace of mind."

We had a great dinner out, followed by a sunset stroll on the beach. The boys splashed in the surf, chased seagulls, threw fistfuls of sand in the water. Jenny was uncharacteristically relaxed. Just knowing Marley was safely secured inside Alcatraz, unable to hurt himself or anything else, was a balm. "What a nice outing this has been," she said as we walked up the front sidewalk to our house.

I was about to agree with her when I noticed something in my peripheral vision, something up ahead that wasn't quite right. I turned my head and stared at the window beside the front door. The miniblinds were shut, as they always were when we left the house. But about a foot up from the bottom of the window the metal slats were bent apart and something was sticking through them.

Something black. And wet. And pressed up against the glass. "What the—?" I said. "How could . . . Marley?"

When I opened the front door, sure enough, there was our one-dog welcoming committee, wiggling all over the foyer, pleased as punch to have us home again. We fanned out across the house, checking every room and closet for telltales of Marley's unsupervised adventure. The house was fine, untouched. We converged on the laundry room. The crate's door stood wide open, swung back like the stone to Jesus' tomb on Easter morning. It was as if some secret accomplice had snuck in and sprung our inmate. I squatted down beside the cage to have a closer look. The two bolt-action barrel locks were slid back in the open position, and—a significant clue—they were dripping with saliva. "It looks like an inside job," I said. "Somehow Houdini here licked his way out of the Big House."

"I can't believe it," Jenny said. Then she uttered a word I was glad the children were not close enough to hear.

We always fancied Marley to be as dumb as algae, but he had been clever enough to figure out how to use his long, strong tongue through the bars to slowly work the barrels free from their slots. He had licked his way to freedom, and he proved over the coming weeks that he was able to easily repeat the trick whenever he wanted. Our maximum-security prison had in fact turned out to be a halfway house. Some days we would return to find him resting peacefully in the cage; other days he'd be waiting at the front window. Involuntary commitment was not a concept Marley was going to take lying down.

We took to wiring both locks in place with heavy electrical cable. That worked for a while, but one day, with distant rumbles on the horizon, we came home to find that the bottom corner of the cage's gate had been peeled back as though with a giant can opener, and a panicky Marley, his paws again bloodied, was firmly stuck around the rib cage, half in and half out of the tight opening. I bent the steel gate back in place as best I could, and we began wiring not only the slide bolts in place but all four corners of the door as well. Pretty soon we were reinforcing the corners of the cage itself as Marley continued to put his brawn into busting out. Within three months the gleaming steel cage we had thought so impregnable looked like it had taken a direct hit from a howitzer. The bars were twisted and bent, the frame pried apart, the door an ill-fitting mess, the sides bulging outward. I continued to reinforce it as best I could, and it continued to hold tenuously against Marley's full-bodied assaults. Whatever false sense of security the contraption had once offered us was gone. Each time we left, even for a half hour, we wondered whether this would be the time that our manic inmate would bust out and go on another couch-shredding, wall-gouging, door-eating rampage. So much for peace of mind.

CHAPTER 18

Alfresco Dining

Marley didn't fit into the Boca Raton scene any better than I did. Boca had (and surely still has) a disproportionate share of the world's smallest, yappiest, most pampered dogs, the kind of pets that the Bocahontas set favored as fashion accessories. They were precious little things, often with bows in their fur and cologne spritzed on their necks, some even with painted toenails, and you would spot them in the most unlikely of places—peeking out of a designer handbag at you as you waited in line at the bagel shop; snoozing on their mistresses' towels at the beach; leading the charge on a rhinestone-studded leash into a pricey antiques store. Mostly, you could find them cruising around town in Lexuses, Mercedes-Benzes, and Jaguars, perched aristocratically behind the steering wheels on their owners' laps. They were to Marley what Grace Kelly was to Gomer Pyle. They were petite, sophisticated, and of discriminating taste. Marley was big, clunky, and a sniffer of genitalia. He wanted so much to have them invite him into their circle; they so much were not about to.

With his recently digested obedience certificate under his belt, Marley was fairly manageable on walks, but if he saw something he liked, he still wouldn't hesitate to lunge for it, threat of strangulation be damned. When we took strolls around town, the high-rent pooches were always worth getting all choked up over. Each time he spotted one, he would break into a gallop, barreling up to it, dragging Jenny or me behind him at the end of the leash, the noose tightening around his throat, making him gasp and cough. Each time Marley would be roundly snubbed, not only by the Boca minidog but by the Boca minidog's owner, who would snatch up young Fifi or Suzi or Cheri as if rescuing her from the jaws of an alligator. Marley didn't seem to mind. The next minidog to come into sight, he would do it all over again, undeterred by his previous jilting. As a guy who was never very good at the rejection part of dating, I admired his perseverance.

Outside dining was a big part of the Boca experience, and many restaurants in town offered alfresco seating beneath palm trees whose trunks and fronds were studded with strings of tiny white lights. These were places to see and be seen, to sip caffè lattes and jabber into cell phones as your companion stared vacantly at the sky. The Boca minidog was an important part of the alfresco ambience. Couples brought their dogs with them and hooked their leashes to the wrought-iron tables where the dogs would contentedly curl up at their feet or sometimes even sit up at the table beside their masters, holding their heads high in an imperious manner as if miffed by the waiters' inattentiveness.

One Sunday afternoon Jenny and I thought it would be fun to take the whole family for an outside meal at one of the popular meeting places. "When in Boca, do as the Boca-lites," I said. We loaded the boys and the dog into the minivan and headed to Mizner Park, the downtown shopping plaza modeled after an Italian piazza with wide sidewalks and endless dining possibilities. We parked and strolled up one side of the three-block strip and down the other, seeing and being seen—and what a sight we must have made. Jenny had the boys strapped into a double stroller that could have been mistaken for a maintenance cart, loaded up in the back with all manner of toddler paraphernalia, from applesauce to wet wipes. I walked beside her, Marley, on full Boca minidog alert, barely contained at my side. He was even wilder than usual, beside himself at the possibility of getting near one of the little purebreds prancing about, and I gripped hard on his leash. His tongue hung out and he panted like a locomotive.

We settled on a restaurant with one of the more affordable menus on the strip and hovered nearby until a sidewalk table opened up. The table was perfect—shaded, with a view of the piazza's central fountain, and heavy enough, we were sure, to secure an excitable hundred-pound Lab. I hooked the end of Marley's leash to one of the legs, and we ordered drinks all around, two beers and two apple juices.

"To a beautiful day with my beautiful family," Jenny said, holding up her glass for a toast. We clicked our beer bottles; the boys smashed their sippy cups together. That's when it happened. So fast, in fact, that we didn't even realize it had happened. All we knew was that one instant we were sitting at a lovely outdoor table toasting the beautiful day, and the next our table was on the move, crashing its way through the sea of other tables, banging into innocent bystanders, and making a horrible, ear-piercing, industrial-grade shriek as it scraped over the concrete pavers. In that first split second, before either of us realized exactly what bad fate had befallen us, it seemed distinctly possible that our table was possessed, fleeing our family of unwashed Boca invaders, which most certainly did not belong here. In the next split second, I saw that it wasn't our table that was haunted, but our dog. Marley was out in front, chugging forward with every ounce of rippling muscle he had, the leash stretched tight as piano wire.

In the fraction of a second after that, I saw just where Marley was heading, table in tow. Fifty feet down the sidewalk, a delicate French poodle lingered at her owner's side, nose in the air. *Damn,* I remember thinking, *what is his thing for poodles?* Jenny and I both sat there for a moment longer, drinks in hand, the boys between us in their stroller, our perfect little Sunday afternoon unblemished except for the fact that our table was now motoring its way through the crowd. An instant later we were on our feet, screaming, running, apologizing to the customers around us as we went. I was the first to reach the runaway table as it surged and scraped down the piazza. I grabbed on, planted my feet, and leaned back with everything I had. Soon Jenny was beside me, pulling back, too. I felt like we were action heroes in a western, giving our all to rein in the runaway train before it jumped the tracks and plunged over a cliff. In the middle of all the bedlam, Jenny actually turned and called over her shoulder, "Be right back, boys!" *Be right back?* She made it sound so ordinary, so expected, so planned, as if we often did this sort of thing, deciding on the spur of the moment that, oh, why not, it might just be fun to let Marley lead us on a little table stroll around town, maybe doing a bit of window-shopping along the way, before we circled back in time for appetizers.

When we finally got the table stopped and Marley reeled in, just feet from the poodle and her mortified owner, I turned back to check on the boys, and that's when I got my first good look at the faces of my fellow alfresco diners. It was like a scene out of one of those E. F. Hutton commercials where an entire bustling crowd freezes in silence, waiting to hear a whispered word of investment advice. Men stopped in midconversation, cell phones in their hands. Women stared with opened mouths. The Bocalites were aghast. It was finally Conor who broke the silence. "Waddy go walk!" he screamed with delight.

A waiter rushed up and helped me drag the table back into place as Jenny held Marley, still fixated on the object of his desire, in a death grip. "Let me get some new place settings," the waiter said.

"That won't be necessary," Jenny said nonchalantly. "We'll just be paying for our drinks and going."

It wasn't long after our excellent excursion into the Boca alfresco-dining scene that I found a book in the library titled *No Bad Dogs* by the acclaimed British dog trainer Barbara Woodhouse. As the title implied, *No Bad Dogs* advanced the same belief that Marley's first instructor, Miss Dominatrix, held so dear—that the only thing standing between an incorrigible canine and greatness was a befuddled, indecisive, weak-willed human master. Dogs weren't the problem,

Woodhouse held; people were. That said, the book went on to describe, chapter after chapter, some of the most egregious canine behaviors imaginable. There were dogs that howled incessantly, dug incessantly, fought incessantly, humped incessantly, and bit incessantly. There were dogs that hated all men and dogs that hated all women; dogs that stole from their masters and dogs that jealously attacked defenseless infants. There were even dogs that ate their own feces. *Thank God*, I thought, *at least he doesn't eat his own feces.*

As I read, I began to feel better about our flawed retriever. We had gradually come to the firm conclusion that Marley was indeed the world's worst dog. Now I was buoyed to read that there were all sorts of horrid behaviors he did *not* have. He didn't have a mean bone in his body. He wasn't much of a barker. Didn't bite. Didn't assault other dogs, except in the pursuit of love. Considered everyone his best friend. Best of all, he didn't eat or roll in scat. Besides, I told myself, there are no bad dogs, only inept, clueless owners like Jenny and me. It was our fault Marley turned out the way he had.

Then I got to chapter 24, "Living with the Mentally Unstable Dog." As I read, I swallowed loudly. Woodhouse was describing Marley with an understanding so intimate I could swear she had been bunking with him in his battered crate. She addressed the manic, bizarre behavior patterns, the destructiveness when left alone, the gouged floors and chewed rugs. She described the attempts by owners of such beasts "to make some place either in the house or yard dogproof." She even addressed the use of tranquilizers as a desperate (and largely ineffective) last measure to try to return these mentally broken mutts to the land of the sane.

"Some are born unstable, some are made unstable by their living conditions, but the result is the same: the dogs, instead of being a joy to their owners, are a worry, an expense, and often bring complete despair to an entire family," Woodhouse wrote. I looked down at Marley snoozing at my feet and said, "Sound familiar?"

In a subsequent chapter, titled "Abnormal Dogs," Woodhouse wrote with a sense of resignation: "I cannot stress often enough that if you wish to keep a dog that is not normal, you must face up to living a slightly restricted existence." *You mean like living in mortal fear of going out for a gallon of milk?* "Although *you* may love a subnormal dog," she continued, "other people must not be inconvenienced by it." *Other people such as, hypothetically speaking, Sunday diners at a sidewalk café in Boca Raton, Florida?*

Woodhouse had nailed our dog and our pathetic, codependent existence. We had it all: the hapless, weak-willed masters; the mentally unstable, out-of-control dog; the trail of destroyed property; the annoyed and inconvenienced strangers and neighbors. We were a textbook case. "Congratulations, Marley," I said to him. "You qualify as subnormal." He opened his eyes at the sound of his name, stretched, and rolled onto his back, paws in the air.

I was expecting Woodhouse to offer a cheery solution for the owners of such defective merchandise, a few helpful tips that, when properly executed, could turn even the most manic of pets into Westminster-worthy show dogs. But she ended her book on a much darker note: "Only the owners of unbalanced dogs can really know where the line can be drawn between a dog that is sane and one that is mentally unsound. No one can make up the owner's mind as to what to do with the last kind. I, as a great dog lover, feel it is kinder to put them to sleep.''

Put them to sleep? Gulp. In case she wasn't making herself clear, she added, "Surely, when all training and veterinary help has been exhausted and there is no hope that the dog will ever live a reasonably normal existence, it is kinder to pet and owner to put the dog to sleep."

Even Barbara Woodhouse, lover of animals, successful trainer of thousands of dogs their owners had deemed hopeless, was conceding that some dogs were simply beyond help. If it were up to her, they would be humanely dispatched to that great canine insane asylum in the sky.

"Don't worry, big guy," I said, leaning down to scratch Marley's belly. "The only sleep we're going to be doing around this house is the kind you get to wake up from."

He sighed dramatically and drifted back to his dreams of French poodles in heat.

It was around this same time that we also learned not all Labs are created equal. The breed actually has two distinct subgroups: English and American. The English line tends to be smaller and stockier than the American line, with blockier heads and gentle, calm dispositions. They are the favored line for showing. Labs belonging to the American line are noticeably larger and stronger, with sleeker, less squat features. They are known for their endless energy and high spirits and favored for use in the field as hunting and sports dogs. The same qualities that make the American line of Labs so unstoppably superb in the woods makes them challenges in the family home. Their exuberant energy level, the literature warned, should not be underestimated.

As the brochure for a Pennsylvania retriever breeder, Endless Mountain Labradors, explains it: "So many people ask us, 'What's the difference between the English and the American (field) Labs?' There is such a big difference that the AKC is considering splitting the breed. There is a difference in build, as well as temperament. If you are looking for strictly a field dog for field trial competition, go for the American field dog. They are athletic, tall, lanky, thin, but have VERY hyper, high-strung personalities, which do not lend themselves to being the best 'family dogs.' On the other hand, the English Labs are very blocky, stocky, shorter in their build. Very sweet, quiet, mellow, lovely dogs."

It didn't take me long to figure out which line Marley belonged to. It was all beginning to make sense. We had blindly picked out a type of Lab best suited to stampeding across the open wilderness all day. If that weren't enough, our specific choice just happened to be mentally unbalanced, unwound, and beyond the reach of training, tranquilizers, or canine psychiatry. The kind of subnormal specimen an experienced dog trainer like Barbara Woodhouse might just consider better off dead. *Great*, I thought. *Now we find out.*

Not long after Woodhouse's book opened our eyes to Marley's crazed mind, a neighbor asked us to take in their cat for a week while they were on vacation. Sure, we said, bring him over. Compared with a dog, cats were easy. Cats ran on autopilot, and this cat in particular was shy and elusive, especially around Marley. He could be counted on to hide beneath the couch all day and only come out after we were asleep to eat his food, kept high out of Marley's reach, and use the kitty-litter box, which we tucked away in a discreet corner of the screened patio that enclosed the pool. There was nothing to it, really. Marley was totally unaware the cat was even in the house.

Midway through the cat's stay with us, I awoke at dawn to a loud, driving beat resonating through the mattress. It was Marley, quivering with excitement beside the bed, his tail slapping the mattress at a furious rate. *Whomp! Whomp! Whomp!* I reached out to pet him, and that sent him into evasive maneuvers. He was prancing and dancing beside the bed. The Marley Mambo. "Okay, what do you have?" I asked him, eyes still shut. As if to answer, Marley proudly plopped his prize onto the crisp sheets, just inches from my face. In my groggy state, it took me a minute to process what exactly it was. The object was small, dark, of indefinable shape, and coated in a coarse, gritty sand. Then the smell reached my nostrils. An acrid, pungent, putrid smell. I bolted upright and pushed backward against Jenny, waking her up. I pointed at Marley's gift to us, glistening on the sheets.

"That's not . . ." Jenny began, revulsion in her voice.

"Yes, it is," I said. "He raided the kitty-litter box."

Marley couldn't have looked more proud had he just presented us with the Hope diamond. As Barbara Woodhouse had so sagely predicted, our mentally unstable, abnormal mutt had entered the feces-eating stage of his life.

CHAPTER 19

Lightning Strikes

*

After Conor's arrival, everyone we knew—with the exception of my very Catholic parents who were praying for dozens of little Grogans—assumed we were done having children. In the two-income, professional crowd in which we ran, one child was the norm, two were considered a bit of an extravagance, and three were simply unheard-of. Especially given the difficult pregnancy we had gone through with Conor, no one could understand why we might want to subject ourselves to the messy process all over again. But we had come a long way since our newly-wed days of killing houseplants. Parenthood became us. Our two boys brought us more joy than we ever thought anyone or anything possibly could. They defined our life now, and while parts of us missed the leisurely vacations, lazy Saturdays reading novels, and romantic dinners that lingered late into the night, we had come to find our pleasures in new ways—in spilled applesauce and tiny nose prints on windowpanes and the soft symphony of bare feet padding down the hallway at dawn. Even on the worst days, we usually managed to find something to smile over, knowing by now what every parent sooner or later figures out, that these wondrous days of early parenthood—of diapered bottoms and first teeth and incomprehensible jabber—are but a brilliant, brief flash in the vastness of an otherwise ordinary lifetime.

We both rolled our eyes when my old-school mother clucked at us, "Enjoy them while you can because they'll be grown up before you know it." Now, even just a few years into it, we were realizing she was right. Hers was a well-worn cliché but one we could already see was steeped in truth. The boys *were* growing up fast, and each week ended another little chapter that could never again be revisited. One week Patrick was sucking his thumb, the next he had weaned himself of it forever. One week Conor was our baby in a crib; the next he was a little boy using a toddler bed for a trampoline. Patrick was unable to pronounce the *L* sound, and when women would coo over him, as they often did, he would put his fists on his hips, stick out his lip, and say, "Dos yadies are yaughing at me." I always meant to get it on videotape, but one day the *L*'s came out perfectly, and that was that. For months we could not get Conor out of his Superman pajamas. He would race through the house, cape flapping behind him, yelling, "Me Stupe Man!" And then it was over, another missed video moment.

Children serve as impossible-to-ignore, in-your-face time-pieces, marking the relentless march of one's life through what otherwise might seem an infinite sea of minutes, hours, days, and years. Our babies were growing up faster than either of us wanted, which partially explains why, about a year after moving to our new house in Boca, we began trying for our third. As I said to Jenny, "Hey, we've got four bedrooms now; why not?" Two tries was all it took. Neither of us would admit we wanted a girl, but of course we did, desperately so, despite our many pronouncements during the pregnancy that having three boys would be just great.

When a sonogram finally confirmed our secret hope, Jenny draped her arms over my shoulders and whispered, "I'm so happy I could give you a little girl." I was so happy, too.

Not all our friends shared our enthusiasm. Most met news of our pregnancy with the same blunt question: "Did you mean to?" They just could not believe a third pregnancy could be anything other than an accident. If indeed it was not, as we insisted, then they had to question our judgment. One acquaintance went so far as to chastise Jenny for allowing me to knock her up again, asking, in a tone best reserved for someone who had just signed over all her worldly possessions to a cult in Guyana: "What *were* you thinking?"

We didn't care. On January 9, 1997, Jenny gave me a belated Christmas present: a pink-cheeked, seven-pound baby girl, whom we named Colleen. Our family only now felt like it was complete. If the pregnancy for Conor had been a litany of stress and worry, this pregnancy was text-book perfect, and delivering at Boca Raton Community Hospital introduced us to a whole new level of pampered customer satisfaction. Just down the hall from our room was a lounge with a free, all-you-can-drink cappuccino station—

so very *Boca*. By the time the baby finally came, I was so jacked up on frothy caffeine, I could barely hold my hands still to snip the umbilical cord.

When Colleen was one week old, Jenny brought her outside for the first time. The day was crisp and beautiful, and the boys and I were in the front yard, planting flowers. Marley was chained to a tree nearby, happy to lie in the shade and watch the world go by. Jenny sat in the grass beside him and placed the sleeping Colleen in a portable bassinet on the ground between them. After several minutes, the boys beckoned for Mom to come closer to see their handiwork, and they led Jenny and me around the garden beds as Colleen napped in the shade beside Marley. We wandered behind some large shrubbery from where we could still see the baby but passersby on the street could not see us. As we turned back, I stopped and motioned for Jenny to look out through the shrubs. Out on the street, an older couple walking by had stopped and were gawking at the scene in our front yard with bewildered expressions. At first, I wasn't sure what had made them stop and stare. Then it hit me: from their vantage point, all they could see was a fragile newborn alone with a large yellow dog, who appeared to be babysitting single-handedly.

We lingered in silence, stifling giggles. There was Marley, looking like an Egyptian sphinx, lying with his front paws crossed, head up, panting contentedly, every few seconds pushing his snout over to sniff the baby's head. The poor couple must have thought they had stumbled on a case of felony child neglect. No doubt the parents were out drinking at a bar somewhere, having left the infant alone in the care of the neighborhood Labrador retriever, who just might attempt to nurse the infant at any second. As if he were in on the ruse, Marley without prompting shifted positions and rested his chin across the baby's stomach, his head bigger than her whole body, and let out a long sigh as if he were saying, *When are those two going to get home?* He appeared to be protecting her, and maybe he was, though I'm pretty sure he was just drinking in the scent of her diaper.

Jenny and I stood there in the bushes and exchanged grins. The thought of Marley as an infant caregiver—Doggie Day Care— was just too good to let go. I was tempted to wait there and see how the scene would play out, but then it occurred to me that one scenario might involve a 911 call to the police. We had gotten away with storing Conor out in the breezeway, but how would we explain this one? ("Well, I know how it must look, Officer, but he's actually surprisingly responsible . . .") We stepped out of the bushes and waved to the couple—and watched the relief wash over their faces. Thank God, that baby hadn't been thrown to the dogs after all.

"You must really trust your dog," the woman said somewhat cautiously, betraying a belief that dogs were fierce and unpredictable and had no place that close to a defenseless newborn.

"He hasn't eaten one yet," I said.

✿

Two months after Colleen arrived home I celebrated my fortieth birthday in a most inauspicious manner, namely, by myself. The Big Four-O is supposed to be a major turning point, the place in life where you bid restless youth farewell and embrace the predictable comforts of middle age. If any birthday merited a blowout celebration, it was the fortieth, but not for me. We were now responsible parents with three children; Jenny had a new baby pressed to her breast. There were more important things to worry about. I arrived home from work, and Jenny was tired and worn down. After a quick meal of leftovers, I bathed the boys and put them to bed while Jenny nursed Colleen. By eight-thirty, all three children were asleep, and so was my wife. I popped a beer and sat out on the patio, staring into the iridescent blue water of the lit swimming pool. As always, Marley was faithfully at my side, and as I scratched his ears, it occurred to me that he was at about the same turning point in life. We had brought him home six years earlier. In dog years, that would put him somewhere in his early forties now. He had crossed unnoticed into middle age but still acted every bit the puppy. Except for a string of stubborn ear infections that required Dr. Jay's repeated intervention, he was healthy. He showed no signs whatsoever of growing up or winding down. I had never thought of Marley as any kind of role model, but sitting there sipping my beer, I was aware that maybe he held the secret for a good life. Never slow down, never look back, live each day with adolescent verve and spunk and curiosity and playfulness. If you think you're still a young pup, then maybe you are, no matter what the calendar says. Not a bad philosophy for life, though I'd take a pass on the part that involved vandalizing couches and laundry rooms.

"Well, big guy," I said, pressing my beer bottle against his cheek in a kind of interspecies toast. "It's just you and me tonight. Here's to forty. Here's to middle age. Here's to running with the big dogs right up until the end." And then he, too, curled up and went to sleep.

I was still moping about my solitary birthday a few days later when Jim Tolpin, my old colleague who had broken Marley of his jumping habit, called unexpectedly and asked if I wanted to grab a beer the next night, a Saturday. Jim had left the newspaper business to pursue a law degree at about the same time we moved to Boca Raton, and we hadn't spoken in months. "Sure," I said, not stopping to wonder why. Jim picked me up at six and took me to an English pub, where we quaffed Bass ale and caught up on each other's lives. We were having a grand old time until the bartender called out, "Is there a John Grogan here? Phone for John Grogan."

It was Jenny, and she sounded very upset and stressed-out. "The baby's crying, the boys are out of control, and I just ripped my contact lens!" she wailed into the phone. "Can you come home right away?"

"Try to calm down," I said. "Sit tight. I'll be right home." I hung up, and the bartender gave me a you-poor-sorry-hen-pecked-bastard kind of a nod and simply said, "My sympathies, mate."

"Come on," Jim said. "I'll drive you home."

When we turned onto my block, both sides of the

street were lined with cars. "Somebody's having a party," I said.

"Looks like it," Jim answered.

"For God's sakes," I said when we reached the house. "Look at that! Someone even parked in my driveway. If that isn't nerve."

We blocked the offender in, and I invited Jim inside. I was still griping about the inconsiderate jerk who parked in my driveway when the front door swung open. It was Jenny with Colleen in her arms. She didn't look upset at all. In fact, she had a big grin on her face. Behind her stood a bagpipe player in kilts. *Good God! What have I walked in on?* Then I looked beyond the bagpipe player and saw that someone had taken down the kiddy fence around the pool and launched floating candles on the water. The deck was crammed with several dozen of my friends, neighbors, and coworkers. Just as I was making the connection that all those cars on the street belonged to all these people in my house, they shouted in unison, "HAPPY BIRTHDAY, OLD MAN!"

My wife had not forgotten after all.

When I was finally able to snap my jaw shut, I took Jenny in my arms, kissed her on the cheek, and whispered in her ear, "I'll get you later for this."

Someone opened the laundry-room door looking for the trash can, and out bounded Marley in prime party mode. He swept through the crowd, stole a mozzarella-and-basil appetizer off a tray, lifted a couple of women's miniskirts with his snout, and made a break for the unfenced swimming pool. I tackled him just as he was launching into his signature running belly flop and dragged him back to solitary confinement. "Don't worry," I said. "I'll save you the leftovers."

It wasn't long after the surprise party—a party whose success was marked by the arrival of the police at midnight to tell us to pipe down—that Marley finally was able to find validation for his intense fear of thunder. I was in the backyard on a Sunday afternoon under brooding, darkening skies, digging up a rectangle of grass to plant yet another vegetable garden. Gardening was becoming a serious hobby for me, and the better I got at it, the more I wanted to grow. Slowly I was taking over the entire backyard. As I worked, Marley paced nervously around me, his internal barometer sensing an impending storm. I sensed it, too, but I wanted to get the project done and figured I would work until I felt the first drops of rain. As I dug, I kept glancing at the sky, watching an ominous black thunderhead forming several miles to the east, out over the ocean. Marley was whining softly, beckoning me to put down the shovel and head inside. "Relax," I told him. "It's still miles away."

The words had barely left my lips when I felt a previously unknown sensation, a kind of quivering tingle on the back of my neck. The sky had turned an odd shade of olive gray, and the air seemed to go suddenly dead as though some heavenly force had grabbed the winds and frozen them in its grip. *Weird,* I thought as I paused, leaning on my shovel to study the sky. That's when I heard it: a buzzing, popping, crackling surge of energy, similar to what you sometimes can hear standing beneath high-tension power lines. A sort of *pffffffffffft* sound filled the air around me, followed by a brief instant of utter silence. In that instant, I knew trouble was coming, but I had no time to react. In the next fraction of a second, the sky went pure, blindingly white, and an explosion, the likes of which I had never heard before, not in any storm, at any fireworks display, at any demolition site, boomed in my ears. A wall of energy hit me in the chest like an invisible linebacker. When I opened my eyes who knows how many seconds later, I was lying facedown on the ground, sand in my mouth, my shovel ten feet away, rain pelting me. Marley was down, too, in his hit-the-deck stance, and when he saw me raise my head he wiggled desperately toward me on his belly like a soldier trying to slide beneath barbed wire. When he reached me he climbed right on my back and buried his snout in my neck, frantically licking me. I looked around for just a second, trying to get my bearings, and I could see where the lightning had struck the power-line pole in the corner of the yard and followed the wire down to the house about twenty feet from where I had been standing. The electrical meter on the wall was in charred ruins.

"Come on!" I yelled, and then Marley and I were on our feet, sprinting through the downpour toward the back door as new bolts of lightning flashed around us. We did not stop until we were safely inside. I knelt on the floor, soaking wet, catching my breath, and Marley clambered on me, licking my face, nibbling my ears, flinging spit and loose fur all over everything. He was beside himself with fear, shaking un-controllably, drool hanging off his chin. I hugged him, tried to calm him down. "Jesus, that was close!" I said, and realized that I was shaking, too. He looked up at me with those big empathetic eyes that I swore could almost talk. I was sure I knew what he was trying to tell me. *I've been trying to warn you for years that this stuff can kill you. But would anyone listen? Now will you take me seriously?*

The dog had a point. Maybe his fear of thunder had not been so irrational after all. Maybe his panic attacks at the first distant rumblings had been his way of telling us that Florida's violent thunderstorms, the deadliest in the country, were not to be dismissed with a shrug. Maybe all those destroyed walls and gouged doors and shredded carpets had been his way of trying to build a lightning-proof den we could all fit into snugly. And how had we rewarded him? With scoldings and tranquilizers.

Our house was dark, the air-conditioning, ceiling fans, televisions, and several appliances all blown out. The circuit breaker was fused into a melted mess. We were about to make some electrician a very happy man. But I was alive and so was my trusty sidekick. Jenny and the kids, tucked safely away in the family room, didn't even know the house had been hit. We were all present and accounted for. What else mattered? I pulled Marley into my lap, all ninety-seven nervous pounds of him, and made him a promise right then and there: Never again would I dismiss his fear of this deadly force of nature.

CHAPTER 20

Dog Beach

As a newspaper columnist, I was always looking for interesting and quirky stories I could grab on to. I wrote three columns each week, which meant that one of the biggest challenges of the job was coming up with a constant stream of fresh topics. Each morning I began my day by scouring the four South Florida daily newspapers, circling and clipping anything that might be worth weighing in on. Then it was a matter of finding an approach or angle that would be mine. My very first column had come directly from the headlines. A speeding car crammed with eight teenagers had flipped into a canal along the edge of the Everglades. Only the sixteen-year-old driver, her twin sister, and a third girl had escaped the submerged car. It was a huge story that I knew I wanted to come in on, but what was the fresh angle I could call my own? I drove out to the lonely crash sight hoping for inspiration, and before I even stopped the car I had found it. The classmates of the five dead children had transformed the pavement into a tapestry of spray-painted eulogies. The blacktop was covered shoulder-to-shoulder for more than a half mile, and the raw emotion of the outpouring was palpable. Notebook in hand, I began copying the words down. "Wasted youth," said one message, accompanied by a painted arrow pointing off the road and into the water. Then, there in the middle of the communal catharsis, I found it: a public apology from the young driver, Jamie Bardol. She wrote in big, loopy letters, a child's scrawl: "I wish it would have been me. I'm sorry." I had found my column.

Not all topics were so dark. When a retiree received an eviction notice from her condo because her pudgy pooch exceeded the weight limit for pets, I swooped in to meet the offending heavyweight. When a confused senior citizen crashed her car into a store while trying to park, fortunately hurting no one, I was close behind, speaking to witnesses. The job would take me to a migrant camp one day, a millionaire's mansion the next, and an inner-city street corner the day after that. I loved the variety; I loved the people I met; and more than anything I loved the near-total freedom I was afforded to go wherever I wanted whenever I wanted in pursuit of whatever topic tickled my curiosity.

What my bosses did not know was that behind my journalistic wanderings was a secret agenda: to use my position as a columnist to engineer as many shamelessly transparent "working holidays" as I possibly could. My motto was "When the columnist has fun, the reader has fun." Why attend a deadening tax-adjustment hearing in pursuit of column fodder when you could be sitting, say, at an outdoor bar in Key West, large alcoholic beverage in hand? Someone had to do the dirty work of telling the story of the lost shakers of salt in Margaritaville; it might as well be me. I lived for any excuse to spend a day goofing around, preferably in shorts and T-shirt, sampling various leisurely and recreational pursuits that I convinced myself the public needed someone to fully investigate. Every profession has its tools of the trade, and mine included a reporter's notebook, a bundle of pens, and a beach towel. I began carrying sunscreen and a bathing suit in my car as a matter of routine.

I spent one day blasting through the Everglades on an airboat and another hiking along the rim of Lake Okeechobee. I spent a day bicycling scenic State Road A1A along the Atlantic Ocean so I could report firsthand on the harrowing proposition of sharing the pavement with confused blueheads and distracted tourists. I spent a day snorkeling above the endangered reefs off Key Largo and another firing off clips of ammunition at a shooting range with a two-time robbery victim who swore he would never be victimized again. I spent a day lolling about on a commercial fishing boat and a day jamming with a band of aging rock musicians. One day I simply climbed a tree and sat for hours enjoying the solitude; a developer planned to bulldoze the grove in which I sat to make way for a high-end housing development, and I figured the least I could do was give this last remnant of nature amid the concrete jungle a proper funeral. My biggest coup of all was when I talked my editors into sending me to the Bahamas so I could be on the forward edge of a brewing hurricane that was making its way toward South Florida. The hurricane veered harmlessly out to sea, and I spent three days beachside at a luxury hotel, sipping piña coladas beneath blue skies.

It was in this vein of journalistic inquiry that I got the idea to take Marley for a day at the beach. Up and down South Florida's heavily used shoreline, various municipalities had banned pets, and for good reason. The last thing beachgoers wanted was a wet, sandy dog pooping and peeing and shaking all over them as they worked on their tans. NO PETS signs bristled along nearly every stretch of sand.

There was one place, though, one small, little-known sliver of beach, where there were no signs, no restrictions, no bans on four-legged water lovers. The beach was tucked away in an unincorporated pocket of Palm Beach County about halfway between West Palm Beach and Boca Raton, stretching for a few hundred yards and hidden behind a grassy dune at the end of a dead-end street. There was no parking, no restroom, no lifeguard, just an unspoiled stretch of unregulated white sand meeting endless water. Over the years, its reputation spread by word of mouth among pet owners as one of South Florida's last safe havens for dogs to come and frolic in the surf without risking a fine. The place had no official name; unofficially, everyone knew it as Dog Beach.

Dog Beach operated on its own set of unwritten rules that had evolved over time, put in place by consensus of the dog owners who frequented it, and enforced by peer pressure and a sort of silent moral code. The dog owners policed themselves so others would not be tempted to, punishing violators with withering stares and, if needed, a few choice words. The rules were simple and few: Aggressive dogs had to stay leashed; all others could run free. Owners were to bring plastic bags with them to pick up any droppings their animal might deposit. All trash, including bagged dog waste, was to be carted out. Each dog should arrive with a supply of fresh drinking water. Above all else, there would be absolutely no fouling of the water. The etiquette called for owners, upon arriving, to walk their dogs along the dune line, far from the ocean's edge, until their pets relieved themselves. Then they could bag the waste and safely proceed to the water.

I had heard about Dog Beach but had never visited. Now I had my excuse. This forgotten vestige of the rapidly disappearing Old Florida, the one that existed before the arrival of waterfront condo towers, metered beach parking, and soaring real estate values, was in the news. A pro-development county commissioner had begun squawking about this unregulated stretch of beach and asking why the same rules that applied to other county beaches should not apply here. She made her intent clear: outlaw the furry critters, improve public access, and open this valuable resource to the masses.

I immediately locked in on the story for what it was: a perfect excuse to spend a day at the beach on company time. On a drop-dead-perfect June morning, I traded my tie and briefcase for swimsuit and flip-flops and headed with Marley across the Intracoastal Waterway. I filled the car with as many beach towels as I could find—and that was just for the drive over. As always, Marley's tongue was hanging out, spit flying everywhere. I felt like I was on a road trip with Old Faithful. My only regret was that the windshield wipers weren't on the inside.

Following Dog Beach protocol, I parked several blocks away, where I wouldn't get a ticket, and began the long hike in through a sleepy neighborhood of sixties-vintage bunga-lows, Marley leading the charge. About halfway there, a gruff voice called out, "Hey, Dog Guy!" I froze, convinced I was about to be busted by an angry neighbor who wanted me to keep my damn dog the hell off his beach. But the voice belonged to another pet owner, who approached me with his own large dog on a leash and handed me a petition to sign urging county commissioners to let Dog Beach stand. Speaking of standing, we would have stood and chatted, but the way Marley and the other dog were circling each other, I knew it was just a matter of seconds before they either (a) lunged at each other in mortal combat or (b) began a family. I yanked Marley away and continued on. Just as we reached the path to the beach, Marley squatted in the weeds and emptied his bowels. Perfect. At least that little social nicety was out of the way. I bagged up the evidence and said, "To the beach!"

When we crested the dune, I was surprised to see several people wading in the shallows with their dogs securely tethered to leashes. What was this all about? I expected the dogs to be running free in unbridled, communal harmony. "A sheriff's deputy was just here," one glum dog owner explained to me. "He said from now on they're enforcing the county leash ordinance and we'll be fined if our dogs are loose." It appeared I had arrived too late to fully enjoy the simple pleasures of Dog Beach. The police, no doubt at the urging of the politically connected anti–Dog Beach forces, were tightening the noose. I obediently walked Marley along the water's edge with the other dog owners, feeling more like I was in a prison exercise yard than on South Florida's last unregulated spit of sand.

I returned with him to my towel and was just pouring Marley a bowl of water from the canteen I had lugged along when over the dune came a shirtless tattooed man in cutoff blue jeans and work boots, a muscular and fierce-looking pit bull terrier on a heavy chain at his side. Pit bulls are known for their aggression, and they were especially notorious during this time in South Florida. They were the dog breed of choice for gang members, thugs, and toughs, and often trained to be vicious. The newspapers were filled with accounts of unprovoked pit bull attacks, sometimes fatal, against both animals and humans. The owner must have noticed me recoiling because he called out, "Don't you worry. Killer's friendly. He don't never fight other dogs." I was just beginning to exhale with relief when he added with obvious pride, "But you should see him rip open a wild hog! I'll tell you, he can get it down and gutted in about fifteen seconds."

Marley and Killer the Pig-Slaying Pit Bull strained at their leashes, circling, sniffing furiously at each other. Marley had never been in a fight in his life and was so much bigger than most other dogs that he had never been intimidated by a challenge, either. Even when a dog attempted to pick a fight, he didn't take the hint. He would merely pounce into a playful stance, butt up, tail wagging, a dumb, happy grin on his face. But he had never before been confronted by a trained killer, a gutter of wild game. I pictured Killer lunging without warning for Marley's throat and not letting go.

Killer's owner was unconcerned. "Unless you're a wild hog, he'll just lick you to death," he said.

I told him the cops had just been here and were going to ticket people who didn't obey the leash ordinance. "I guess they're cracking down," I said.

"That's bullshit!" he yelled, and spit into the sand. "I've been bringing my dogs to this beach for years. You don't need no leash at Dog Beach. Bullshit!" With that he unclipped the heavy chain, and Killer galloped across the sand and into the water. Marley reared back on his hind legs, bouncing up and down. He looked at Killer and then up at me. He looked back at Killer and back at me. His paws padded nervously on the sand, and he let out a soft, sustained whimper. If he could talk, I knew what he would have asked. I scanned the dune line; no cops anywhere in sight. I looked at Marley. *Please! Please! Pretty please! I'll be good. I promise.*

"Go ahead, let him loose," Killer's owner said. "A dog ain't meant to spend his life on the end of a rope."

"Oh, what the hell," I said, and unsnapped the leash. Marley dashed for the water, kicking sand all over us as he blasted off. He crashed into the surf just as a breaker rolled in, tossing him under the water. A second later his head reappeared, and the instant he regained his footing he threw a cross-body block at Killer the Pig-Slaying Pit Bull, knocking both of them off their feet. Together they rolled beneath a wave, and I held my breath, wondering if Marley had just crossed the line that would throw Killer into a homicidal, Lab-butchering fury. But when they popped back up again, their tails were wagging, their mouths grinning. Killer

jumped on Marley's back and Marley on Killer's, their jaws
clamping playfully around each other's throats. They chased
each other up the waterline and back again, sending plumes
of spray flying on either side of them. They pranced, they
danced, they wrestled, they dove. I don't think I had ever
before, or have ever since, witnessed such unadulterated
joy.

The other dog owners took our cue, and pretty soon all
the dogs, about a dozen in total, were running free. The dogs
all got along splendidly; the owners all followed the rules. It
was Dog Beach as it was meant to be. This was the real
Florida, unblemished and unchecked, the Florida of a forgotten, simpler time and place, immune to the march of
progress.

There was only one small problem. As the morning
progressed, Marley kept lapping up salt water. I followed
behind him with the bowl of fresh water, but he was too
distracted to drink. Several times I led him right up to the
bowl and stuck his nose into it, but he spurned the fresh
water as if it were vinegar, wanting only to return to his new
best friend, Killer, and the other dogs.

Out in the shallows, he paused from his play to lap up
even more salt water. "Stop that, you dummy!" I yelled at
him. "You're going to make yourself . . ." Before I could
finish my thought, it happened. A strange glaze settled over
his eyes and a horrible churning sound began to erupt from
his gut. He arched his back high and opened and shut his
mouth several times, as if trying to clear something from his
craw. His shoulders heaved; his abdomen contorted. I
hurried to finish my sentence: ". . . sick."

The instant the word left my lips, Marley fulfilled the prophecy, committing the ultimate Dog Beach heresy. *GAAAAAAAAACK!*

I raced to pull him out of the water, but it was too late. Everything was coming up. *GAAAAAAAAACK!* I could see last night's dog chow floating on the water's surface, looking surprisingly like it had before it went in. Bobbing among the nuggets were undigested corn kernels he had swiped off the kids' plates, a milk-jug cap, and the severed head of a tiny plastic soldier. The entire evacuation took no more than three seconds, and the instant his stomach was emptied he looked up brightly, apparently fully recovered with no lingering aftereffects, as if to say, *Now that I've got that taken care of, who wants to bodysurf?* I glanced nervously around, but no one had seemed to notice. The other dog owners were occupied with their own dogs farther down the beach, a mother not far away was focused on helping her toddler make a sandcastle, and the few sunbathers scattered about were lying flat on their backs, eyes closed. *Thank God!* I thought, as I waded into Marley's puke zone, roiling the water with my feet as nonchalantly as I could to disperse the evidence. *How embarrassing would that have been?* At any rate, I told myself, despite the technical violation of the No. 1 Dog Beach Rule, we had caused no real harm. After all, it was just undigested food; the fish would be thankful for the meal, wouldn't they? I even picked out the milk-jug cap and soldier's head and put them in my pocket so as not to litter.

"Listen, you," I said sternly, grabbing Marley around the snout and forcing him to look me in the eye. "Stop drinking salt water. What kind of a dog doesn't know enough to not drink salt water?'' I considered yanking him off the beach and cutting our adventure short, but he seemed fine now. There couldn't possibly be anything left in his stomach. The damage was done, and we had gotten away with it unde- tected. I released him and he streaked down the beach to rejoin Killer.

What I had failed to consider was that, while Marley's stomach may have been completely emptied, his bowels were not. The sun was reflecting blindingly off the water, and I squinted to see Marley frolicking among the other dogs. As I watched, he abruptly disengaged from the play and began turning in tight circles in the shallow water. I knew the circling maneuver well. It was what he did every morning in the backyard as he prepared to defecate. It was a ritual for him, as though not just any spot would do for the gift he was about to bestow on the world. Sometimes the circling could go on for a minute or more as he sought just the perfect patch of earth. And now he was circling in the shallows of Dog Beach, on that brave frontier where no dog had dared to poop before. He was entering his squatting position. And this time, he had an audience. Killer's dad and several other dog owners were standing within a few yards of him. The mother and her daughter had turned from their sandcastle to gaze out to sea. A couple approached, walking hand in hand along the water's edge. "No," I whispered. "Please, God, no."

"Hey!" someone yelled out. "Get your dog!"

"Stop him!" someone else shouted.

As alarmed voices cried out, the sunbathers propped themselves up to see what all the commotion was about.

I burst into a full sprint, racing to get to him before it was too late. If I could just reach him and yank him out of his squat before his bowels began to move, I might be able to interrupt the whole awful humiliation, at least long enough to get him safely up on the dune. As I raced toward him, I had what can only be described as an out-of-body experience. Even as I ran, I was looking down from above, the scene unfolding one frozen frame at a time. Each step seemed to last an eternity. Each foot hit the sand with a dull thud. My arms swung through the air; my face contorted in a sort of agonized grimace. As I ran, I absorbed the slow-mo frames around me: a young woman sunbather, holding her top in place over her breasts with one hand, her other hand plastered over her mouth; the mother scooping up her child and retreating from the water's edge; the dog owners, their faces twisted with disgust, pointing; Killer's dad, his leathery neck bulging, yelling. Marley was done circling now and in full squat position, looking up to the heavens as if saying a little prayer. And I heard my own voice rising above the din and uncoiling in an oddly guttural, distorted, drawn-out scream: *"Nooooooooooooooooo!"*

I was almost there, just feet from him. "Marley, no!" I screamed. "No, Marley, no! No! No! No!" It was no use. Just as I reached him, he exploded in a burst of watery diarrhea. Everyone was jumping back now, recoiling, fleeing to higher ground. Owners were grabbing their dogs. Sunbathers scooped up their towels. Then it was over. Marley trotted out of the water onto the beach, shook off with gusto, and turned to look at me, panting happily. I pulled a plastic bag out of my pocket and held it helplessly in the air. I could see immediately it would do no good. The waves crashed in, spreading Marley's mess across the water and up onto the beach.

"Dude," Killer's dad said in a voice that made me appreciate how the wild hogs must feel at the instant of Killer's final, fatal lunge. "That was not cool."

No, it wasn't cool at all. Marley and I had violated the sacred rule of Dog Beach. We had fouled the water, not once but twice, and ruined the morning for everyone. It was time to beat a quick retreat.

"Sorry," I mumbled to Killer's owner as I snapped the leash on Marley. "He swallowed a bunch of seawater."

Back at the car, I threw a towel over Marley and vigorously rubbed him down. The more I rubbed, the more he shook, and soon I was covered in sand and spray and fur. I wanted to be mad at him. I wanted to strangle him. But it was too late now. Besides, who wouldn't get sick drinking a half gallon of salt water? As with so many of his misdeeds, this one was not malicious or premeditated. It wasn't as though he had disobeyed a command or set out to intentionally humiliate me. He simply had to go and he went. True, at the wrong place and the wrong time and in front of all the wrong people. I knew he was a victim of his own diminished mental capacity. He was the only beast on the whole beach dumb enough to guzzle seawater. The dog was defective. How could I hold that against him?

"You don't have to look so pleased with yourself," I said as I loaded him into the backseat. But pleased he was. He could not have looked happier had I bought him his own Caribbean island. What he did not know was that this would be his last time setting a paw in any body of salt water. His days—or rather, hours—as a beach bum were behind him. "Well, Salty Dog," I said on the drive home, "you've done it this time. If dogs are banned from Dog Beach, we'll know why." It would take several more years, but in the end that's exactly what happened.

CHAPTER 21

A Northbound Plane

S hortly after Colleen turned two, I inadvertently set off a fateful series of events that would lead us to leave Florida. And I did it with the click of a mouse. I had wrapped up my column early for the day and found myself with a half hour to kill as I waited for my editor. On a whim I decided to check out the website of a magazine I had been subscribing to since not long after we bought our West Palm Beach house. The magazine was *Organic Gardening*, which was launched in 1942 by the eccentric J. I. Rodale and went on to become the bible of the back-to-the-earth movement that blossomed in the 1960s and 1970s.

Rodale had been a New York City businessman specializing in electrical switches when his health began to fail. Instead of turning to modern medicine to solve his problems, he moved from the city to a small farm outside the tiny borough of Emmaus, Pennsylvania, and began playing in the dirt. He had a deep distrust of technology and believed the modern farming and gardening methods sweeping the country, nearly all of them relying on chemical pesticides and fertilizers, were not the saviors of American agriculture they purported to be. Rodale's theory was that the chemicals were gradually poisoning the earth and all of its inhabitants. He began experimenting with farming techniques that mimicked nature. On his farm, he built huge compost piles of decaying plant matter, which, once the material had turned to rich black humus, he used as fertilizer and a natural soil builder. He covered the dirt in his garden rows with a thick carpet of straw to suppress weeds and retain moisture. He planted cover crops of clover and alfalfa and then plowed them under to return nutrients to the soil. Instead of spraying for insects, he unleashed thousands of ladybugs and other beneficial insects that devoured the destructive ones. He was a bit of a kook, but his theories proved themselves. His garden flourished and so did his health, and he trumpeted his successes in the pages of his magazine.

By the time I started reading *Organic Gardening*, J. I. Rodale was long dead and so was his son, Robert, who had built his father's business, Rodale Press, into a multimillion-dollar publishing company. The magazine was not very well written or edited; reading it, you got the impression it was put out by a group of dedicated but amateurish devotees of J. I.'s philosophy, serious gardeners with no professional training as journalists; later I would learn this was exactly the case. Regardless, the organic philosophy increasingly made sense to me, especially after Jenny's miscarriage and our suspicion that it might have had something to do with the pesticides we had used. By the time Colleen was born, our yard was a little organic oasis in a suburban sea of chemical weed-and-feed applications and pesticides. Passersby often stopped to admire our thriving front garden, which I tended with increasing passion, and they almost always asked the same question: "What do you put on it to make it look so good?" When I answered, "I don't," they looked at me uncomfortably, as though they had just stumbled upon something unspeakably subversive going on in well-ordered, homogeneous, conformist Boca Raton.

That afternoon in my office, I clicked through the screens at *organicgardening.com* and eventually found my way to a button that said "Career Opportunities." I clicked on it, why I'm still not sure. I loved my job as a columnist; loved the daily interaction I had with readers; loved the freedom to pick my own topics and be as serious or as flippant as I wanted to be. I loved the newsroom and the quirky, brainy, neurotic, idealistic people it attracted. I loved being in the middle of the biggest story of the day. I had no desire to leave newspapers for a sleepy publishing company in the middle of nowhere. Still, I began scrolling through the Rodale job postings, more idly curious than anything, but midway down the list I stopped cold. *Organic Gardening*, the company's flagship magazine, was seeking a new managing editor. My heart skipped a beat. I had often daydreamed about the huge difference a decent journalist could make at the magazine, and now here was my chance. It was crazy; it was ridiculous. A career editing stories about cauliflower and compost? Why would I want to do that?

That night I told Jenny about the opening, fully expecting her to tell me I was insane for even considering it. Instead she surprised me by encouraging me to send a résumé. The idea of leaving the heat and humidity and congestion and crime of South Florida for a simpler life in the country appealed to her. She missed four seasons and hills. She missed falling leaves and spring daffodils. She missed icicles and apple cider. She wanted our kids and, as ridiculous as it sounds, our dog to experience the wonders of a winter blizzard. "Marley's never even chased a snowball," she said, stroking his fur with her bare foot.

"Now, there's a good reason for changing careers," I said.

"You should do it just to satisfy your curiosity," she said. "See what happens. If they offer it to you, you can always turn them down."

I had to admit I shared her dream about moving north again.

As much as I enjoyed our dozen years in South Florida, I was a northern native who had never learned to stop missing three things: rolling hills, changing seasons, and open land. Even as I grew to love Florida with its mild winters, spicy food, and comically irascible mix of people, I did not stop dreaming of someday escaping to my own private paradise—not a postage-stamp-sized lot in the heart of hyperprecious Boca Raton but a real piece of land where I could dig in the dirt, chop my own firewood, and tromp through the forest, my dog at my side.

I applied, fully convincing myself it was just a lark. Two weeks later the phone rang and it was J. I. Rodale's grand-daughter, Maria Rodale. I had sent my letter to "Dear Human Resources" and was so surprised to be hearing from the owner of the company that I asked her to repeat her last name. Maria had taken a personal interest in the magazine her grandfather had founded, and she was intent on returning it to its former glory. She was convinced she needed a professional journalist, not another earnest organic gardener, to do that, and she wanted to take on more challenging and important stories about the environment, genetic engineering, factory farming, and the burgeoning organic movement.

I arrived for the job interview fully intending to play hard to get, but I was hooked the moment I drove out of the airport and onto the first curving, two-lane country road. At every turn was another postcard: a stone farmhouse here, a covered bridge there. Icy brooks gurgled down hillsides, and furrowed farmland stretched to the horizon like God's own golden robes. It didn't help that it was spring and every last tree in the Lehigh Valley was in full, glorious bloom. At a lonely country stop sign, I stepped out of my rental car and stood in the middle of the pavement. For as far as I could see in any direction, there was nothing but woods and meadows. Not a car, not a person, not a building. At the first pay phone I could find, I called Jenny. "You're not going to believe this place," I said.

Two months later the movers had the entire contents of our Boca house loaded into a gigantic truck. An auto carrier arrived to haul off our car and minivan. We turned the house keys over to the new owners and spent our last night in Florida sleeping on the floor of a neighbor's home, Marley sprawled out in the middle of us. "Indoor camping!" Patrick shrieked.

The next morning I arose early and took Marley for what would be his last walk on Florida soil. He sniffed and tugged and pranced as we circled the block, stopping to lift his leg on every shrub and mailbox we came to, happily oblivious to the abrupt change I was about to foist on him. I had bought a sturdy plastic travel crate to carry him on the airplane, and following Dr. Jay's advice, I clamped open Marley's jaws after our walk and slipped a double dose of tranquilizers down his throat. By the time our neighbor dropped us off at Palm Beach International Airport, Marley was red-eyed and exceptionally mellow. We could have strapped him to a rocket and he wouldn't have minded.

In the terminal, the Grogan clan cut a fine form: two wildly excited little boys racing around in circles, a hungry baby in a stroller, two stressed-out parents, and one very stoned dog. Rounding out the lineup was the rest of our menagerie: two frogs, three goldfish, a hermit crab, a snail named Sluggy, and a box of live crickets for feeding the frogs. As we waited in line at check-in, I assembled the plastic pet carrier. It was the biggest one I could find, but when we reached the counter, a woman in uniform looked at Marley, looked at the crate, looked back at Marley, and said, "We can't allow that dog aboard in that container. He's too big for it."

"The pet store said this was the 'large dog' size," I pleaded.

"FAA regulations require that the dog can freely stand up inside and turn fully around," she explained, adding skeptically, "Go ahead, give it a try."

I opened the gate and called Marley, but he was not about

to voluntarily walk into this mobile jail cell. I pushed and prodded, coaxed and cajoled; he wasn't budging. Where were the dog biscuits when I needed them? I searched my pockets for something to bribe him with, finally fishing out a tin of breath mints. This was as good as it was going to get. I took one out and held it in front of his nose. "Want a mint, Marley? Go get the mint!" and I tossed it into the crate. Sure enough, he took the bait and blithely entered the box.

The lady was right; he didn't quite fit. He had to scrunch down so his head wouldn't hit the ceiling; even with his nose touching the back wall, his butt stuck out the open door. I scrunched his tail down and closed the gate, nudging his rear inside. "What did I tell you?" I said, hoping she would consider it a comfortable fit.

"He's got to be able to turn around," she said.

"Turn around, boy," I beckoned to him, giving a little whistle. "Come on, turn around." He shot a glance over his shoulder at me with those doper eyes, his head scraping the ceiling, as if awaiting instructions on just how to accomplish such a feat.

If he could not turn around, the airline was not letting him aboard the flight. I checked my watch. We had twelve minutes left to get through security, down the concourse, and onto the plane. "Come here, Marley!" I said more desperately. "Come on!" I snapped my fingers, rattled the metal gate, made kissy-kissy sounds. "Come on," I pleaded. "Turn around." I was about to drop to my knees and beg when I heard a crash, followed almost immediately by Patrick's voice.

"Oops," he said.

"The frogs are loose!" Jenny screamed, jumping into action.

"Froggy! Croaky! Come back!" the boys yelled in unison.

My wife was on all fours now, racing around the terminal as the frogs cannily stayed one hop ahead of her. Passersby began to stop and stare. From a distance you could not see the frogs at all, just the crazy lady with the diaper bag hanging from her neck, crawling around like she had started the morning off with a little too much moonshine. From their expressions, I could tell they fully expected her to start howling at any moment.

"Excuse me a second," I said as calmly as I could to the airline worker, then joined Jenny on my hands and knees.

After doing our part to entertain the early-morning travel crowd, we finally captured Froggy and Croaky just as they were ready to make their final leap for freedom out the automatic doors. As we turned back, I heard a mighty ruckus coming from the dog crate. The entire box shivered and lurched across the floor, and when I peered in I saw that Marley had somehow gotten himself turned around. "See?" I said to the baggage supervisor. "He can turn around, no problem."

"Okay," she said with a frown. "But you're really pushing it."

Two workers lifted Marley and his crate onto a dolly and wheeled him away. The rest of us raced for our plane, arriving at the gate just as the flight attendants were closing the hatch. It occurred to me that if we missed the flight, Marley would be arriving alone in Pennsylvania, a scene of potential pandemonium I did not even want to contemplate. "Wait! We're here!" I shouted, pushing Colleen ahead of me, the boys and Jenny trailing by fifty feet.

As we settled into our seats, I finally allowed myself to exhale. We had gotten Marley squared away. We had captured the frogs. We had made the flight. Next stop, Allentown, Pennsylvania. I could relax now. Through the window I watched as a tram pulled up with the dog crate sitting on it. "Look," I said to the kids. "There's Marley." They waved out the window and called, "Hi, Waddy!"

As the engines revved and the flight attendant went over the safety precautions, I pulled out a magazine. That's when I noticed Jenny freeze in the row in front of me. Then I heard it, too. From below our feet, deep in the bowels of the plane, came a sound, muffled but undeniable. It was pitifully mournful sound, a sort of primal call that started low and rose as it went. *Oh, dear Jesus, he's down there howling*. For the record, Labrador retrievers do not howl. Beagles howl. Wolves howl. Labs do not howl, at least not well. Marley had attempted to howl twice before, both times in answer to a passing police siren, tossing back his head, forming his mouth into an *O* shape, and letting loose the most pathetic sound I have ever heard, more like he was gargling than answering the call of the wild. But now, no question about it, he was howling.

The passengers began to look up from their newspapers and novels. A flight attendant handing out pillows paused and cocked her head quizzically. A woman across the aisle from us looked at her husband and asked: "Listen. Do you hear that? I think it's a dog." Jenny stared straight ahead. I stared into my magazine. If anyone asked, we were denying ownership.

"Waddy's sad," Patrick said.

No, son, I wanted to correct him, *some strange dog we have never seen before and have no knowledge of is sad.* But I just pulled my magazine higher over my face, following the advice of the immortal Richard Milhous Nixon: plausible deniability. The jet engines whined and the plane taxied down the runway, drowning out Marley's dirge. I pictured him down below in the dark hold, alone, scared, confused, stoned, not even able to fully stand up. I imagined the roaring engines, which in Marley's warped mind might be just another thunderous assault by random lightning bolts determined to take him out. The poor guy. I wasn't willing to admit he was mine, but I knew I would be spending the whole flight worrying about him.

The airplane was barely off the ground when I heard another little crash, and this time it was Conor who said, "Oops." I looked down and then, once again, stared straight into my magazine. *Plausible deniability*. After several seconds, I furtively glanced around. When I was pretty sure no one was staring, I leaned forward and whispered into Jenny's ear: "Don't look now, but the crickets are loose."

CHAPTER 22

In the Land of Pencils

✳

We settled into a rambling house on two acres perched on the side of a steep hill. Or perhaps it was a small mountain; the locals seemed to disagree on this point. Our property had a meadow where we could pick wild raspberries, a woods where I could chop logs to my heart's content, and a small, spring-fed creek where the kids and Marley soon found they could get exceptionally muddy. There was a fireplace and endless garden possibilities and a white-steepled church on the next hill, visible from our kitchen window when the leaves dropped in the fall.

Our new home even came with a neighbor right out of Central Casting, an orange-bearded bear of a man who lived in a 1790s stone farmhouse and on Sundays enjoyed sitting on his back porch and shooting his rifle into the woods just for fun, much to Marley's unnerved dismay. On our first day in our new house, he walked over with a bottle of home-made wild-cherry wine and a basket of the biggest black-berries I had ever seen. He introduced himself as Digger. As we surmised from the nickname, Digger made his living as an excavator. If we had any holes we needed dug or earth we wanted moved, he instructed, we were to just give a shout and he'd swing by with one of his big machines. "And if you hit a deer with your car, come get me," he said with a wink. "We'll butcher it up and split the meat before the game officer knows a thing." No doubt about it, we weren't in Boca anymore.

There was only one thing missing from our new bucolic existence. Minutes after we pulled into the driveway of our new house, Conor looked up at me, big tears rolling out of his eyes, and declared: "I thought there were going to be pencils in Pencilvania." For our boys, now ages seven and five, this was a near deal breaker. Given the name of the state we were adopting, both of them arrived fully expecting to see bright yellow writing implements hanging like berries from every tree and shrub, there for the plucking. They were crushed to learn otherwise.

What our property lacked in school supplies, it made up for in skunks, opossums, woodchucks, and poison ivy, which flourished along the edge of our woods and snaked up the trees, giving me hives just to look at it. One morning I glanced out the kitchen window as I fumbled with the coffeemaker and there staring back at me was a magnificent eight-point buck. Another morning a family of wild turkeys gobbled its way across the backyard. As Marley and I walked through the woods down the hill from our house one Saturday, we came upon a mink trapper laying snares. A mink trapper! Almost in my backyard! What the Bocahontas set would have given for that connection.

Living in the country was at once peaceful, charming—and just a little lonely. The Pennsylvania Dutch were polite but cautious of outsiders. And we were definitely outsiders. After South Florida's legion crowds and lines, I should have been ecstatic about the solitude. Instead, at least in the early months, I found myself darkly ruminating over our decision to move to a place where so few others apparently wanted to live.

Marley, on the other hand, had no such misgivings. Except for the crack of Digger's gun going off, the new country lifestyle fit him splendidly. For a dog with more energy than sense, what wasn't to like? He raced across the lawn, crashed through the brambles, splashed through the creek. His life's mission was to catch one of the countless rabbits that considered my garden their own personal salad bar. He would spot a rabbit munching the lettuce and barrel off down the hill in hot pursuit, ears flapping behind him, paws pounding the ground, his bark filling the air. He was about as stealthy as a marching band and never got closer than a dozen feet before his intended prey scampered off into the woods to safety. True to his trademark, he remained eternally optimistic that success waited just around the bend. He would loop back, tail wagging, not discouraged in the least, and five minutes later do it all over again. Fortunately, he was no better at sneaking up on the skunks.

Autumn came and with it a whole new mischievous game: Attack the Leaf Pile. In Florida, trees did not shed their leaves in the fall, and Marley was positively convinced the foliage drifting down from the skies now was a gift meant just for him. As I raked the orange and yellow leaves into giant heaps, Marley would sit and watch patiently, biding his time, waiting until just the right moment to strike. Only after I had gathered a mighty towering pile would he slink forward, crouched low. Every few steps, he would stop, front paw raised, to sniff the air like a lion on the Serengeti stalking an unsuspecting gazelle. Then, just as I leaned on my rake to admire my handiwork, he would lunge, charging across the lawn in a series of bounding leaps, flying for the last several feet and landing in a giant belly flop in the middle of the pile, where he growled and rolled and flailed and scratched and snapped, and, for reasons not clear to me, fiercely chased his tail, not stopping until my neat leaf pile was scattered across the lawn again. Then he would sit up amid *his* handiwork, the shredded remains of leaves clinging to his fur, and give me a self-satisfied look, as if his contribution were an integral part of the leaf-gathering process.

Our first Christmas in Pennsylvania was supposed to be white. Jenny and I had had to do a sales job on Patrick and Conor to convince them that leaving their home and friends in Florida was for the best, and one of the big selling points was the promise of snow. Not just any kind of snow, but deep, fluffy, made-for-postcards snow, the kind that fell from the sky in big silent flakes, piled into drifts, and was of just the right consistency for shaping into snowmen. And snow for Christmas Day, well, that was best of all, the Holy Grail of northern winter experiences. We wantonly spun a Currier and Ives image for them of waking up on Christmas morning to a starkly white landscape, unblemished except for the solitary tracks of Santa's sleigh outside our front door.

In the week leading up to the big day, the three of them sat in the window together for hours, their eyes glued on the leaden sky as if they could will it to open and discharge its load. "Come on, snow!" the kids chanted. They had never seen it; Jenny and I hadn't seen it for the last quarter of our lives. We wanted snow, but the clouds would not give it up. A few days before Christmas, the whole family piled into the minivan and drove to a farm a half mile away where we cut a spruce tree and enjoyed a free hayride and hot apple cider around a bonfire. It was the kind of classic northern holiday moment we had missed in Florida, but one thing was absent. Where was the damn snow? Jenny and I were beginning to regret how recklessly we had hyped the inevitable first snowfall. As we hauled our fresh-cut tree home, the sweet scent of its sap filling the van, the kids complained about getting gypped. First no pencils, now no snow; what else had their parents lied to them about?

Christmas morning found a brand-new toboggan beneath the tree and enough snow gear to outfit an excursion to Antarctica, but the view out our windows remained all bare branches, dormant lawns, and brown cornfields. I built a cheery fire in the fireplace and told the children to be patient. The snow would come when the snow would come.

New Year's arrived and still it did not come. Even Marley seemed antsy, pacing and gazing out the windows, whimpering softly, as if he too felt he had been sold a bill of goods. The kids returned to school after the holiday, and still nothing. At the breakfast table they gazed sullenly at me, the father who had betrayed them. I began making lame excuses, saying things like "Maybe little boys and girls in some other place need the snow more than we do."

"Yeah, right, Dad," Patrick said.

Three weeks into the new year, the snow finally rescued me from my purgatory of guilt. It came during the night after everyone was asleep, and Patrick was the first to sound the alarm, running into our bedroom at dawn and yanking open the blinds. "Look! Look!" he squealed. "It's here!" Jenny and I sat up in bed to behold our vindication. A white blanket covered the hillsides and cornfields and pine trees and rooftops, stretching to the horizon. "Of course, it's here," I answered nonchalantly. "What did I tell you?"

The snow was nearly a foot deep and still coming down. Soon Conor and Colleen came chugging down the hall, thumbs in mouths, blankies trailing behind them. Marley was up and stretching, banging his tail into everything, sensing the excitement. I turned to Jenny and said, "I guess going back to sleep isn't an option," and when she confirmed it was not, I turned to the kids and shouted, "Okay, snow bunnies, let's suit up!"

For the next half hour we wrestled with zippers and leggings and buckles and hoods and gloves. By the time we were done, the kids looked like mummies and our kitchen like the staging area for the Winter Olympics. And competing in the Goof on Ice Downhill Competition, Large Canine Division, was . . . Marley the Dog. I opened the front door and before anyone else could step out, Marley blasted past us, knocking the well-bundled Colleen over in the process.

The instant his paws hit the strange white stuff—*Ah, wet! Ah, cold!*—he had second thoughts and attempted an abrupt about-face. As anyone who has ever driven a car in snow knows, sudden braking coupled with tight U-turns is never a good idea.

Marley went into a full skid, his rear end spinning out in front of him. He dropped down on one flank briefly before bouncing upright again just in time to somersault down the front porch steps and headfirst into a snowdrift. When he popped back up a second later, he looked like a giant powdered doughnut. Except for a black nose and two brown eyes, he was completely dusted in white. The Abominable Snowdog. Marley did not know what to make of this foreign substance. He jammed his nose deep into it and let loose a violent sneeze. He snapped at it and rubbed his face in it. Then, as if an invisible hand reached down from the heavens and jabbed him with a giant shot of adrenaline, he took off at full throttle, racing around the yard in a series of giant, loping leaps interrupted every several feet by a random somersault or nosedive. Snow was almost as much fun as raiding the neighbors' trash.

To follow Marley's tracks in the snow was to begin to understand his warped mind. His path was filled with abrupt twists and turns and about-faces, with erratic loops and figure-eights, with corkscrews and triple lutzes, as though he were following some bizarre algorithm that only he could understand. Soon the kids were taking his lead, spinning and rolling and frolicking, snow packing into every crease and crevice of their outerwear. Jenny came out with buttered toast, mugs of hot cocoa, and an announcement: school was canceled. I knew there was no way I was getting my little two-wheel-drive Nissan out the driveway anytime soon, let alone up and down the unplowed mountain roads, and I declared an official snow day for me, too.

I scraped the snow away from the stone circle I had built that fall for backyard campfires and soon had a crackling blaze going. The kids glided screaming down the hill in the toboggan, past the campfire and to the edge of the woods, Marley chasing behind them. I looked at Jenny and asked, "If someone had told you a year ago that your kids would be sledding right out their back door, would you have believed them?"

"Not a chance," she said, then wound up and unleashed a snowball that thumped me in the chest. The snow was in her hair, a blush in her cheeks, her breath rising in a cloud above her.

"Come here and kiss me," I said.

Later, as the kids warmed themselves by the fire, I decided to try a run on the toboggan, something I hadn't done since I was a teenager. "Care to join me?" I asked Jenny.

"Sorry, Jean Claude, you're on your own," she said.

I positioned the toboggan at the top of the hill and lay back on it, propped up on my elbows, my feet tucked inside its nose. I began rocking to get moving. Not often did Marley have the opportunity to look down at me, and having me prone like that was tantamount to an invitation. He sidled up to me and sniffed my face. "What do you want?" I asked, and that was all the welcome he needed. He clambered aboard, straddling me and dropping onto my chest. "Get off me, you big lug!" I screamed. But it was too late. We were already creeping forward, gathering speed as we began our descent.

"Bon voyage!" Jenny yelled behind us.

Off we went, snow flying, Marley plastered on top of me, licking me lustily all over my face as we careered down the slope. With our combined weight, we had considerably more momentum than the kids had, and we barreled past the point where their tracks petered out. "Hold on, Marley!" I screamed. "We're going into the woods!"

We shot past a large walnut tree, then between two wild cherry trees, miraculously avoiding all unyielding objects as we crashed through the underbrush, brambles tearing at us. It suddenly occurred to me that just up ahead was the bank leading down several feet to the creek, still unfrozen. I tried to kick my feet out to use as brakes, but they were stuck. The bank was steep, nearly a sheer drop-off, and we were going over. I had time only to wrap my arms around Marley, squeeze my eyes shut, and yell, "Whoaaaaaa!"

Our toboggan shot over the bank and dropped out from beneath us. I felt like I was in one of those classic cartoon moments, suspended in midair for an endless second before falling to ruinous injury. Only in this cartoon I was welded to a madly salivating Labrador retriever. We clung to each other as we crash-landed into a snowbank with a soft *poof* and, hanging half off the toboggan, slid to the water's edge. I opened my eyes and took stock of my condition. I could wiggle my toes and fingers and rotate my neck; nothing was broken. Marley was up and prancing around me, eager to do it all over again. I stood up with a groan and, brushing myself off, said, "I'm getting too old for this stuff." In the months ahead it would become increasingly obvious that Marley was, too.

Sometime toward the end of that first winter in Pennsylvania I began to notice Marley had moved quietly out of middle age and into retirement. He had turned nine that December, and ever so slightly he was slowing down. He still had his bursts of unbridled, adrenaline-pumped energy, as he did on the day of the first snowfall, but they were briefer now and farther apart. He was content to snooze most of the day, and on walks he tired before I did, a first in our relationship. One late-winter day, the temperature above freezing and the scent of spring thaw in the air, I walked him down our hill and up the next one, even steeper than ours, where the white church perched on the crest beside an old cemetery filled with Civil War veterans. It was a walk I took often and one that even the previous fall Marley had made without visible effort, despite the angle of the climb, which always got us both panting. This time, though, he was falling behind. I coaxed him along, calling out words of encouragement, but it was like watching a toy slowly wind down as its battery went dead. Marley just did not have the oomph needed to make it to the top. I stopped to let him rest before continuing, something I had never had to do before. "You're not going soft on me, are you?" I asked, leaning over and stroking his face with my gloved hands. He looked up at me, his eyes bright, his nose wet, not at all concerned about his flagging energy. He had a contented but tuckered-out look on his face, as though life got no better than this, sitting along the side of a country road on a crisp late-winter's day with your master at your side. "If you think I'm carrying you," I said, "forget it."

The sun bathed over him, and I noticed just how much gray had crept into his tawny face. Because his fur was so light, the effect was subtle but undeniable. His whole muzzle and a good part of his brow had turned from buff to white. Without us quite realizing it, our eternal puppy had become a senior citizen.

That's not to say he was any better behaved. Marley was still up to all his old antics, simply at a more leisurely pace. He still stole food off the children's plates. He still flipped open the lid of the kitchen trash can with his nose and rummaged inside. He still strained at his leash. Still swallowed a wide assortment of household objects. Still drank out of the bathtub and trailed water from his gullet. And when the skies darkened and thunder rumbled, he still panicked and, if alone, turned destructive. One day we arrived home to find Marley in a lather and Conor's mattress splayed open down to the coils.

Over the years, we had become philosophical about the damage, which had become much less frequent now that we were away from Florida's daily storm patterns. In a dog's life, some plaster would fall, some cushions would open, some rugs would shred. Like any relationship, this one had its costs. They were costs we came to accept and balance against the joy and amusement and protection and companionship he gave us. We could have bought a small yacht with what we spent on our dog and all the things he destroyed. Then again, how many yachts wait by the door all day for your return? How many live for the moment they can climb in your lap or ride down the hill with you on a toboggan, licking your face?

Marley had earned his place in our family. Like a quirky but beloved uncle, he was what he was. He would never be Lassie or Benji or Old Yeller; he would never reach Westminster or even the county fair. We knew that now. We accepted him for the dog he was, and loved him all the more for it.

"You old geezer," I said to him on the side of the road that late-winter day, scruffing his neck. Our goal, the cemetery, was still a steep climb ahead. But just as in life, I was figuring out, the destination was less important than the journey. I dropped to one knee, running my hands down his sides, and said, "Let's just sit here for a while." When he was ready, we turned back down the hill and poked our way home.

CHAPTER 23

Poultry on Parade

That spring we decided to try our hand at animal husbandry. We owned two acres in the country now; it only seemed right to share it with a farm animal or two. Besides, I was editor of *Organic Gardening*, a magazine that had long celebrated the incorporation of animals—and their manure—into a healthy, well-balanced garden. "A cow would be fun," Jenny suggested.

"A cow?" I asked. "Are you crazy? We don't even have a barn; how can we have a cow? Where do you suggest we keep it, in the garage next to the minivan?"

"How about sheep?" she said. "Sheep are cute." I shot her my well-practiced you're-not-being-practical look.

"A goat? Goats are adorable."

In the end we settled on poultry. For any gardener who has sworn off chemical pesticides and fertilizers, chickens made a lot of sense. They were inexpensive and relatively low-maintenance. They needed only a small coop and a few cups of cracked corn each morning to be happy. Not only did they provide fresh eggs, but, when let loose to roam, they spent their days studiously scouring the property, eating bugs and grubs, devouring ticks, scratching up the soil like efficient little rototillers, and fertilizing with their high-nitrogen droppings as they went. Each evening at dusk they returned to their coop on their own. What wasn't to like? A chicken was an organic gardener's best friend. Chickens made perfect sense. Besides, as Jenny pointed out, they passed the cuteness test.

Chickens it was. Jenny had become friendly with a mom from school who lived on a farm and said she'd be happy to give us some chicks from the next clutch of eggs to hatch. I told Digger about our plans, and he agreed a few hens around the place made sense. Digger had a large coop of his own in which he kept a flock of chickens for both eggs and meat.

"Just one word of warning," he said, folding his meaty arms across his chest. "Whatever you do, don't let the kids name them. Once you name 'em, they're no longer poultry, they're pets."

"Right," I said. Chicken farming, I knew, had no room for sentimentality. Hens could live fifteen years or more but only produced eggs in their first couple of years. When they stopped laying, it was time for the stewing pot. That was just part of managing a flock.

Digger looked hard at me, as if divining what I was up against, and added, "Once you name them, it's all over."

"Absolutely," I agreed. "No names."

The next evening I pulled into the driveway from work, and the three kids raced out of the house to greet me, each cradling a newborn chick. Jenny was behind them with a fourth in her hands. Her friend, Donna, had brought the baby birds over that afternoon. They were barely a day old and peered up at me with cocked heads as if to ask, "Are you my mama?"

Patrick was the first to break the news. "I named mine Feathers!" he proclaimed.

"Mine is Tweety," said Conor.

"My wicka Wuffy," Colleen chimed in.

I shot Jenny a quizzical look.

"Fluffy," Jenny said. "She named her chicken Fluffy."

"Jenny," I protested. "What did Digger tell us? These are farm animals, not pets."

"Oh, get real, Farmer John," she said. "You know as well as I do that you could never hurt one of these. Just look at how cute they are."

"Jenny," I said, the frustration rising in my voice.

"By the way," she said, holding up the fourth chick in her hands, "meet Shirley."

Feathers, Tweety, Fluffy, and Shirley took up residence in a box on the kitchen counter, a lightbulb dangling above them for warmth. They ate and they pooped and they ate some more—and grew at a breathtaking pace. Several weeks after we brought the birds home, something jolted me awake before dawn. I sat up in bed and listened. From downstairs came a weak, sickly call. It was croaky and hoarse, more like a tubercular cough than a proclamation of dominance. It sounded again: *Cock-a-doodle-do!* A few seconds ticked past and then came an equally sickly, but distinct, reply: *Rook-ru-rook-ru-roo!*

I shook Jenny and, when she opened her eyes, asked:

"When Donna brought the chicks over, you did ask her to check to make sure they were hens, right?"

"You mean you can do that?" she asked, and rolled back over, sound asleep.

It's called sexing. Farmers who know what they are doing can inspect a newborn chicken and determine, with about 80 percent accuracy, whether it is male or female. At the farm store, sexed chicks command a premium price. The cheaper option is to buy "straight run" birds of unknown gender. You take your chances with straight run, the idea being that the males will be slaughtered young for meat and the hens will be kept to lay eggs. Playing the straight-run gamble, of course, assumes you have what it takes to kill, gut, and pluck any excess males you might end up with. As anyone who has ever raised chickens knows, two roosters in a flock is one rooster too many.

As it turned out, Donna had not attempted to sex our four chicks, and three of our four "laying hens" were males. We had on our kitchen counter the poultry equivalent of Boys Town U.S.A. The thing about roosters is they're never content to play second chair to any other rooster. If you had equal numbers of roosters and hens, you might think they would pair off into happy little Ozzie and Harriet–style couples. But you would be wrong. The males will fight endlessly, bloodying one another gruesomely, to determine who will dominate the roost. Winner takes all.

As they grew into adolescents, our three roosters took to posturing and pecking and, most distressing considering they were still in our kitchen as I raced to finish their coop in the backyard, crowing their testosterone-pumped hearts out. Shirley, our one poor, overtaxed female, was getting way more attention than even the most lusty of women could want.

I had thought the constant crowing of our roosters would drive Marley insane. In his younger years, the sweet chirp of a single tiny songbird in the yard would set him off on a frenetic barking jag as he raced from one window to the next, hopping up and down on his hind legs. Three crowing roosters a few steps from his food bowl, however, had no effect on him at all. He didn't seem to even know they were there. Each day the crowing grew louder and stronger, rising up from the kitchen to echo through the house at five in the morning. *Cock-a-doodle-dooooo!* Marley slept right through the racket. That's when it first occurred to me that maybe he wasn't just ignoring the crowing; maybe he couldn't hear it. I walked up behind him one afternoon as he snoozed in the kitchen and said, "Marley?" Nothing. I said it louder: "Marley!" Nothing. I clapped my hands and shouted, "MARLEY!" He lifted his head and looked blankly around, his ears up, trying to figure out what it was his radar had detected. I did it again, clapping loudly and shouting his name. This time he turned his head enough to catch a glimpse of me standing behind him. *Oh, it's you!* He bounced up, tail wagging, happy—and clearly surprised— to see me. He bumped up against my legs in greeting and gave me a sheepish look as if to ask, *What's the idea sneaking up on me like that?* My dog, it seemed, was going deaf.

It all made sense. In recent months Marley seemed to simply ignore me in a way he never had before. I would call

for him and he would not so much as glance my way. I
would take him outside before turning in for the night, and
he would sniff his way across the yard, oblivious to my
whistles and calls to get him to turn back. He would be
asleep at my feet in the family room when someone would
ring the doorbell—and he would not so much as open an
eye.

Marley's ears had caused him problems from an early age.
Like many Labrador retrievers, he was predisposed to ear
infections, and we had spent a small fortune on antibiotics,
ointments, cleansers, drops, and veterinarian visits. He even
underwent surgery to shorten his ear canals in an attempt to
correct the problem. It had not occurred to me until after
we brought the impossible-to-ignore roosters into our house
that all those years of problems had taken their toll and our
dog had gradually slipped into a muffled world of faraway
whispers.

Not that he seemed to mind. Retirement suited Marley just
fine, and his hearing problems didn't seem to impinge on his
leisurely country lifestyle. If anything, deafness proved for-
tuitous for him, finally giving him a doctor-certified excuse for
disobeying. After all, how could he heed a command that he
could not hear? As thick-skulled as I always insisted he was, I
swear he figured out how to use his deafness to his advantage.
Drop a piece of steak into his bowl, and he would come
trotting in from the next room. He still had the ability to detect
the dull, satisfying thud of meat on metal. But yell for him to
come when he had somewhere else he'd rather be going, and
he'd stroll blithely away from you, not even glancing guiltily
over his shoulder as he once would have.

"I think the dog's scamming us," I told Jenny. She agreed his hearing problems seemed selective, but every time we tested him, sneaking up, clapping our hands, shouting his name, he would not respond. And every time we dropped food into his bowl, he would come running. He appeared to be deaf to all sounds except the one that was dearest to his heart or, more accurately, his stomach: the sound of dinner.

Marley went through life insatiably hungry. Not only did we give him four big scoops of dog chow a day—enough food to sustain an entire family of Chihuahuas for a week—but we began freely supplementing his diet with table scraps, against the better advice of every dog guide we had ever read. Table scraps, we knew, simply programmed dogs to prefer human food to dog chow (and given the choice between a half-eaten hamburger and dry kibble, who could blame them?). Table scraps were a recipe for canine obesity. Labs, in particular, were prone to chubbiness, especially as they moved into middle age and beyond. Some Labs, especially those of the English variety, were so rotund by adulthood, they looked like they'd been inflated with an air hose and were ready to float down Fifth Avenue in the Macy's Thanksgiving Day Parade.

Not our dog. Marley had many problems, but obesity was not among them. No matter how many calories he devoured, he always burned more. All that unbridled high-strung exuberance consumed vast amounts of energy. He was like a high-kilowatt electric plant that instantly converted every ounce of available fuel into pure, raw power. Marley was an amazing physical specimen, the kind of dog passersby stopped to admire. He was huge for a Labrador retriever, considerably bigger than the average male of his breed, which runs sixty-five to eighty pounds. Even as he aged, the bulk of his mass was pure muscle—ninety-seven pounds of rippled, sinewy brawn with nary an ounce of fat anywhere on him. His rib cage was the size of a small beer keg, but the ribs themselves stretched just beneath his fur with no spare padding. We were not worried about obesity; exactly the opposite. On our many visits to Dr. Jay before leaving Florida, Jenny and I would voice the same concerns: We were feeding him tremendous amounts of food, but still he was so much thinner than most Labs, and he always appeared famished, even immediately after wolfing down a bucket of kibble that looked like it was meant for a draft horse. Were we slowly starving him? Dr. Jay always responded the same way. He would run his hands down Marley's sleek sides, setting him off on a desperately happy Labrador evader journey around the cramped exam room, and tell us that, as far as physical attributes went, Marley was just about perfect. "Just keep doing what you're doing," Dr. Jay would say. Then, as Marley lunged between his legs or snarfed a cotton ball off the counter, Dr. Jay would add: "Obviously, I don't need to tell you that Marley burns a lot of nervous energy."

Each evening after we finished dinner, when it came time to give Marley his meal, I would fill his bowl with chow and then freely toss in any tasty leftovers or scraps I could find. With three young children at the table, half-eaten food was something we had in plentiful supply. Bread crusts, steak trimmings, pan drippings, chicken skins, gravy, rice, carrots, puréed prunes, sandwiches, three-day-old pasta—into the bowl it went. Our pet may have behaved like the court jester, but he ate like the Prince of Wales. The only foods we kept from him were those we knew to be unhealthy for dogs, such as dairy products, sweets, potatoes, and choco-late. I have a problem with people who buy human food for their pets, but larding Marley's meals with scraps that would otherwise be thrown out made me feel thrifty—waste not, want not—and charitable. I was giving always-appreciative Marley a break from the endless monotony of dog-chow hell.

When Marley wasn't acting as our household garbage disposal, he was on duty as the family's emergency spill-response team. No mess was too big a job for our dog. One of the kids would flip a full bowl of spaghetti and meatballs on the floor, and we'd simply whistle and stand back while Old Wet Vac sucked up every last noodle and then licked the floor until it gleamed. Errant peas, dropped celery, runaway rigatoni, spilled applesauce, it didn't matter what it was. If it hit the floor, it was history. To the amazement of our friends, he even wolfed down salad greens.

Not that food had to make it to the ground before it ended up in Marley's stomach. He was a skilled and unremorseful thief, preying mostly on unsuspecting children and always after checking to make sure neither Jenny nor I was watch-ing. Birthday parties were bonanzas for him. He would make his way through the crowd of five-year-olds, shamelessly snatching hot dogs right out of their little hands. During one party, we estimated he ended up getting two-thirds of the birthday cake, nabbing piece after piece off the paper plates the children held on their laps.

It didn't matter how much food he devoured, either

through legitimate means or illicit activities. He always wanted more. When deafness came, we weren't completely surprised that the only sound he could still hear was the sweet, soft thud of falling food.

One day I arrived home from work to find the house empty. Jenny and the kids were out somewhere, and I called for Marley but got no response. I walked upstairs, where he sometimes snoozed when left alone, but he was nowhere in sight. After I changed my clothes, I returned downstairs and found him in the kitchen up to no good. His back to me, he was standing on his hind legs, his front paws and chest resting on the kitchen table as he gobbled down the remains of a grilled cheese sandwich. My first reaction was to loudly scold him. Instead I decided to see how close I could get before he realized he had company. I tiptoed up behind him until I was close enough to touch him. As he chewed the crusts, he kept glancing at the door that led into the garage, knowing that was where Jenny and the kids would enter upon their return. The instant the door opened, he would be on the floor under the table, feigning sleep. Apparently it had not occurred to him that Dad would be arriving home, too, and just might sneak in through the front door.

"Oh, Marley?" I asked in a normal voice. "What do you think you're doing?" He just kept gulping the sandwich down, clueless to my presence. His tail was wagging languidly, a sign he thought he was alone and getting away with a major food heist. Clearly he was pleased with himself.

I cleared my throat loudly, and he still didn't hear me. I made kissy noises with my mouth. Nothing. He polished off one sandwich, nosed the plate out of the way, and stretched forward to reach the crusts left on a second plate. "You are such a bad dog," I said as he chewed away. I snapped my fingers twice and he froze midbite, staring at the back door. *What was that? Did I hear a car door slam?* After a moment, he convinced himself that whatever he heard was nothing and went back to his purloined snack.

That's when I reached out and tapped him once on the butt. I might as well have lit a stick of dynamite. The old dog nearly jumped out of his fur coat. He rocketed backward off the table and, as soon as he saw me, dropped onto the floor, rolling over to expose his belly to me in surrender. "Busted!" I told him. "You are so busted." But I didn't have it in me to scold him. He was old; he was deaf; he was beyond reform. I wasn't going to change him. Sneaking up on him had been great fun, and I laughed out loud when he jumped. Now as he lay at my feet begging for forgiveness I just found it a little sad. I guess secretly I had hoped he'd been faking all along.

I finished the chicken coop, an A-frame plywood affair with a drawbridge-style gangplank that could be raised at night to keep out predators. Donna kindly took back two of our three roosters and exchanged them for hens from her flock. We now had three girls and one testosterone-pumped guy bird that spent every waking minute doing one of three things: pursuing sex, having sex, or crowing boastfully about the sex he had just scored. Jenny observed that roosters are what men would be if left to their own devices, with no social conventions to rein in their baser instincts, and I couldn't disagree. I had to admit, I kind of admired the lucky bastard.

We let the chickens out each morning to roam the yard, and Marley made a few gallant runs at them, charging ahead barking for a dozen paces or so before losing steam and giving up. It was as though some genetic coding deep inside him was sending an urgent message: "You're a retriever; they are birds. Don't you think it might be a good idea to chase them?" He just did not have his heart in it. Soon the birds learned the lumbering yellow beast was no threat whatsoever, more a minor annoyance than anything else, and Marley learned to share the yard with these new, feathered interlopers. One day I looked up from weeding in the garden to see Marley and the four chickens making their way down the row toward me as if in formation, the birds pecking and Marley sniffing as they went. It was like old friends out for a Sunday stroll. "What kind of self-respecting hunting dog are you?" I chastised him. Marley lifted his leg and peed on a tomato plant before hurrying to rejoin his new pals.

CHAPTER 24

The Potty Room

A person can learn a few things from an old dog. As the months slipped by and his infirmities mounted, Marley taught us mostly about life's uncompromising finiteness. Jenny and I were not quite middle-aged. Our children were young, our health good, and our retirement years still an unfathomable distance off on the horizon. It would have been easy to deny the inevitable creep of age, to pretend it might somehow pass us by. Marley would not afford us the luxury of such denial. As we watched him grow gray and deaf and creaky, there was no ignoring his mortality—or ours. Age sneaks up on us all, but it sneaks up on a dog with a swiftness that is both breathtaking and sobering. In the brief span of twelve years, Marley had gone from bubbly puppy to awkward adolescent to muscular adult to doddering senior citizen. He aged roughly seven years for every one of ours, putting him, in human years, on the downward slope to ninety.

His once sparkling white teeth had gradually worn down to brown nubs. Three of his four front fangs were missing, broken off one by one during crazed panic attacks as he tried to chew his way to safety. His breath, always a bit on the fishy side, had taken on the bouquet of a sun-baked Dumpster. The fact that he had acquired a taste for that little appreciated delicacy known as chicken manure didn't help, either. To our complete revulsion, he gobbled the stuff up like it was caviar.

His digestion was not what it once had been, and he became as gassy as a methane plant. There were days I swore that if I lit a match, the whole house would go up. Marley was able to clear an entire room with his silent, deadly flatulence, which seemed to increase in direct correlation to the number of dinner guests we had in our home. "Marley! Not again!" the children would scream in unison, and lead the retreat. Sometimes he drove even himself away. He would be sleeping peacefully when the smell would reach his nostrils; his eyes would pop open and he'd furl his brow as if asking, *"Good God! Who dealt it?"* And he would stand up and nonchalantly move into the next room.

When he wasn't farting, he was outside pooping. Or at least thinking about it. His choosiness about where he squatted to defecate had grown to the point of compulsive obsession. Each time I let him out, he took longer and longer to decide on the perfect spot. Back and forth he would promenade; round and round he went, sniffing, pausing, scratching, circling, moving on, the whole while sporting a ridiculous grin on his face. As he combed the grounds in search of squatting nirvana, I stood outside, sometimes in the rain, sometimes in the snow, sometimes in the dark of night, often barefoot, occasionally just in my boxer shorts, knowing from experience that I didn't dare leave him unsupervised lest he decide to meander up the hill to visit the dogs on the next street.

Sneaking away became a sport for him. If the opportunity presented itself and he thought he could get away with it, he would bolt for the property line. Well, not exactly bolt. He would more sniff and shuffle his way from one bush to the next until he was out of sight. Late one night I let him out the front door for his final walk before bed. Freezing rain was forming an icy slush on the ground, and I turned around to grab a slicker out of the front closet. When I walked out onto the sidewalk less than a minute later, he was nowhere to be found. I walked out into the yard, whistling and clapping, knowing he couldn't hear me, though pretty sure all the neighbors could. For twenty minutes I prowled through our neighbors' yards in the rain, making quite the fashion statement dressed in boots, raincoat, and boxer shorts. I prayed no porch lights would come on. The more I hunted, the angrier I got. *Where the hell did he mosey off to this time?* But as the minutes passed, my anger turned to worry. I thought of those old men you read about in the newspaper who wander away from nursing homes and are found frozen in the snow three days later. I returned home, walked upstairs, and woke up Jenny. "Marley's disappeared," I said. "I can't find him anywhere. He's out there in the freezing rain." She was on her feet instantly, pulling on jeans, slipping into a sweater and boots. Together we broadened the search. I could hear her way up the side of the hill, whistling and clucking for him as I crashed through the woods in the dark, half expecting to find him lying unconscious in a creek bed.

Eventually our paths met up. "Anything?" I asked.

"Nothing," Jenny said.

We were soaked from the rain, and my bare legs were stinging from the cold. "Come on," I said. "Let's go home and get warm and I'll come back out with the car." We walked down the hill and up the driveway. That's when we saw him, standing beneath the overhang out of the rain and overjoyed to have us back. I could have killed him. Instead, I brought him inside and toweled him off, the unmistakable smell of wet dog filling the kitchen. Exhausted from his late-night jaunt, Marley conked out and did not budge till nearly noon the next day.

Marley's eyesight had grown fuzzy, and bunnies could now scamper past a dozen feet in front of him without him noticing. He was shedding his fur in vast quantities, forcing Jenny to vacuum every day—and still she couldn't keep up with it. Dog hair insinuated itself into every crevice of our home, every piece of our wardrobe, and more than a few of our meals. He had always been a shedder, but what had once been light flurries had grown into full-fledged blizzards. He would shake and a cloud of loose fur would rise around him, drifting down onto every surface. One night as I watched television, I dangled my leg off the couch and absently stroked his hip with my bare foot. At the commercial break, I looked down to see a sphere of fur the size of a grapefruit near where I had been rubbing. His hairballs rolled across the wood floors like tumbleweeds on a windblown plain.

Most worrisome of all were his hips, which had mostly forsaken him. Arthritis had snuck into his joints, weakening them and making them ache. The same dog that once could ride me bronco-style on his back, the dog that could lift the entire dining room table on his shoulders and bounce it around the room, could now barely pull himself up. He groaned in pain when he lay down, and groaned again when he struggled to his feet. I did not realize just how weak his hips had become until one day when I gave his rump a light pat and his hindquarters collapsed beneath him as though he had just received a cross-body block. Down he went. It was painful to watch.

Climbing the stairs to the second floor was becoming increasingly difficult for him, but he wouldn't think of sleeping alone on the main floor, even after we put a dog bed at the foot of the stairs for him. Marley loved people, loved being underfoot, loved resting his chin on the mattress and panting in our faces as we slept, loved jamming his head through the shower curtain for a drink as we bathed, and he wasn't about to stop now. Each night when Jenny and I retired to our bedroom, he would fret at the foot of the stairs, whining, yipping, pacing, tentatively testing the first step with his front paw as he mustered his courage for the ascent that not long before had been effortless. From the top of the stairs, I would beckon, "Come on, boy. You can do it." After several minutes of this, he would disappear around the corner in order to get a running start and then come charging up, his front shoulders bearing most of his weight. Sometimes he made it; sometimes he stalled midflight and had to return to the bottom and try again. On his most pitiful attempts he would lose his footing entirely and slide ingloriously backward down the steps on his belly. He was too big for me to carry, but increasingly I found myself following him up the stairs, lifting his rear end up each step as he hopped forward on his front paws.

Because of the difficulty stairs now posed for him, I assumed Marley would try to limit the number of trips he made up and down. That would be giving him far too much credit for common sense. No matter how much trouble he had getting up the stairs, if I returned downstairs, say to grab a book or turn off the lights, he would be right on my heels, clomping heavily down behind me. Then, seconds later, he would have to repeat the torturous climb. Jenny and I both took to sneaking around behind his back once he was upstairs for the night so he would not be tempted to follow us back down. We assumed sneaking downstairs without his knowledge would be easy now that his hearing was shot and he was sleeping longer and more heavily than ever. But he always seemed to know when we had stolen away. I would be reading in bed and he would be asleep on the floor beside me, snoring heavily. Stealthily, I would pull back the covers, slide out of bed, and tiptoe past him out of the room, turning back to make sure I hadn't disturbed him. I would be downstairs for only a few minutes when I would hear his heavy steps on the stairs, coming in search of me. He might be deaf and half blind, but his radar apparently was still in good working order.

This went on not only at night but all day long, too. I would be reading the newspaper at the kitchen table with Marley curled up at my feet when I would get up for a refill from the coffeepot across the room. Even though I was within sight and would be coming right back, he would lumber with difficulty to his feet and trudge over to be with me. No sooner had he gotten comfortable at my feet by the coffeepot than I would return to the table, where he would again drag himself and settle in. A few minutes later I would walk into the family room to turn on the stereo, and up again he would struggle, following me in, circling around and collapsing with a moan beside me just as I was ready to walk away. So it would go, not only with me but with Jenny and the kids, too.

As age took its toll, Marley had good days and bad days. He had good minutes and bad minutes, too, sandwiched so close together sometimes it was hard to believe it was the same dog.

One evening in the spring of 2002, I took Marley out for a short walk around the yard. The night was cool, in the high forties, and windy. Invigorated by the crisp air, I started to run, and Marley, feeling frisky himself, galloped along beside me just like in the old days. I even said out loud to him, "See, Marl, you still have some of the puppy in you." We trotted together back to the front door, his tongue out as he panted happily, his eyes alert. At the porch stoop, Marley gamely tried to leap up the two steps—but his rear hips collapsed on him as he pushed off, and he found himself awkwardly stuck, his front paws on the stoop, his belly resting on the steps and his butt collapsed flat on the sidewalk. There he sat, looking up at me like he didn't know what had caused such an embarrassing display. I whistled and slapped my hands on my thighs, and he flailed his front legs valiantly, trying to get up, but it was no use. He could not lift his rear off the ground. "Come on, Marley!" I called, but he was immobilized. Finally, I grabbed him under the front shoulders and turned him sideways so he could get all four legs on the ground. Then, after a few failed tries, he was able to stand. He backed up, looked apprehensively at the stairs for a few seconds, and loped up and into the house. From that day on, his confidence as a champion stair climber was shot; he never attempted those two small steps again without first stopping and fretting.

No doubt about it, getting old was a bitch. And an undignified one at that.

Marley reminded me of life's brevity, of its fleeting joys and missed opportunities. He reminded me that each of us gets just one shot at the gold, with no replays. One day you're swimming halfway out into the ocean convinced this is the day you will catch that seagull; the next you're barely able to bend down to drink out of your water bowl. Like Patrick Henry and everyone else, I had but one life to live. I kept coming back to the same question: What in God's name was I doing spending it at a gardening magazine? It wasn't that my new job did not have its rewards. I was proud of what I had done with the magazine. But I missed newspapers desperately. I missed the people who read them and the people who write them. I missed being part of the big story of the day, and the feeling that I was in my own small way helping to make a difference. I missed the adrenaline surge of writing on deadline and the satisfaction of waking up the next morning to find my in-box filled with e-mails responding to my words. Mostly, I missed telling stories. I wondered why I had ever walked away from a gig that so perfectly fit my disposition to wade into the treacherous waters of magazine management with its bare-bones budgets, relentless advertising pressures, staffing headaches, and thankless behind-the-scenes editing chores.

When a former colleague of mine mentioned in passing that the *Philadelphia Inquirer* was seeking a metropolitan columnist, I leapt without a second's hesitation. Columnist positions are extremely hard to come by, even at smaller papers, and when a position does open up it's almost always filled internally, a plum handed to veteran staffers who've proved themselves as reporters. The *Inquirer* was well respected, winner of seventeen Pulitzer Prizes over the years and one of the country's great newspapers. I was a fan, and now the *Inquirer*'s editors were asking to meet me. I wouldn't even have to relocate my family to take the job. The office I would be working in was just forty-five minutes down the Pennsylvania Turnpike, a tolerable commute. I don't put much stock in miracles, but it all seemed too good to be true, like an act of divine intervention.

In November 2002, I traded in my gardening togs for a *Philadelphia Inquirer* press badge. It quite possibly was the happiest day of my life. I was back where I belonged, in a newsroom as a columnist once again.

I had only been in the new job for a few months when the first big snowstorm of 2003 hit. The flakes began to fall on a Sunday night, and by the time they stopped the next day, a blanket two feet deep covered the ground. The children were off school for three days as our community slowly dug out, and I filed my columns from home. With a snowblower I borrowed from my neighbor, I cleared the driveway and opened a narrow canyon to the front door. Knowing Marley could never climb the sheer walls to get out into the yard, let alone negotiate the deep drifts once he was off the path, I cleared him his own "potty room," as the kids dubbed it—a small plowed space off the front walkway where he could do his business. When I called him outside to try out the new facilities, though, he just stood in the clearing and sniffed the snow suspiciously. He had very particular notions about what constituted a suitable place to answer nature's call, and this clearly was not what he had in mind. He was willing to lift his leg and pee, but that's where he drew the line. *Poop right here? Smack in front of the picture window? You can't be serious.* He turned and, with a mighty heave to climb up the slippery porch steps, went back inside.

That night after dinner I brought him out again, and this time Marley no longer could afford the luxury of waiting. He had to go. He nervously paced up and down the cleared walkway, into the potty room and out onto the driveway, sniffing the snow, pawing at the frozen ground. *No, this just won't do.* Before I could stop him, he somehow clambered up and over the sheer snow wall the snowblower had cut and began making his way across the yard toward a stand of white pines fifty feet away. I couldn't believe it; my arthritic, geriatric dog was off on an alpine trek. Every couple of steps his back hips collapsed on him and he sank down into the snow, where he rested on his belly for a few seconds before struggling back to his feet and pushing on. Slowly, painfully, he made his way through the deep snow, using his still-strong front shoulders to pull his body forward. I stood in the driveway, wondering how I was going to rescue him when he finally got stuck and could go no farther. But he trudged on and finally made it to the closest pine tree. Suddenly I saw what he was up to. The dog had a plan. Beneath the dense branches of the pine, the snow was just a few inches deep. The tree acted like an umbrella, and once underneath it Marley was free to move about and squat comfortably to relieve himself. I had to admit, it was pretty brilliant. He circled and sniffed and scratched in his customary way, trying to locate a worthy shrine for his daily offering. Then, to my amazement, he abandoned the cozy shelter and lunged back into the deep snow en route to the next pine tree. The first spot looked perfect to me, but clearly it was just not up to his sterling standards.

With difficulty he reached the second tree, but again, after considerable circling, found the area beneath its branches unsuitable. So he set off to the third tree, and then the fourth and the fifth, each time getting farther from the driveway. I tried calling him back, though I knew he couldn't hear me. "Marley, you're going to get stuck, you dumbo!" I yelled. He just plowed ahead with single-minded determination. The dog was on a quest. Finally, he reached the last tree on our property, a big spruce with a dense canopy of branches out near where the kids waited for the school bus. It was here he found the frozen piece of ground he had been looking for, private and barely dusted with snow. He circled a few times and creakily squatted down on his old, shot, arthritis-riddled haunches. There he finally found relief. Eureka!

With mission accomplished, he set off on the long journey home. As he struggled through the snow, I waved my arms and clapped my hands to encourage him. "Keep coming, boy! You can make it!" But I could see him tiring, and he still had a long way to go. "Don't stop now!" I yelled. A dozen yards from the driveway, that's just what he did. He was done. He stopped and lay down in the snow, exhausted. Marley did not exactly look distressed, but he didn't look at ease, either. He shot me a worried look. *Now what do we do, boss?* I had no idea. I could wade through the snow to him, but then what? He was too heavy for me to pick up and carry. For several minutes I stood there, calling and cajoling, but Marley wouldn't budge.

"Hang on," I said. "Let me get my boots on and I'll come get you." It had dawned on me that I could wrestle him up onto the toboggan and pull him back to the house. As soon as he saw me approaching with the toboggan, my plan became moot. He jumped up, reenergized. The only thing I could think was that he remembered our infamous ride into the woods and over the creek bank and was hoping for a repeat. He lurched forward toward me like a dinosaur in a tar pit. I waded out into the snow, stomping down a path for him as I went, and he inched ahead. Finally we scrambled over the snowbank and onto the driveway together. He shook the snow off and banged his tail against my knees, prancing about, all frisky and cocky, flush with the bravado of an adventurer just back from a jaunt through uncharted wilderness. To think, I had doubted he could do it.

The next morning I shoveled a narrow path out to the far spruce tree on the corner of the property for him, and Marley adopted the space as his own personal powder room for the duration of the winter. The crisis had been averted, but bigger questions loomed. How much longer could he continue like this? And at what point would the aches and indignities of old age outstrip the simple contentment he found in each sleepy, lazy day?

CHAPTER 25

Beating the Odds

❖

When school let out for the summer, Jenny packed the kids into the minivan and headed to Boston for a week to visit her sister. I stayed behind to work. That left Marley with no one at home to keep him company and let him out. Of the many little embarrassments old age inflicted on him, the one that seemed to bother him most was the diminished control he had over his bowels. For all Marley's bad behavior over the years, his bathroom habits had always been surefire. It was the one Marley feature we could brag about. From just a few months of age, he never, ever, had accidents in the house, even when left alone for ten or twelve hours. We joked that his bladder was made of steel and his bowels of stone.

That had changed in recent months. He no longer could go more than a few hours between pit stops. When the urge called, he had to go, and if we were not home to let him out, he had no choice but to go inside. It killed him to do it, and we always knew the second we walked into the house when he had had an accident. Instead of greeting us at the door in his exuberant manner, he would be standing far back in the room, his head hanging nearly to the floor, his tail flat between his legs, the shame radiating off him. We never punished him for it. How could we? He was nearly thirteen, about as old as Labs got. We knew he couldn't help it, and he seemed to know it, too. I was sure if he could talk, he would profess his humiliation and assure us that he had tried, really tried, to hold it in.

Jenny bought a steam cleaner for the carpet, and we began arranging our schedules to make sure we were not away from the house for more than a few hours at a time. Jenny would rush home from school, where she volunteered, to let Marley out. I would leave dinner parties between the main course and dessert to give him a walk, which, of course, Marley dragged out as long as possible, sniffing and circling his way around the yard. Our friends teasingly wondered aloud who was the real master over at the Grogan house.

With Jenny and the kids away, I knew I would be putting in long days. This was my chance to stay out after work, wandering around the region and exploring the towns and neighborhoods I was now writing about. With my long commute, I would be away from home ten to twelve hours a day. There was no question Marley couldn't be alone that long, or even half that long. We decided to board him at the local kennel we used every summer when we went on vacation. The kennel was attached to a large veterinarian practice that offered professional care if not the most personal service. Each time we went there, it seemed, we saw a different doctor who knew nothing about Marley except what was printed in his chart. We never even learned their names. Unlike our beloved Dr. Jay in Florida, who knew Marley almost as well as we did and who truly had become a family friend by the time we left, these were strangers—competent strangers but strangers nonetheless. Marley didn't seem to mind.

"Waddy go doggie camp!" Colleen screeched, and he perked up as though the idea had possibilities. We joked about the activities the kennel staff would have for him: hole digging from 9:00 to 10:00; pillow shredding from 10:15 to 11:00; garbage raiding from 11:05 to noon, and so on. I dropped him off on a Sunday evening and left my cell phone number with the front desk. Marley never seemed to fully relax when he was boarded, even in the familiar surroundings of Dr. Jay's office, and I always worried a little about him. After each visit, he returned looking gaunter, his snout often rubbed raw from where he had fretted it against the grating of his cage, and when he got home he would collapse in the corner and sleep heavily for hours, as if he had spent the entire time away pacing his cage with insomnia.

That Tuesday morning, I was near Independence Hall in downtown Philadelphia when my cell phone rang. "Could you please hold for Dr. So-and-so?" the woman from the kennel asked. It was yet another veterinarian whose name I had never heard before. A few seconds later the vet came on the phone. "We have an emergency with Marley," she said.

My heart rose in my chest. "An emergency?"

The vet said Marley's stomach had bloated with food, water, and air and then, stretched and distended, had flipped over on itself, twisting and trapping its contents. With nowhere for the gas and other contents to escape, his stomach had swelled painfully in a life-threatening condition known as gastric dilatation-volvulus. It almost always required surgery to correct, she said, and if left untreated could result in death within a few hours.

She said she had inserted a tube down his throat and released much of the gas that had built up in his stomach, which relieved the swelling. By manipulating the tube in his stomach, she had worked the twist out of it, or as she put it, "unflipped it," and he was now sedated and resting comfortably.

"That's a good thing, right?" I asked cautiously.

"But only temporary," the doctor said. "We got him through the immediate crisis, but once their stomachs twist like that, they almost always will twist again."

"Like how almost always?" I asked.

"I would say he has a one percent chance that it won't flip again," she said. *One percent? For God's sake*, I thought, *he has better odds of getting into Harvard.*

"One percent? That's it?"

"I'm sorry," she said. "It's very grave."

If his stomach did flip again—and she was telling me it was a virtual certainty—we had two choices. The first was to operate on him. She said she would open him up and attach the stomach to the cavity wall with sutures to prevent it from flipping again. "The operation will cost about two thousand dollars," she said. I gulped. "And I have to tell you, it's very invasive. It will be tough going for a dog his age." The recovery would be long and difficult, assuming he made it through the operation at all. Sometimes older dogs like him did not survive the trauma of the surgery, she explained.

"If he was four or five years old, I would be saying by all means let's operate," the vet said. "But at his age, you have to ask yourself if you really want to put him through that."

"Not if we can help it," I said. "What's the second option?"

"The second option," she said, hesitating only slightly, "would be putting him to sleep."

"Oh," I said.

I was having trouble processing it all. Five minutes ago I was walking to the Liberty Bell, assuming Marley was happily relaxing in his kennel run. Now I was being asked to decide whether he should live or die. I had never even heard of the condition she described. Only later would I learn that bloat was fairly common in some breeds of dogs, especially those, such as Marley, with deep barrel chests. Dogs who scarfed down their entire meal in a few quick gulps—Marley, once again—also seemed to be at higher risk. Some dog owners suspected the stress of being in a kennel could trigger bloat, but I later would see a professor of veterinarian medicine quoted as saying his research showed no connection between kennel stress and bloat. The vet on the phone acknowledged Marley's excitement around the other dogs in the kennel could have brought on the attack. He had gulped down his food as usual and was panting and salivating heavily, worked up by all the other dogs around him. She thought he might have swallowed so much air and saliva that his stomach began to dilate on its long axis, making it vulnerable to twisting. "Can't we just wait and see how he does?" I asked. "Maybe it won't twist again."

"That's what we're doing right now," she said, "waiting and watching." She repeated the one percent odds and added, "If his stomach flips again, I'll need you to make a quick decision. We can't let him suffer."

"I need to speak with my wife," I told her. "I'll call you back."

When Jenny answered her cell phone she was on a crowded tour boat with the kids in the middle of Boston Harbor. I could hear the boat's engine chugging and the guide's voice booming through a loudspeaker in the background. We had a choppy, awkward conversation over a bad connection. Neither of us could hear the other well. I shouted to try to communicate what we were up against. She was only getting snippets. Marley . . . emergency . . . stomach . . . surgery . . . put to sleep.

There was silence on the other end. "Hello?" I said. "Are you still there?"

"I'm here," Jenny said, then went quiet again. We both knew this day would come eventually; we just did not think it would be today. Not with her and the kids out of town where they couldn't even have their good-byes; not with me ninety minutes away in downtown Philadelphia with work commitments. By the end of the conversation, through shouts and blurts and pregnant pauses, we decided there was really no decision at all. The vet was right. Marley was fading on all fronts. It would be cruel to put him through a traumatic surgery to simply try to stave off the inevitable.

We could not ignore the high cost, either. It seemed obscene, almost immoral, to spend that kind of money on an old dog at the end of his life when there were unwanted dogs put down every day for lack of a home, and more important, children not getting proper medical attention for lack of financial resources. If this was Marley's time, then it was his time, and we would see to it he went out with dignity and without suffering. We knew it was the right thing, yet neither of us was ready to lose him.

I called the veterinarian back and told her our decision. "His teeth are rotted away, he's stone-deaf, and his hips have gotten so bad he can barely get up the porch stoop anymore," I told her as if she needed convincing. "He's having trouble squatting to have a bowel movement."

The vet, whom I now knew as Dr. Hopkinson, made it easy on me. "I think it's time," she said.

"I guess so," I answered, but I didn't want her to put him down without calling me first. I wanted to be there with him if possible. "And," I reminded her, "I'm still holding out for that one percent miracle."

"Let's talk in an hour," she said.

An hour later Dr. Hopkinson sounded slightly more optimistic. Marley was still holding his own, resting with an intravenous drip in his front leg. She raised his odds to five percent. "I don't want you to get your hopes up," she said. "He's a very sick dog."

The next morning the doctor sounded brighter still. "He had a good night," she said. When I called back at noon, she had removed the IV from his paw and started him on a slurry of rice and meat. "He's famished," she reported. By the next call, he was up on his feet. "Good news," she said. "One of our techs just took him outside and he pooped and peed." I cheered into the phone as though he had just taken Best in Show. Then she added: "He must be feeling better. He just gave me a big sloppy kiss on the lips." Yep, that was our Marley.

"I wouldn't have thought it possible yesterday," the doc said, "but I think you'll be able to take him home tomorrow." The following evening after work, that's just what I did. He looked terrible—weak and skeletal, his eyes milky and crusted with mucus, as if he had been to the other side of death and back, which in a sense I guess he had. I must have looked a little ill myself after paying the eight-hundred-dollar bill. When I thanked the doctor for her good work, she replied, "The whole staff loves Marley. Everyone was rooting for him."

I walked him out to the car, my ninety-nine-to-one-odds miracle dog, and said, "Let's get you home where you belong." He just stood there looking woefully into the backseat, knowing it was as unattainable as Mount Olympus. He didn't even try to hop in. I called to one of the kennel workers, who helped me gingerly lift him into the car, and I drove him home with a box of medicines and strict instructions. Marley would never again gulp a huge meal in one sitting, or slurp unlimited amounts of water. His days of playing submarine with his snout in the water bowl were over. From now on, he was to receive four small meals a day and only limited rations of water—a half cup or so in his bowl at a time. In this way, the doctor hoped, his stomach would stay calm and not bloat and twist again. He also was never again to be boarded in a large kennel surrounded by barking, pacing dogs. I was convinced, and Dr. Hopkinson seemed to be, too, that that had been the precipitating factor in his close call with death.

That night, after I got him home and inside, I spread a sleeping bag on the floor in the family room beside him. He was not up to climbing the stairs to the bedroom, and I didn't have the heart to leave him alone and helpless. I knew he would fret all night if he was not at my side. "We're having a sleepover, Marley!" I proclaimed, and lay down next to him. I stroked him head to tail until huge clouds of fur rolled off his back. I wiped the mucus from the corners of his eyes and scratched his ears until he moaned with pleasure. Jenny and the kids would be home in the morning; she would pamper him with frequent minimeals of boiled hamburger and rice. It had taken him thirteen years, but Marley had finally merited people food, not leftovers but a stovetop meal made just for him. The children would throw their arms around him, unaware of how close they had come to never seeing him again.

Tomorrow the house would be loud and boisterous and full of life again. For tonight, it was just the two of us, Marley and me. Lying there with him, his smelly breath in my face, I couldn't help thinking of our first night together all those years ago after I brought him home from the breeder, a tiny puppy whimpering for his mother. I remembered how I dragged his box into the bedroom and the way we had fallen asleep together, my arm dangling over the side of the bed to comfort him. Thirteen years later, here we were, still inseparable. I thought about his puppyhood and adolescence, about the shredded couches and eaten mattresses, about the wild walks along the Intracoastal and the cheek-to-jowl dances with the stereo blaring. I thought about the swallowed objects and purloined paychecks and sweet moments of canine-human empathy. Mostly I thought about what a good and loyal companion he had been all these years. What a trip it had been.

"You really scared me, old man," I whispered as he stretched out beside me and slid his snout beneath my arm to encourage me to keep petting him. "It's good to have you home."

We fell asleep together, side by side on the floor, his rump half on my sleeping bag, my arm draped across his back. He woke me once in the night, his shoulders flinching, his paws twitching, little baby barks coming from deep in his throat, more like coughs than anything else. He was dreaming. Dreaming, I imagined, that he was young and strong again. And running like there was no tomorrow.

CHAPTER 26

Borrowed Time

❖

Over the next several weeks, Marley bounced back from the edge of death. The mischievous sparkle returned to his eyes, the cool wetness to his nose, and a little meat to his bones. For all he'd been through, he seemed none the worse off. He was content to snooze his days away, favoring a spot in front of the glass door in the family room where the sun flooded in and baked his fur. On his new low-bulk diet of petite meals, he was perpetually ravenous and was begging and thieving food more shamelessly than ever. One evening I caught him alone in the kitchen up on his hind legs with his front paws on the kitchen counter, stealing Rice Krispies Treats from a platter. How he got up there on his frail hips, I'll never know. Infirmities be damned; when the will called, Marley's body answered. I wanted to hug him, I was so happy at the surprise display of strength.

The scare of that summer should have snapped Jenny and me out of our denial about Marley's advancing age, but we quickly returned to the comfortable assumption that the crisis was a one time fluke, and his eternal march into the sunset could resume once again. Part of us wanted to believe he could chug on forever. Despite all his frailties, he was still the same happy-go-lucky dog. Each morning after his breakfast, he trotted into the family room to use the couch as a giant napkin, walking along its length, rubbing his snout and mouth against the fabric as he went and flipping up the cushions in the process. Then he would turn around and come back in the opposite direction so he could wipe the other side. From there he would drop to the floor and roll onto his back, wiggling from side to side to give himself a back rub. He liked to sit and lick the carpeting with lust, as if it had been larded with the most delectable gravy he had ever tasted. His daily routine included barking at the mailman, visiting the chickens, staring at the bird feeder, and making the rounds of the bathtub faucets to check for any drips of water he could lap up. Several times a day he flipped the lid up on the kitchen trash can to see what goodies he could scavenge. On a daily basis, he launched into Labrador evader mode, banging around the house, tail thumping the walls and furniture, and on a daily basis I continued to pry open his jaws and extract from the roof of his mouth all sorts of flotsam from our daily lives—potato skins and muffin wrappers, discarded Kleenex and dental floss. Even in old age, some things did not change.

As September 11, 2003, approached, I drove across the state to the tiny mining town of Shanksville, Pennsylvania, where United Flight 93 had crashed into an empty field on that infamous morning two years earlier amid a passenger uprising. The hijackers who had seized the flight were

believed to be heading for Washington, D.C. , to crash the
plane into the White House or the Capitol, and the passengers who rushed the cockpit almost certainly saved countless lives on the ground. To mark the second anniversary of
the attacks, my editors wanted me to visit the site and take
my best shot at capturing that sacrifice and the lasting effect
it had on the American psyche.

I spent the entire day at the crash site, lingering at the
impromptu memorial that had risen there. I talked to the
steady stream of visitors who showed up to pay their
respects, interviewed locals who remembered the force
of the explosion, sat with a woman who had lost her
daughter in a car accident and who came to the crash site
to find solace in communal grief. I documented the many
mementoes and notes that filled the gravel parking lot. Still I
was not feeling the column. What could I say about this
immense tragedy that had not been said already? I went to
dinner in town and pored over my notes. Writing a newspaper column is a lot like building a tower out of blocks;
each nugget of information, each quote and captured moment, is a block. You start by building a broad foundation,
strong enough to support your premise, then work your way
up toward the pinnacle. My notebook was full of solid
building blocks, but I was missing the mortar to hold them
all together. I had no idea what to do with them.

After I finished my meat loaf and iced tea, I headed back to
the hotel to try to write. Halfway there, on an impulse, I
pulled a U-turn and drove back out to the crash site, several
miles outside town, arriving just as the sun was slipping
behind the hillside and the last few visitors were pulling

away. I sat out there alone for a long time, as sunset turned to dusk and dusk to night. A sharp wind blew down off the hills, and I pulled my Windbreaker tight around me. Towering overhead, a giant American flag snapped in the breeze, its colors glowing almost iridescent in the last smoldering light. Only then did the emotion of this sacred place envelop me and the magnitude of what happened in the sky above this lonely field begin to sink in. I looked out on the spot where the plane hit the earth and then up at the flag, and I felt tears stinging my eyes. For the first time in my life, I took the time to count the stripes. Seven red and six white. I counted the stars, fifty of them on a field of blue. It meant more to us now, this American flag. To a new generation, it stood once again for valor and sacrifice. I knew what I needed to write.

I shoved my hands into my pockets and walked out to the edge of the gravel lot, where I stared into the growing blackness. Standing out there in the dark, I felt many different things. One of them was pride in my fellow Americans, ordinary people who rose to the moment, knowing it was their last. One was humility, for I was alive and untouched by the horrors of that day, free to continue my happy life as a husband and father and writer. In the lonely blackness, I could almost taste the finiteness of life and thus its preciousness. We take it for granted, but it is fragile, precarious, uncertain, able to cease at any instant without notice. I was reminded of what should be obvious but too often is not, that each day, each hour and minute, is worth cherishing.

I felt something else, as well—an amazement at the boundless capacity of the human heart, at once big enough to absorb a tragedy of this magnitude yet still find room for the little moments of personal pain and heartache that are part of any life. In my case, one of those little moments was my failing dog. With a tinge of shame, I realized that even amid the colossus of human heartbreak that was Flight 93, I could still feel the sharp pang of the loss I knew was coming.

Marley was living on borrowed time; that much was clear. Another health crisis could come any day, and when it did, I would not fight the inevitable. Any invasive medical procedure at this stage in his life would be cruel, something Jenny and I would be doing more for our sake than his. We loved that crazy old dog, loved him despite everything—or perhaps *because* of everything. But I could see now the time was near for us to let him go. I got back in the car and returned to my hotel room.

The next morning, my column filed, I called home from the hotel. Jenny said, "I just want you to know that Marley really misses you."

"Marley?" I asked. "How about the rest of you?"

"Of course we miss you, dingo," she said. "But I mean Marley really, really misses you. He's driving us all bonkers."

The night before, unable to find me, Marley had paced and sniffed the entire house over and over, she said, poking through every room, looking behind doors and in closets. He struggled to get upstairs and, not finding me there, came back down and began his search all over again. "He was really out of sorts," she said.

He even braved the steep descent into the basement,

where, until the slippery wooden stairs put it off-limits to him, Marley had happily kept me company for long hours in my workshop, snoozing at my feet as I built things, the sawdust floating down and covering his fur like a soft snowfall. Once down there, he couldn't get back up the stairs, and he stood yipping and whining until Jenny and the kids came to his rescue, holding him beneath the shoulders and hips and boosting him up step by step.

At bedtime, instead of sleeping beside our bed as he normally did, Marley camped out on the landing at the top of the stairs where he could keep watch on all the bedrooms and the front door directly at the bottom of the stairs in case I either (1) came out of hiding; or (2) arrived home during the night, on the chance I had snuck out without telling him. That's where he was the next morning when Jenny went downstairs to make breakfast. A couple of hours passed before it dawned on her that Marley still had not shown his face, which was highly unusual; he almost always was the first one down the steps each morning, charging ahead of us and banging his tail against the front door to go out. She found him sleeping soundly on the floor tight against my side of the bed. Then she saw why. When she had gotten up, she had inadvertently pushed her pillows—she sleeps with three of them— over to my side of the bed, beneath the covers, forming a large lump where I usually slept. With his Mr. Magoo eyesight, Marley could be forgiven for mistaking a pile of feathers for his master. "He absolutely thought you were in there," she said. "I could just tell he did. He was convinced you were sleeping in!"

We laughed together on the phone, and then Jenny said, "You've got to give him points for loyalty." That I did. Devotion had always come easily to our dog.

I had been back from Shanksville for only a week when the crisis we knew could come at any time arrived. I was in the bedroom getting dressed for work when I heard a terrible clatter followed by Conor's scream: "Help! Marley fell down the stairs!" I came running and found him in a heap at the bottom of the long staircase, struggling to get to his feet. Jenny and I raced to him and ran our hands over his body, gently squeezing his limbs, pressing his ribs, massaging his spine. Nothing seemed to be broken. With a groan, Marley made it to his feet, shook off, and walked away without so much as a limp. Conor had witnessed the fall. He said Marley had started down the stairs but, after just two steps, realized everyone was still upstairs and attempted an about-face. As he tried to turn around, his hips dropped out from beneath him and he tumbled in a free fall down the entire length of the stairs.

"Wow, was he lucky," I said. "A fall like that could have killed him."

"I can't believe he didn't get hurt," Jenny said. "He's like a cat with nine lives."

But he had gotten hurt. Within minutes he was stiffening up, and by the time I arrived home from work that night, Marley was completely incapacitated, unable to move. He seemed to be sore everywhere, as though he had been worked over by thugs. What really had him laid up, though, was his front left leg; he was unable to put any weight at all on it. I could squeeze it without him yelping, and I suspected he had pulled a tendon. When he saw me, he tried to struggle to his feet to greet me, but it was no use. His left front paw was useless, and with his weak back legs, he just had no power to do anything. Marley was down to one good limb, lousy odds for any four-legged beast. He finally made it up and tried to hop on three paws to get to me, but his back legs caved in and he collapsed back to the floor. Jenny gave him an aspirin and held a bag of ice to his front leg. Marley, playful even under duress, kept trying to eat the ice cubes.

By ten-thirty that night, he was no better, and he hadn't been outside to empty his bladder since one o'clock that afternoon. He had been holding his urine for nearly ten hours. I had no idea how to get him outside and back in again so he could relieve himself. Straddling him and clasping my hands beneath his chest, I lifted him to his feet. Together we waddled our way to the front door, with me holding him up as he hopped along. But out on the porch stoop he froze. A steady rain was falling, and the porch steps, his nemesis, loomed slick and wet before him. He looked unnerved. "Come on," I said. "Just a quick pee and we'll go right back inside." He would have no part of it. I wished I could have persuaded him to just go right on the porch and be done with it, but there was no teaching this old dog that new trick. He hopped back inside and stared morosely up at me as if apologizing for what he knew was coming. "We'll try again later," I said. As if hearing his cue, he half squatted on his three remaining legs and emptied his full bladder on the foyer floor, a puddle spreading out around him. It was the first time since he was a tiny puppy that Marley had urinated in the house.

The next morning Marley was better, though still hobbling about like an invalid. We got him outside, where he urinated and defecated without a problem. On the count of three, Jenny and I together lifted him up the porch stairs to get him back inside. "I have a feeling," I told her, "that Marley will never see the upstairs of this house again." It was apparent he had climbed his last staircase. From now on, he would have to get used to living and sleeping on the ground floor.

I worked from home that day and was upstairs in the bedroom, writing a column on my laptop computer, when I heard a commotion on the stairs. I stopped typing and listened. The sound was instantly familiar, a sort of loud clomping noise as if a shod horse were galloping up a gangplank. I looked at the bedroom doorway and held my breath. A few seconds later, Marley popped his head around the corner and came sauntering into the room. His eyes brightened when he spotted me. *So there you are!* He smashed his head into my lap, begging for an ear rub, which I figured he had earned.

"Marley, you made it!" I exclaimed. "You old hound! I can't believe you're up here!"

Later, as I sat on the floor with him and scruffed his neck, he twisted his head around and gamely gummed my wrist in his jaws. It was a good sign, a telltale of the playful puppy still in him. The day he sat still and let me pet him without trying to engage me would be the day I knew he had had enough. The previous night he had seemed on death's door, and I again had braced myself for the worst. Today he was panting and pawing and trying to slime my hands off. Just when I thought his long, lucky run was over, he was back.

I pulled his head up and made him look me in the eyes. "You're going to tell me when it's time, right?" I said, more a statement than a question. I didn't want to have to make the decision on my own. "You'll let me know, won't you?"

CHAPTER 27

The Big Meadow

✳

Winter arrived early that year, and as the days grew short and the winds howled through the frozen branches, we cocooned into our snug home. I chopped and split a winter's worth of firewood and stacked it by the back door. Jenny made hearty soups and homemade breads, and the children once again sat in the window and waited for the snow to arrive. I anticipated the first snowfall, too, but with a quiet sense of dread, wondering how Marley could possibly make it through another tough winter. The previous one had been hard enough on him, and he had weakened markedly, dramatically, in the ensuing year. I wasn't sure how he would navigate ice-glazed sidewalks, slippery stairs, and a snow-covered landscape. It was dawning on me why the elderly retired to Florida and Arizona.

On a blustery Sunday night in mid-December, when the children had finished their homework and practiced their musical instruments, Jenny started the popcorn on the stove and declared a family movie night. The kids raced to pick out a video, and I whistled for Marley, taking him outside with me to fetch a basket of maple logs off the woodpile. He poked around in the frozen grass as I loaded up the wood, standing with his face into the wind, wet nose sniffing the icy air as if divining winter's descent. I clapped my hands and waved my arms to get his attention, and he followed me inside, hesitating at the front porch steps before summoning his courage and lurching forward, dragging his back legs up behind him.

Inside, I got the fire humming as the kids queued up the movie. The flames leapt and the heat radiated into the room, prompting Marley, as was his habit, to claim the best spot for himself, directly in front of the hearth. I lay down on the floor a few feet from him and propped my head on a pillow, more watching the fire than the movie. Marley didn't want to lose his warm spot, but he couldn't resist this opportunity. His favorite human was at ground level in the prone position, utterly defenseless. Who was the alpha male now? His tail began pounding the floor. Then he started wiggling his way in my direction. He sashayed from side to side on his belly, his rear legs stretched out behind him, and soon he was pressed up against me, grinding his head into my ribs. The minute I reached out to pet him, it was all over. He pushed himself up on his paws, shook hard, showering me in loose fur, and stared down at me, his billowing jowls hanging immediately over my face. When I started to laugh, he took this as a green light to advance, and before I quite knew what was happening, he had straddled my chest with his front paws and, in one big free fall, collapsed on top of me in a heap. "Ugh!" I screamed under his weight. "Full-frontal Lab attack!'' The kids squealed. Marley could not believe his good fortune. I wasn't even trying to get him off me. He squirmed, he drooled, he licked me all over the face and nuzzled my neck. I could barely breathe under his weight, and after a few minutes I slid him half off me, where he remained through most of the movie, his head, shoulder, and one paw resting on my chest, the rest of him pressed against my side.

I didn't say so to anyone in the room, but I found myself clinging to the moment, knowing there would not be too many more like it. Marley was in the quiet dusk of a long and eventful life. Looking back on it later, I would recognize that night in front of the fire for what it was, our farewell party. I stroked his head until he fell asleep, and then I stroked it some more.

Four days later, we packed the minivan in preparation for a family vacation to Disney World in Florida. It would be the children's first Christmas away from home, and they were wild with excitement. That evening, in preparation for an early-morning departure, Jenny delivered Marley to the veterinarian's office, where she had arranged for him to spend our week away in the intensive care unit where the doctors and workers could keep their eyes on him around the clock and where he would not be riled by the other dogs. After his close call on their watch the previous summer, they were happy to give him the Cadillac digs and extra attention at no extra cost.

That night as we finished packing, both Jenny and I commented on how strange it felt to be in a dog-free zone. There was no oversized canine constantly underfoot, shadowing our every move, trying to sneak out the door with us each time we carried a bag to the garage. The freedom was liberating, but the house seemed cavernous and empty, even with the kids bouncing off the walls.

The next morning before the sun was over the tree line, we piled into the minivan and headed south. Ridiculing the whole Disney experience is a favorite sport in the circle of parents I run with. I've lost track of how many times I've said, "We could take the whole family to Paris for the same amount of money." But the whole family had a wonderful time, even naysayer Dad. Of the many potential pitfalls—sickness, fatigue-induced tantrums, lost tickets, lost children, sibling fistfights—we escaped them all. It was a great family vacation, and we spent much of the long drive back north recounting the pros and cons of each ride, each meal, each swim, each moment. When we were halfway through Maryland, just four hours from home, my cell phone rang. It was one of the workers from the veterinarian's office. Marley was acting lethargic, she said, and his hips had begun to droop worse than usual. He seemed to be in discomfort. She said the vet wanted our permission to give him a steroid shot and pain medication. Sure, I said. Keep him comfortable, and we'd be there to pick him up the next day.

When Jenny arrived to take him home the following afternoon, December 29, Marley looked tired and a little out of sorts but not visibly ill. As we had been warned, his hips were weaker than ever. The doctor talked to her about putting him on a regimen of arthritis medications, and a worker helped Jenny lift him into the minivan. But within a half hour of getting him home, he was retching, trying to clear thick mucus from his throat. Jenny let him out into the front yard, and he simply lay on the frozen ground and could not or would not budge. She called me at work in a panic. "I can't get him back inside," she said. "He's lying out there in the cold, and he won't get up." I left immediately, and by the time I arrived home forty-five minutes later, she had managed to get him to his feet and back into the house. I found him sprawled on the dining room floor, clearly distressed and clearly not himself.

In thirteen years I had not been able to walk into the house without him bounding to his feet, stretching, shaking, panting, banging his tail into everything, greeting me like I'd just returned from the Hundred Years' War. Not on this day. His eyes followed me as I walked into the room, but he did not move his head. I knelt down beside him and rubbed his snout. No reaction. He did not try to gum my wrist, did not want to play, did not even lift his head. His eyes were far away, and his tail lay limp on the floor.

Jenny had left two messages at the animal hospital and was waiting for a vet to call back, but it was becoming obvious this was turning into an emergency. I put a third call in. After several minutes, Marley slowly stood up on shaky legs and tried to retch again, but nothing would come out. That's when I noticed his stomach; it looked bigger than usual, and it was hard to the touch. My heart sank; I knew what this meant. I called back the veterinarian's office, and this time I described Marley's bloated stomach. The receptionist put me on hold for a moment, then came back and said, "The doctor says to bring him right in."

Jenny and I did not have to say a word to each other; we both understood that the moment had arrived. We braced the kids, telling them Marley had to go to the hospital and the doctors were going to try to make him better, but that he was very sick. As I was getting ready to go, I looked in, and Jenny and the kids were huddled around him as he lay on the floor so clearly in distress, making their good-byes. They each got to pet him and have a few last moments with him. The children remained bullishly optimistic that this dog who had been a constant part of their lives would soon be back, good as new. "Get all better, Marley," Colleen said in her little voice.

With Jenny's help, I got him into the back of my car. She gave him a last quick hug, and I drove off with him, promising to call as soon as I learned something. He lay on the floor in the backseat with his head resting on the center hump, and I drove with one hand on the wheel and the other stretched behind me so I could stroke his head and shoulders. "Oh, Marley," I just kept saying.

In the parking lot of the animal hospital, I helped him out of the car, and he stopped to sniff a tree where the other dogs all pee—still curious despite how ill he felt. I gave him a minute, knowing this might be his last time in his beloved outdoors, then tugged gently at his choker chain and led him into the lobby. Just inside the front door, he decided he had gone far enough and gingerly let himself down on the tile floor. When the techs and I were unable to get him back to his feet, they brought out a stretcher, slid him onto it, and disappeared with him behind the counter, heading for the examining area.

A few minutes later, the vet, a young woman I had never met before, came out and led me into an exam room where she put a pair of X-ray films up on a light board. She showed me how his stomach had bloated to twice its normal size. On the film, near where the stomach meets the intestines, she traced two fist-sized dark spots, which she said indicated a twist. Just as with the last time, she said she would sedate him and insert a tube into his stomach to release the gas causing the bloating. She would then use the tube to manually feel for the back of the stomach. "It's a long shot," she said, "but I'm going to try to use the tube to massage his stomach back into place." It was exactly the same one percent gamble Dr. Hopkinson had given over the summer. It had worked once, it could work again. I remained silently optimistic.

"Okay," I said. "Please give it your best shot."

A half hour later she emerged with a grim face. She had tried three times and was unable to open the blockage. She had given him more sedatives in the hope they might relax his stomach muscles. When none of that worked, she had inserted a catheter through his ribs, a last-ditch attempt to clear the blockage, also without luck. "At this point," she said, "our only real option is to go into surgery." She paused, as if gauging whether I was ready to talk about the inevitable, and then said, "Or the most humane thing might be to put him to sleep."

Jenny and I had been through this decision five months earlier and had already made the hard choice. My visit to Shanksville had only solidified my resolve not to subject Marley to any more suffering. Yet standing in the waiting

room, the hour upon me once again, I stood frozen. The
doctor sensed my agony and discussed the complications
that could likely be expected in operating on a dog of
Marley's age. Another thing troubling her, she said, was a
bloody residue that had come out on the catheter, indicating
problems with the stomach wall. "Who knows what we
might find when we get in there," she said.

I told her I wanted to step outside to call my wife. On the
cell phone in the parking lot, I told Jenny that they had tried
everything short of surgery to no avail. We sat silently on the
phone for a long moment before she said, "I love you,
John."

"I love you, too, Jenny," I said.

I walked back inside and asked the doctor if I could have a
couple of minutes alone with him. She warned me that he
was heavily sedated. "Take all the time you need," she said. I
found him unconscious on the stretcher on the floor, an IV
shunt in his forearm. I got down on my knees and ran my
fingers through his fur, the way he liked. I ran my hand
down his back. I lifted each floppy ear in my hands—those
crazy ears that had caused him so many problems over the
years and cost us a king's ransom—and felt their weight. I
pulled his lip up and looked at his lousy, worn-out teeth.
I picked up a front paw and cupped it in my hand. Then I
dropped my forehead against his and sat there for a long
time, as if I could telegraph a message through our two
skulls, from my brain to his. I wanted to make him understand some things.

"You know all that stuff we've always said about you?" I
whispered. "What a total pain you are? Don't believe it.

Don't believe it for a minute, Marley." He needed to know that, and something more, too. There was something I had never told him, that no one ever had. I wanted him to hear it before he went.

"Marley," I said. "You are a *great* dog."

I found the doctor waiting at the front counter. "I'm ready," I said. My voice was cracking, which surprised me because I had really believed I'd braced myself months earlier for this moment. I knew if I said another word, I would break down, and so I just nodded and signed as she handed me release forms. When the paperwork was completed, I followed her back to the unconscious Marley, and I knelt in front of him again, my hands cradling his head as she prepared a syringe and inserted it into the shunt. "Are you okay?" she asked. I nodded, and she pushed the plunger. His jaw shuddered ever so slightly. She listened to his heart and said it had slowed way down but not stopped. He was a big dog. She prepared a second syringe and again pushed the plunger. A minute later, she listened again and said, "He's gone." She left me alone with him, and I gently lifted one of his eyelids. She was right; Marley was gone.

I walked out to the front desk and paid the bill. She discussed "group cremation" for $75 or individual crema- tion, with the ashes returned, for $170. No, I said; I would be taking him home. A few minutes later, she and an assistant wheeled out a cart with a large black bag on it and helped me lift it into the backseat. The doctor shook my hand, told me how sorry she was. She had done her best, she said. It was his time, I said, then thanked her and drove away.

In the car on the way home, I started to cry, something I almost never do, not even at funerals. It only lasted a few minutes. By the time I pulled into the driveway, I was dry-eyed again. I left Marley in the car and went inside where Jenny was sitting up, waiting. The children were all in bed asleep; we would tell them in the morning. We fell into each other's arms and both started weeping. I tried to describe it to her, to assure her he was already deeply asleep when the end came, that there was no panic, no trauma, no pain. But I couldn't find the words. So we simply rocked in each other's arms. Later, we went outside and together lifted the heavy black bag out of the car and into the garden cart, which I rolled into the garage for the night.

CHAPTER 28

Beneath the Cherry Trees

✳

Sleep came fitfully that night, and an hour before dawn I slid out of bed and dressed quietly so as not to wake Jenny. In the kitchen I drank a glass of water—coffee could wait—and walked out into a light, slushy drizzle. I grabbed a shovel and pickax and walked to the pea patch, which hugged the white pines where Marley had sought potty refuge the previous winter. It was here I had decided to lay him to rest.

The temperature was in the mid-thirties and the ground blessedly unfrozen. In the half dark, I began to dig. Once I was through a thin layer of topsoil, I hit heavy, dense clay studded with rocks—the backfill from the excavation of our basement—and the going was slow and arduous. After fifteen minutes I peeled off my coat and paused to catch my breath. After thirty minutes I was in a sweat and not yet down two feet. At the forty-five-minute mark, I struck water. The hole began to fill. And fill. Soon a foot of muddy cold water covered the bottom. I fetched a bucket and tried to bail it, but more water just seeped in. There was no way I could lay Marley down in that icy swamp. No way.

Despite the work I had invested in it—my heart was pounding like I had just run a marathon—I abandoned the location and scouted the yard, stopping where the lawn meets the woods at the bottom of the hill. Between two big native cherry trees, their branches arching above me in the gray light of dawn like an open-air cathedral, I sunk my shovel. These were the same trees Marley and I had narrowly missed on our wild toboggan ride, and I said out loud, "This feels right." The spot was beyond where the bulldozers had spread the shale substrata, and the native soil was light and well drained, a gardener's dream. Digging went easily, and I soon had an oval hole roughly two by three feet around and four feet deep. I went inside and found all three kids up, sniffling quietly. Jenny had just told them.

Seeing them grieving—their first up-close experience with death—deeply affected me. Yes, it was only a dog, and dogs come and go in the course of a human life, sometimes simply because they become an inconvenience. It was only a dog, and yet every time I tried to talk about Marley to them, tears welled in my eyes. I told them it was okay to cry, and that owning a dog always ended with this sadness because dogs just don't live as long as people do. I told them how Marley was sleeping when they gave him the shot and that he didn't feel a thing. He just drifted off and was gone. Colleen was upset that she didn't have a chance to say a real good-bye to him; she thought he would be coming home. I told her I had said good-bye for all of us. Conor, our budding author, showed me something he had made for Marley, to go in the grave with him. It was a drawing of a big red heart beneath which he had written: "To Marley, I hope you know how much I loved you all of my life. You were always there when I needed you. Through life or death, I will always love you. Your brother, Conor Richard Grogan." Then Colleen drew a picture of a girl with a big yellow dog and beneath it, with spelling help from her brother, she wrote, "P. S.—I will never forget you."

I went out alone and wheeled Marley's body down the hill, where I cut an armful of soft pine boughs that I laid on the floor of the hole. I lifted the heavy body bag off the cart and down into the hole as gently as I could, though there was really no graceful way to do it. I got into the hole, opened the bag to see him one last time, and positioned him in a comfortable, natural way—just as he might be lying in front of the fireplace, curled up, head tucked around to his side. "Okay, big guy, this is it," I said. I closed the bag up and returned to the house to get Jenny and the kids.

As a family, we walked down to the grave. Conor and Colleen had sealed their notes back-to-back in a plastic bag, and I placed it right beside Marley's head. Patrick used his jackknife to cut five pine boughs, one for each of us. One by one, we dropped them in the hole, their scent rising around us. We paused for a moment, then all together, as if we had rehearsed it, said, "Marley, we love you." I picked up the shovel and tossed the first scoop of dirt in. It slapped heavily on the plastic, making an ugly sound, and Jenny began to weep. I kept shoveling. The kids stood watching in silence.

When the hole was half filled, I took a break and we all walked up to the house, where we sat around the kitchen table and told funny Marley stories. One minute tears were welling in our eyes, the next we were laughing. Jenny told the story of Marley going bonkers during the filming of *The Last Home Run* when a stranger picked up baby Conor. I told about all the leashes he had severed and the time he peed on our neighbor's ankle. We described all the things he had destroyed and the thousands of dollars he had cost us. We could laugh about it now. To make the kids feel better, I told them something I did not quite believe. "Marley's spirit is up in dog heaven now," I said. "He's in a giant golden meadow, running free. And his hips are good again. And his hearing is back, and his eyesight is sharp, and he has all his teeth. He's back in his prime—chasing rabbits all day long."

Jenny added, "And having endless screen doors to crash through." The image of him barging his way oafishly through heaven got a laugh out of everyone.

The morning was slipping away, and I still needed to go to work. I went back down to his grave alone and finished filling the hole, gently, respectfully, using my boot to tamp down the loose earth. When the hole was flush with the ground, I placed two large rocks from the woods on top of it, then went inside, took a hot shower, and drove to the office.

In the days immediately after we buried Marley, the whole family went silent. The animal that was the amusing target of so many hours of conversation and stories over the years had become a taboo topic. We were trying to return our lives to normal, and speaking of him only made it harder. Colleen in particular could not bear to hear his name or see his photo. Tears would well in her eyes and she would clench her fists and say angrily, "I don't want to talk about him!"

I resumed my schedule, driving to work, writing my column, coming home again. Every night for thirteen years he had waited for me at the door. Walking in now at the end of the day was the most painful part of all. The house seemed silent, empty, not quite a home anymore. Jenny vacuumed like a fiend, determined to get up the bucketsful of Marley fur that had been falling out in massive clumps for the past couple of years, insinuating itself into every crevice and fold. Slowly, the signs of the old dog were being erased. One morning I went to put my shoes on, and inside them, covering the insoles, lay a carpet of Marley fur, picked up by my socks from walking on the floors and gradually deposited inside the shoes. I just sat and looked at it—actually petted it with two fingers—and smiled. I held it up to show Jenny and said, "We're not getting rid of him that easy." She laughed, but that evening in our bedroom, Jenny—who had not said much all week— blurted out: "I miss him. I mean I really, *really* miss him. I ache-inside miss him."

"I know," I said. "I do, too."

I wanted to write a farewell column to Marley, but I was afraid all my emotion would pour out into a gushy, maudlin piece of self-indulgence that would only humiliate me. So I stuck with topics less dear to my heart. I did, however, carry a tape recorder with me, and when a thought came to me, I would get it down. I knew I wanted to portray him as he was and not as some impossibly perfect reincarnation of Old Yeller or Rin Tin Tin, as if there were any danger of that. So many people remake their pets in death, turning them into supernatural, noble beasts that in life did everything for their masters except fry eggs for breakfast. I wanted to be honest. Marley was a funny, bigger-than-life pain in the ass who never quite got the hang of the whole chain-of-command thing. Honestly, he might well have been the world's worst-behaved dog. Yet he intuitively grasped from the start what it meant to be man's best friend.

During the week after his death, I walked down the hill several times to stand by his grave. Partly, I wanted to make sure no wild animals were coming around at night. The grave remained undisturbed, but already I could see that in the spring I would need to add a couple of wheelbarrows of soil to fill the depression where it was settling. Mostly I just wanted to commune with him. Standing there, I found myself replaying random snippets from his life. I was embarrassed by how deep my grief went for this dog, deeper than for some humans I had known. It's not that I equated a dog's life with a human's, but outside my immediate family few people had given themselves so selflessly to me. Secretly, I brought Marley's choker chain in from the car, where it had sat since his final ride to the hospital, and stashed it beneath the underwear in my dresser, where each morning I could reach down and touch it.

I walked around all week with a dull ache inside. It was actually physical, not unlike a stomach virus. I was lethargic, unmotivated. I couldn't even muster the energy to indulge my hobbies—playing guitar, woodworking, reading. I felt out of sorts, not sure what to do with myself. I ended up going to bed early most nights, at nine-thirty, ten o'clock.

On New Year's Eve we were invited to a neighbor's house
for a party. Friends quietly expressed their condolences, but
we all tried to keep the conversation light and moving. This
was, after all, New Year's Eve. At dinner, Sara and Dave
Pandl, a pair of landscape architects who had moved back to
Pennsylvania from California to turn an old stone barn into
their home, and who had become our dear friends, sat at
one corner of the table with me, and we talked at length
about dogs and love and loss. Dave and Sara had put down
their cherished Nelly, an Australian shepherd, five years
earlier and buried her on the hill beside their farmhouse.
Dave is one of the most unsentimental people I have ever
met, a quiet stoic cut from taciturn Pennsylvania Dutch
stock. But when it came to Nelly, he, too, struggled with a
deep inner grief. He told me how he combed the rocky
woods behind his home for days until he found the perfect
stone for her grave. It was naturally shaped like a heart, and
he took it to a stone carver who inscribed "Nelly" into its
surface. All these years later, the death of that dog still
touched them profoundly. Their eyes misted up as they told
me about her. As Sara said, blinking back her tears, sometimes a dog comes along that really touches your life, and
you can never forget her.

That weekend I took a long walk through the woods, and
by the time I arrived at work on Monday, I knew what I
wanted to say about the dog that touched my life, the one I
would never forget.

I began the column by describing my walk down the hill
with the shovel at dawn and how odd it was to be outdoors
without Marley, who for thirteen years had made it his

business to be at my side for any excursion. "And now here I was alone," I wrote, "digging him this hole."

I quoted my father who, when I told him I had to put the old guy down, gave the closest thing to a compliment my dog had ever received: "There will never be another dog like Marley."

I gave a lot of thought to how I should describe him, and this is what I settled on: "No one ever called him a great dog—or even a good dog. He was as wild as a banshee and as strong as a bull. He crashed joyously through life with a gusto most often associated with natural disasters. He's the only dog I've ever known to get expelled from obedience school." I continued: "Marley was a chewer of couches, a slasher of screens, a slinger of drool, a tipper of trash cans. As for brains, let me just say he chased his tail till the day he died, apparently convinced he was on the verge of a major canine breakthrough." There was more to him than that, however, and I described his intuition and empathy, his gentleness with children, his pure heart.

What I really wanted to say was how this animal had touched our souls and taught us some of the most important lessons of our lives. "A person can learn a lot from a dog, even a loopy one like ours," I wrote. "Marley taught me about living each day with unbridled exuberance and joy, about seizing the moment and following your heart. He taught me to appreciate the simple things—a walk in the woods, a fresh snowfall, a nap in a shaft of winter sunlight. And as he grew old and achy, he taught me about optimism in the face of adversity. Mostly, he taught me about friendship and self-lessness and, above all else, unwavering loyalty."

It was an amazing concept that I was only now, in the wake of his death, fully absorbing: Marley as mentor. As teacher and role model. Was it possible for a dog—any dog, but especially a nutty, wildly uncontrollable one like ours— to point humans to the things that really mattered in life? I believed it was. Loyalty. Courage. Devotion. Simplicity. Joy. And the things that did not matter, too. A dog has no use for fancy cars or big homes or designer clothes. Status symbols mean nothing to him. A waterlogged stick will do just fine. A dog judges others not by their color or creed or class but by who they are inside. A dog doesn't care if you are rich or poor, educated or illiterate, clever or dull. Give him your heart and he will give you his. It was really quite simple, and yet we humans, so much wiser and more sophisticated, have always had trouble figuring out what really counts and what does not. As I wrote that farewell column to Marley, I realized it was all right there in front of us, if only we opened our eyes. Sometimes it took a dog with bad breath, worse manners, and pure intentions to help us see.

I finished my column, turned it in to my editor, and drove home for the night, feeling somehow lighter, almost buoy- ant, as though a weight I did not even know I had been carrying was lifted from me.

CHAPTER 29

The Bad Dog Club

When I arrived at work the next morning, the red message light on my telephone was blinking. I punched in my access code and received a recorded warning I had never heard before. "Your mailbox is full," the voice said. "Please delete all unneeded messages."

I logged on to my computer and opened my e-mail. Same story. The opening screen was filled with new messages, and so was the next screen, and the one after that, and after that, too. The morning e-mail was a ritual for me, a visceral, if inexact, barometer of the impact that day's column had made. Some columns brought as few as five or ten responses, and on those days I knew I had not connected. Others brought several dozen, a good day. A few brought even more. But this morning there were hundreds, far more than anything I had received before. The headers at the top of the e-mails said things like "Deepest condolences," "About your loss," or simply "Marley."

Animal lovers are a special breed of human, generous of

spirit, full of empathy, perhaps a little prone to sentimentality, and with hearts as big as a cloudless sky. Most who wrote and called simply wanted to express their sympathies, to tell me they, too, had been down this road and knew what my family was going through. Others had dogs whose lives were drawing to their inevitable ends; they dreaded what they knew was coming, just as we had dreaded it, too.

One couple wrote, "We fully understand and we mourn for your loss of Marley, and for our loss of Rusty. They'll always be missed, never truly replaced." A reader named Joyce wrote, "Thanks for reminding us of Duncan, who lies buried in our own backyard." A suburbanite named Debi added: "Our family understands how you feel. This past Labor Day we had to put our golden retriever Chewy to sleep. He was thirteen and had many of the same afflictions you named with your dog. When he couldn't even get up to go outside to relieve himself that last day, we knew we couldn't let him keep suffering. We, too, had a burial in our backyard, under a red maple that will always be his memorial."

An employment recruiter named Monica, owner of Katie the Lab, wrote: "My condolences and tears to you. My girl Katie is only two and I always think, 'Monica, why did you go and let this wonderful creature steal your heart like this?'" From Carmela: "Marley must have been a great dog to have a family that loved him so much. Only dog owners can understand the unconditional love they give and the tremendous heartache when they are gone." From Elaine: "Such short little lives our pets have to spend with us, and they spend most of it waiting for us to come home each day. It is amazing how much love and laughter they bring into our lives and even how much closer we become with each other because of them." From Nancy: "Dogs are one of the wonders of life and add so very much to ours." From MaryPat: "To this day I miss the sound of Max's tags jingling as he padded through the house checking things out; that silence will drive you nuts for a while, especially at night." From Connie: "It's just the most amazing thing to love a dog, isn't it? It makes our relationships with people seem as boring as a bowl of oatmeal."

When the messages finally stopped coming several days later, I counted them up. Nearly eight hundred people, animal lovers all, had been moved to contact me. It was an incredible outpouring, and what a catharsis it was for me. By the time I had plowed through them all—and answered as many as I could—I felt better, as though I was part of a giant cyber-support group. My private mourning had become a public therapy session, and in this crowd there was no shame in admitting a real, piercing grief for something as seemingly inconsequential as an old, smelly dog.

My correspondents wrote and called for another reason, too. They wanted to dispute the central premise of my report, the part in which I insisted Marley was the world's worst-behaved animal. "Excuse me," the typical response went, "but yours couldn't have been the world's worst dog—because mine was." To make their case, they regaled me with detailed accounts of their pets' woeful behavior. I heard about shredded curtains, stolen lingerie, devoured birthday cakes, trashed auto interiors, great escapes, even a swallowed diamond engagement ring, which made Marley's taste for gold chains seem positively lowbrow by comparison. My in-box resembled a television talk show, *Bad Dogs and the People Who Love Them*, with the willing victims lining up to proudly brag, not about how wonderful their dogs were but about just how awful. Oddly enough, most of the horror stories involved large loopy retrievers just like mine. We weren't alone after all.

A woman named Elyssa described how her Lab Mo always broke out of the house when left alone, usually by crashing through window screens. Elyssa and her husband thought they had foiled Mo's wandering ways by closing and locking all the ground-floor windows. It hadn't occurred to them to close the upstairs windows, as well. "One day my husband came home and saw the second-floor screen hanging loose. He was scared to death to look for him," she wrote. Just as her husband began to fear the worst, "Mo all of a sudden came around the corner of the house with his head down. He knew he was in trouble, but we were amazed he was not hurt. He had flown through the window and landed on a sturdy bush that broke his fall."

Larry the Lab swallowed his mistress's bra and then burped it up in one piece ten days later. Gypsy, another Lab with adventurous tastes, devoured a jalousie window. Jason, a retriever–Irish setter mix, downed a five-foot vacuum cleaner hose, "interior reinforcing wire and all," his owner, Mike, reported. "Jason also ate a two-by-three-foot hole in a plaster wall and backhoed a three-foot-long trench in the carpet, stretching back from his favorite spot by the window," Mike wrote, adding, "but I loved that beast."

Phoebe, a Lab mix, was kicked out of two different boarding kennels and told never to return, owner Aimee wrote. "It seems she was the gang leader in breaking out of not only her cage but doing the favor for two other dogs, too. They then helped themselves to all kinds of snacks during the overnight hours." Hayden, a hundred-pound Lab, ate just about anything he could get his jaws around, owner Carolyn reported, including a whole box of fish food, a pair of suede loafers, and a tube of superglue, "not in the same sitting." She added: "His finest hour, though, was when he tore the garage-door frame out of the wall because I had foolishly attached his leash to it so he could lie in the sunshine."

Tim reported his yellow Lab Ralph was every bit as much a food thief as Marley, only smarter. One day before going out, Tim placed a large chocolate centerpiece on top of the refrigerator where it would be safely out of Ralph's reach. The dog, his owner reported, pawed open the cupboard drawers, then used them as stairs to climb onto the counter, where he could balance on his hind legs and reach the chocolate, which was gone without a trace when his master returned home. Despite the chocolate overdose, Ralph showed no ill effects. "Another time," Tim wrote, "Ralph opened the refrigerator and emptied its contents, including things in jars."

Nancy clipped my column to save because Marley reminded her so much of her retriever Gracie. "I left the article on the kitchen table and turned to put away the scissors," Nancy wrote. "When I turned back, sure enough, Gracie had eaten the column."

Wow, I was feeling better by the minute. Marley no longer sounded all that terrible. If nothing else, he certainly had plenty of company in the Bad Dog Club. I brought several of the messages home to share with Jenny, who laughed for the first time since Marley's death. My new friends in the Secret Brotherhood of Dysfunctional Dog Owners had helped us more than they ever would know.

The days turned into weeks and winter melted into spring. Daffodils pushed up through the earth and bloomed around Marley's grave, and delicate white cherry blossoms floated down to rest on it. Gradually, life without our dog became more comfortable. Days would float by without me even thinking of him, and then some little cue—one of his hairs on my sweater, the rattle of his choker chain as I reached into my drawer for a pair of socks— would bring him abruptly back. As time passed, the recollections were more pleasant than painful. Long-forgotten moments flashed in my head with vivid clarity like clips being rerun from old home videos: The way Lisa the stabbing victim had leaned over and kissed Marley on the snout after she got out of the hospital. The way the crew on the movie set fawned over him. The way the mail lady slipped him a treat each day at the front door. The way he held mangoes in his front paws as he nibbled out the flesh. The way he

snapped at the babies' diapers with that look of narcotic
bliss on his face, and the way he begged for his tranquilizers like they were steak bits. Little moments hardly
worth remembering, and yet here they were, randomly
playing out on my mental movie screen at the least likely
times and places. Most of them made me smile; a few
made me bite my lip and pause.

I was in a staff meeting at the office when this one came
to me: It was back in West Palm Beach when Marley was
still a puppy and Jenny and I were still dreamy-eyed
newlyweds. We were strolling along the Intracoastal
Waterway on a crisp winter's day, holding hands, Marley
out in front, tugging us along. I let him hop up on the
concrete breakwater, which was about two feet wide and
three feet above the water's surface. "John," Jenny protested. "He could fall in." I looked at her dubiously. "How
dumb do you think he is?" I asked. "What do you think
he'll do? Just walk right off the edge into thin air?" Ten
seconds later, that's exactly what he did, landing in the
water with a huge splash and requiring a complicated
rescue operation on our part to get him back up the wall
and onto land again.

A few days later I was driving to an interview when out of
nowhere came another early scene from our marriage: a
romantic getaway weekend to a beachfront cottage on
Sanibel Island before children arrived. The bride, the
groom—and Marley. I had completely forgotten about that
weekend, and here it was again, replaying in living color:
driving across the state with him wedged between us, his
nose occasionally bumping the gearshift lever into neutral.

Bathing him in the tub of our rental place after a day on the beach, suds and water and sand flying everywhere. And later, Jenny and I making love beneath the cool cotton sheets, an ocean breeze wafting over us, Marley's otter tail thumping against the mattress.

He was a central player in some of the happiest chapters of our lives. Chapters of young love and new beginnings, of budding careers and tiny babies. Of heady successes and crushing disappointments; of discovery and freedom and self-realization. He came into our lives just as we were trying to figure out what they would become. He joined us as we grappled with what every couple must eventually confront, the sometimes painful process of forging from two distinct pasts one shared future. He became part of our melded fabric, a tightly woven and inseparable strand in the weave that was us. Just as we had helped shape him into the family pet he would become, he helped to shape us, as well—as a couple, as parents, as animal lovers, as adults. Despite everything, all the disappointments and unmet expectations, Marley had given us a gift, at once priceless and free. He taught us the art of unqualified love. How to give it, how to accept it. Where there is that, most of the other pieces fall into place.

The summer after his death we installed a swimming pool, and I could not help thinking how much Marley, our tireless water dog, would have loved it, loved it more than any of us possibly could, even as he gouged the liner with his claws and clogged the filter with his fur. Jenny marveled at how easy it was to keep the house clean without a dog shedding and drooling and tracking in dirt. I admitted how nice it was to walk barefoot in the grass without watching where I stepped. The garden was definitely better off without a big, heavy-pawed rabbit chaser crashing through it. No doubt about it, life without a dog was easier and immensely simpler. We could take a weekend jaunt without arranging boarding. We could go out to dinner without worrying what family heirloom was in jeopardy. The kids could eat without having to guard their plates. The trash can didn't have to go up on the kitchen counter when we left. Once again we could sit back and enjoy in peace the wondrous show of a good lightning storm. I especially liked the freedom of moving around the house without a giant yellow magnet glued to my heels.

Still, as a family, we were not quite whole.

One morning in late summer I came down for breakfast, and Jenny handed me a section of the newspaper folded over to expose an inside page. "You're not going to believe this," she said.

Once a week, our local paper featured a dog from a rescue shelter that needed a home. The profile always featured a photograph of the dog, its name, and a brief description, written as if the dog were speaking in the first person, making its own best case. It was a gimmick the shelter people used to make the animals seem charming and adorable. We always found the doggie résumés amusing, if for no other reason than the effort made to put the best shine on unwanted animals that had already struck out at least once.

On this day, staring up from the page at me was a face I instantly recognized. Our Marley. Or at least a dog that could have been his identical twin. He was a big male yellow Lab with an anvil head, furrowed brow, and floppy ears cocked back at a comical angle. He stared directly into the camera lens with a quivering intensity that made you just know that seconds after the picture was snapped he had knocked the photographer to the ground and tried to swallow the camera. Beneath the photo was the name: Lucky. I read his sales pitch aloud. This is what Lucky had to say about himself: "Full of zip! I would do well in a home that is quiet while I am learning how to control my energy level. I have not had an easy life so my new family will need to be patient with me and continue to teach me my doggie manners."

"My God," I exclaimed. "It's him. He's back from the dead."

"Reincarnation," Jenny said.

It was uncanny how much Lucky looked like Marley and how much the description fit him, too. Full of zip? Problem controlling energy? Working on doggie manners? Patience required? We were well familiar with those euphemisms, having used them ourselves. Our mentally unbalanced dog was back, young and strong again, and wilder than ever. We both stood there, staring at the newspaper, not saying anything.

"I guess we could go look at him," I finally said.

"Just for the fun of it," Jenny added.

"Right. Just out of curiosity."

"What's the harm of looking?"

"No harm at all," I agreed.

"Well then," she said, "why not?"

"What do we have to lose?"

The following column appeared in the
Philadelphia Inquirer, *January 6, 2004*

SAYING FAREWELL TO A FAITHFUL PAL
John Grogan, *Inquirer* columnist

I n the gray of dawn, I found the shovel in the garage and walked down the hill to where the lawn meets the woods. There, beneath a wild cherry tree, I began to dig.

The earth was loose and blessedly unfrozen, and the work went fast. It was odd being out in the backyard without Marley, the Labrador retriever who for 13 years made it his business to be tight by my side for every excursion out the door, whether to pick a tomato, pull a weed, or fetch the mail. And now here I was alone, digging him this hole.

"There will never be another dog like Marley," my father said when I told him the news, that I finally had to put the old guy down. It was as close to a compliment as our pet ever received.

No one ever called him a great dog—or even a good dog. He was as wild as a banshee and as strong as a bull. He crashed joyously through life with a gusto most often associated with natural disasters.

He's the only dog I've ever known to get expelled from obedience school.

Marley was a chewer of couches, a slasher of screens, a slinger of drool, a tipper of trash cans. He was so big he could eat off the kitchen table with all four paws planted on the floor—and did so whenever we weren't looking.

Marley shredded more mattresses and dug through more drywall than I care to remember, almost always out of sheer terror brought on by his mortal enemy, thunder.

CUTE BUT DUMB

He was a majestic animal, nearly 100 pounds of quivering muscle wrapped in a luxurious fur coat the color of straw. As for brains, let me just say he chased his tail till the day he died, apparently convinced he was on the verge of a major canine breakthrough.

That tail could clear a coffee table in one swipe. We lost track of the things he swallowed, including my wife's gold necklace, which we eventually recovered, shinier than ever. We took him with us once to a chi-chi outdoor cafe and tied him to the heavy wrought-iron table. Big mistake. Marley spotted a cute poodle and off he bounded, table in tow.

But his heart was pure.

When I brought my wife home from the doctor after our first pregnancy ended in a miscarriage, that wild beast gently rested his blocky head in her lap and just whimpered. And when babies finally arrived, he somehow understood they were something special and let them climb all over him, tugging his ears and pulling out little fistfuls of fur. One day when a stranger tried to hold one of the children, our jolly giant showed a ferocity we never imagined was inside him.

As the years passed, Marley mellowed, and sleeping

became his favorite pastime. By the end, his hearing was shot, his teeth were gone, his hips so riddled with arthritis he barely could stand. Despite the infirmities, he greeted each day with the mischievous glee that was his hallmark. Just days before his death, I caught him with his head stuck in the garbage pail.

LIFE LESSONS LEARNED

A person can learn a lot from a dog, even a loopy one like ours.

Marley taught me about living each day with unbridled exuberance and joy, about seizing the moment and following your heart. He taught me to appreciate the simple things—a walk in the woods, a fresh snowfall, a nap in a shaft of winter sunlight. And as he grew old and achy, he taught me about optimism in the face of adversity.

Mostly, he taught me about friendship and selflessness and, above all else, unwavering loyalty.

When his time came last week, I knelt beside him on the floor of the animal hospital, rubbing his gray snout as the veterinarian discussed cremation with me. No, I told her, I would be taking him home with me.

The next morning, our family would stand over the hole I had dug and say goodbye. The kids would tuck drawings in beside him. My wife would speak for us all when she'd say: "God, I'm going to miss that big, dumb lug."

But now I had a few minutes with him before the doctor returned. I thought back over his 13 years—the destroyed furniture and goofy antics; the sloppy kisses and utter devotion. All in all, not a bad run.

I didn't want him to leave this world believing all his bad press. I rested my forehead against his and said: "Marley, you are a great dog."

Acknowledgments

No man is an island, authors included, and I would like to thank the many people whose support helped me bring this book to fruition. At the top of the list, let me start by expressing my deep appreciation to my agent, the talented and indefatigable Laurie Abkemeier of DeFiore and Company, who believed in this story and my ability to tell it even before I fully did myself. I am convinced that without her unflagging enthusiasm and coaching, this book would still be locked in my head. Thank you, Laurie, for being my confidante, my advocate, my friend.

My heartfelt thanks to my wonderful editor, Mauro DiPreta, whose judicious and intelligent editing made this a better book, and to the always cheerful Joelle Yudin, who kept track of all the details. Thanks also to Michael Morrison, Lisa Gallagher, Seale Ballenger, Ana Maria Allessi, Christine Tanigawa, Richard Aquan, and everyone in the HarperCollins group for falling in love with Marley and his story, and making my dream a reality.

I owe a debt to my editors at the *Philadelphia Inquirer* for rescuing me from my self-imposed exile from the newspaper business that I love so much, and for giving me the priceless gift of my own column in one of America's greatest newspapers.

I am beyond grateful to Anna Quindlen whose early enthusiasm and encouragement meant more to me than she will ever know.

A hearty thank-you to Jon Katz, who gave me valuable advice and feedback, and whose books, especially *A Dog Year: Twelve Months, Four Dogs, and Me*, inspired me.

To Jim Tolpin, a busy lawyer who always found the time to give me free and sage advice. To Pete and Maureen Kelly, whose companionship—and cottage overlooking Lake Huron—was the tonic I needed. To Ray and JoAnn Smith for being there when I needed them most, and to Timothy R. Smith for the beautiful music that made me cry. To Digger Dan for the steady supply of smoked meats, and to my siblings, Marijo, Timothy, and Michael Grogan, for the cheerleading. To Maria Rodale for trusting me with a beloved family heirloom and helping me find my balance. To all those friends and colleagues too numerous to mention for their kindness, support, and good wishes . . . thank you all.

I could not have even contemplated this project without my mother, Ruth Marie Howard Grogan, who taught me early on the joy of a good tale well told and shared her gift for storytelling with me. With sadness, I remember and honor my biggest fan of all, my father Richard Frank Grogan, who died on December 23, 2004, as this book was going into production. He did not get the chance to read it, but I was able to sit with him one night as his health failed and read the few opening chapters aloud, even making him laugh. That smile, I will remember forever.

I owe a huge debt to my lovely and patient wife, Jenny, and my children, Patrick, Conor, and Colleen, for allowing me to trot them out into the public spotlight, sharing the most intimate of details. You guys are good sports, and I love you beyond words.

Finally (yes, last once again), I need to thank that pain-in-the-ass four-legged friend of mine, without whom there would be no *Marley & Me*. He'd be happy to know that his debt for all the shredded mattresses, gouged drywall, and swallowed valuables is now officially satisfied in full.

Praise for *Marley & Me*

❈ ❈ ❈

"The reason *Marley & Me* has proved to be a bestseller is that it is not just a funny dog story . . . it's also an honest and raw account of a young couple's desire to have children, their fears they won't be able to and their never ending quest to do the right thing by the family they have created. It's a universal story of family life, and a publishing sensation."
Catherine O'Brien, *The Times*

"A brilliant memoir"
Henry Sutton, *The Mirror*

"John Grogan brings the tale of Marley vividly to life, and readers won't be disappointed. With a light and humorous touch, John Grogan has crafted a loving tribute. A book for dog lovers definitely, but well worth a read even if you have never owned one of our canine friends."
Andrew Martin, *Birmingham Post*

"A beguiling and funny read"
Choice Magazine

"As the owner of a 90-pound Bouvier who as a puppy routinely had me screaming on all fours in front of our entire obedience class, I laughed out loud reading John Grogan's hilarious description of his attempts to train his Lab Marley. As they say, No pain, no gain. Grogan's gain – and the reader's too – is Marley, a Hall of Fame dog if there ever was one."
John Burnham Schwartz, author of *Reservation Road*

"Labrador retrievers are generally considered even-tempered, calm and reliable—and then there's Marley, the subject of this delightful tribute to one Lab who doesn't fit the mould . . . Grogan's chronicle of the . . . overly energetic but endearing dog is delivered with great humor. Dog lovers will love this account of Grogan's much loved canine."
Publishers Weekly

"Grogan . . . offers a humorous and loving tribute to Marley (after Bob Marley), his late 100-pound yellow Labrador . . . Readers will delight in this tribute; recommended."
Library Journal

About the Author

John Grogan has spent more than 25 years as a newspaper journalist, most recently as metropolitan columnist for the *Philadelphia Inquirer*. Previously he worked as a reporter, bureau chief, and columnist at newspapers in Michigan and Florida. He also is the former editor in chief of Rodale's *Organic Gardening* magazine. His work has won numerous awards, including the National Press Club's Consumer Journalism Award. He lives in the Pennsylvania countryside with his wife, Jenny, and their three children.

Author photo © Adam Nadel